PLANETS ON THE MOVE

PLANETS
ON THE MOVE

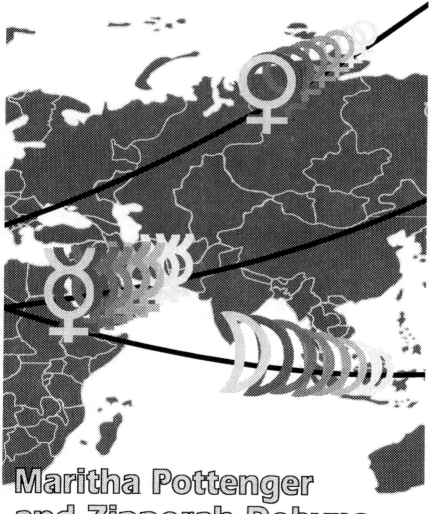

Maritha Pottenger
and Zipporah Dobyns

International Standard Book Number 0-935127-23-2

Library of Congress Catalog Card Number: 95-75852

Cover Design by Maria Kay Simms and Daryl S Fuller

Printed in the United States of America

Published by ACS Publications
5521 Ruffin Road
San Diego, CA 92123

First Printing, March 1995
Second Printing, May 1997

Also by ACS Publications

All About Astrology Series of booklets
The American Atlas, Expanded Fifth Edition (Shanks)
The American Ephemeris for the 20th Century [Noon or Midnight] 1900 to 2000, Rev. 5th Edition
The American Ephemeris for the 21st Century [Noon or Midnight] 2000-2050, Rev. 2nd Edition
The American Heliocentric Ephemeris 1901-2000
The American Heliocentric Ephemeris 2001-2050
The American Midpoint Ephemeris 1996-2000
The American Sidereal Ephemeris 1976-2000, 2nd Edition
The American Sidereal Ephemeris 2001-2025
Asteroid Goddesses (George & Bloch)
Astro-Alchemy (Negus)
Astrological Insights into Personality (Lundsted)
Astrology for the Light Side of the Brain (Rogers-Gallagher)
Basic Astrology: A Guide for Teachers & Students (Negus)
Basic Astrology: A Workbook for Students (Negus)
The Book of Jupiter (Waram)
The Book of Neptune (Waram)
The Book of Pluto (Forrest)
The Book of Saturn (Dobyns)
The Book of Uranus (Negus)
The Changing Sky (Forrest)
Complete Horoscope Interpretation (Pottenger)
Cosmic Combinations (Negus)
Dial Detective (Simms)
Easy Astrology Guide (Pottenger)
Easy Tarot Guide (Masino)
Expanding Astrology's Universe (Dobyns)
Finding our Way Through the Dark (George)
Future Signs (Simms)
Hands That Heal, 2nd Edition (Bodine)
Healing with the Horoscope (Pottenger)
The Inner Sky (Forrest)
The International Atlas, Revised Fourth Edition (Shanks)
New Insights into Astrology (Press)
The Night Speaks (Forrest)
The Only Way to... Learn Astrology, Vols. I-VI (March & McEvers)
    Volume I - Basic Principles, 2nd Edition
    Volume II - Math & Interpretation Techniques
    Volume III - Horoscope Analysis
    Volume IV- Learn About Tomorrow: Current Patterns
    Volume V - Learn About Relationships: Synastry Techniques
    Volume VI - Learn About Horary and Electional Astrology
Past Lives Future Choices (Pottenger)
Planetary Heredity (M. Gauquelin)
Psychology of the Planets (F. Gauquelin)
Spirit Guides: We Are Not Alone (Belhayes)
Tables of Planetary Phenomena (Michelsen)
Twelve Wings of the Eagle (Simms)
Your Magical Child (Simms)
Your Starway to Love, 2nd Edition (Pottenger)

Also by ACS Publications

All About Astrology Series of booklets
The American Atlas, Expanded Fifth Edition (Shanks)
The American Ephemeris for the 20th Century [Noon or Midnight] 1900 to 2000,
    Rev. 5th Edition
The American Ephemeris for the 21st Century [Noon or Midnight] 2000-2050,
    Rev. 2nd Edition
The American Heliocentric Ephemeris 1901-2000
The American Heliocentric Ephemeris 2001-2050
The American Midpoint Ephemeris 1996-2000
The American Sidereal Ephemeris 1976-2000, 2nd Edition
The American Sidereal Ephemeris 2001-2025
Asteroid Goddesses (George & Bloch)
Astro-Alchemy (Negus)
Astrological Insights into Personality (Lundsted)
Astrology for the Light Side of the Brain (Rogers-Gallagher)
Basic Astrology: A Guide for Teachers & Students (Negus)
Basic Astrology: A Workbook for Students (Negus)
The Book of Jupiter (Waram)
The Book of Neptune (Waram)
The Book of Pluto (Forrest)
The Book of Saturn (Dobyns)
The Book of Uranus (Negus)
The Changing Sky (Forrest)
Complete Horoscope Interpretation (Pottenger)
Cosmic Combinations (Negus)
Dial Detective (Simms)
Easy Astrology Guide (Pottenger)
Easy Tarot Guide (Masino)
Expanding Astrology's Universe (Dobyns)
Finding our Way Through the Dark (George)
Future Signs (Simms)
Hands That Heal, 2nd Edition (Bodine)
Healing with the Horoscope (Pottenger)
The Inner Sky (Forrest)
The International Atlas, Revised Fourth Edition (Shanks)
New Insights into Astrology (Press)
The Night Speaks (Forrest)
The Only Way to... Learn Astrology, Vols. I-VI (March & McEvers)
    Volume I - Basic Principles, 2nd Edition
    Volume II - Math & Interpretation Techniques
    Volume III - Horoscope Analysis
    Volume IV- Learn About Tomorrow: Current Patterns
    Volume V - Learn About Relationships: Synastry Techniques
    Volume VI - Learn About Horary and Electional Astrology
Past Lives Future Choices (Pottenger)
Planetary Heredity (M. Gauquelin)
Psychology of the Planets (F. Gauquelin)
Spirit Guides: We Are Not Alone (Belhayes)
Tables of Planetary Phenomena (Michelsen)
Twelve Wings of the Eagle (Simms)
Your Magical Child (Simms)
Your Starway to Love, 2nd Edition (Pottenger)

TABLE OF CONTENTS

Chapter Three: Aspects to Angles
Ascendant/Descendant Aspects

Midheaven/IC Aspects

Chapter Four:
Aspects to the Angles from House Rulers

Chapter Five: Rulers Changing Houses
Rulers of the Ascendant (1st House)

Rulers of the Midheaven (10th House)

Chapter Seven:
Changing Signs on the Midheaven

Chapter Eight:
"Instant" Relocation for Specific Questions

CHAPTER ONE

THE ASTROLOGY OF RELOCATION

Have you ever noticed how you can be a very different person when associating with different friends? With one group, you are sociable and outgoing. With another group, you are more retiring and reticent. You've also probably discovered that differing sides of your personality seem to predominate in different parts of the country (or the world). Certain events occur more readily in some areas than others. **Relocational astrology is a valuable tool for understanding the changes you experience as you move from place to place**.

What Will This Book Teach You about Your Place on Earth?

This book is designed to offer information which can be used by a wide range of people: from astrological novices who want information about their places of residence to practicing astrologers who want examples, input, ideas, and stimulation about how to interpret and use Relocation Charts.

FOR THE NOVICE ONLY

The easiest way to use this book is to examine your Relocation Chart for the city where you live. You can order a **free** Relocation

Chart with a printout telling you exactly what factors to look up in this book (and the page numbers!) from Astro Communications using the coupon in the back of this book. With your Astro Relocation Chart in hand, you simply turn to the correct page (in each of five sections) and read about the themes with which you are dealing in your current location. Everything is explained in English and you don't even have to understand the nuances of astrology! (This book also includes a number of examples to help "bring to life" relocation issues. Since astrological technicalities will be discussed, you may wish to skip the case illustrations.) But everything you need to know about your potentials in different parts of the world is supplied by your Astro Relocation Chart and this book.

FOR THE ASTROLOGICAL STUDENT

What is a Relocated (or Relocation) Chart?
A relocated chart is a horoscope which has been erected for a place of current (or potential) residence (as opposed to one's place of birth). It is a tool for examining issues in high focus in different parts of the world. Your chart—relocated to an area where you are living (or thinking about moving or visiting for an extended period of time)— offers important information about the **themes likely to pervade your life in that area**. The astrology of relocation helps to explain the different facets of our personalities which are highlighted in different places.

How Do You Calculate a Relocated Chart?
The easiest way to get a relocated chart is to have a computer calculate it. The focus of this book is **interpreting** a relocated chart—knowing what it **means**. If you're not interested in the calculation, skip this section.

Whether done by "hand" or by computer, the erection of a relocated chart is simple: one merely calculates the houses of the horoscope **as if** the individual had been born in the new place of residence. The time (in terms of Greenwich) is kept constant. Thus, an individual who was born at 4:30 PM in New York City (during Eastern Standard time) would have a Greenwich birth time of 9:30 PM. If we wanted to relocate the horoscope to Los Angeles, California, that 4:30 PM EST is equivalent to 1:30 PM PST (Pacific Standard Time). We would go through the usual steps to calculate house cusps (laid out clearly in *The American Book of Tables*) using the birth day, month, and year, but with the Pacific Standard Time and the latitude and longitude for Los Angeles.

Actually, if you follow the procedures outlined in *The American Book of Tables,* there is an even simpler method of calculation. To determine the sign, degree, and minute of the house cusps of a horoscope, you need to figure out the Local Sidereal Time of Birth (LST). The next-to-last step in figuring LST is to get the Greenwich Sidereal Time of Birth (GST). Once you have the Greenwich Sidereal Time of Birth for a particular chart, it does not change. The final step in getting the LST (local sidereal time) is to add or subtract the longitude correction from the GST. The longitude correction is the hours, minutes, and seconds that a birthplace is away from Greenwich. (One can convert longitude into hours and minutes and seconds or use tables or a computer). To calculate a relocated chart, simply make the longitude correction **for the place of relocation** instead of for the birthplace. The LST (local sidereal time) you obtain will be for the relocated place. The house cusps you figure (following usual procedures) will be for that relocation.

Since the time is constant, one's **planets do not change position in regard to signs**. They occupy the same degrees in each sign and make the same aspects to one another. Therefore, you need not repeat any math for figuring out planetary placements. What does change, in a relocation, is one's houses— because they are dependent on place (as well as time) of birth. **Planets will move to different houses if you move far enough from your birthplace**. Planets will also **change aspects to the major angles** (Ascendant, Descendant, Midheaven, IC) of the horoscope. An individual may move, for example, from a natal Saturn square Midheaven to a relocated Saturn trine Midheaven (or Saturn not aspecting the Midheaven). One might have no aspect in the natal chart, but gain an aspect (e.g., Sun sextile Ascendant) in the relocation. A general "rule of thumb" is that your Midheaven will move approximately one degree in the zodiac for every degree of longitude you move east or west from your birthplace. (The Midheaven moves earlier in the zodiac as you move west and later in the zodiac as you move east.)

FOR THE NOVICE, STUDENT, AND PROFESSIONAL ASTROLOGER

Why Look at a Relocated Chart?

Some astrologers feel the birth chart is sufficient for their purposes. If you examine relocated horoscopes, however, you will be impressed by the important information which they provide. Here are just a few examples.

A child born with **Neptune exactly on her Midheaven** had a mysterious illness from birth. Several local doctors were unable to diagnose the problem or offer a solution. The family moved to a different state, hoping that a change of climate might help. In the new location, of course, the local MC (Midheaven) was moved away from Neptune. In that new location, the first doctor to whom the child was taken recognized the very obscure problem and provided treatment which took care of it.

Two women were born in countries where women are usually dependent upon and subordinate to men. The women moved to cities in the U.S. where they had **Saturn closely conjunct the Ascendant**. One of the women has developed a very successful career and become totally financially independent. The other, who made the move quite recently, is working to achieve control over her life.

A man with a natal emphasis on independence moved to a city which put his **local MC on Uranus**. At age 30, he remains unmarried in a job which satisfies his need for personal freedom and constant change.

A man had been married for years to an alcoholic wife. He chose to leave both his home and his wife when his **progressed Moon was crossing his local Midheaven**.

A seventeen-year-old woman eloped and married when her **progressed Venus was entering her local 7th house** of marriage.

Nancy Kerrigan engaged in the supreme contest in her skating career when she won the silver medal in the 1994 Olympics. Her **progressed Mars was crossing her Descendant in Lillehammer**, Norway. The 7th house can be manifested in either cooperation or competition. With Venus, an individual is more likely to choose the former, and with Mars the latter, but details are always subject to personal choices.

Historical Background

The idea of "relocating" a horoscope is at least 40 years old. In our increasingly mobile society, astrologers wondered whether the place of residence—if different from the place of birth—ought to be taken into account astrologically. As with any new theory, the way to find out if it works is to test it. People began to work with "relocated" charts—and significant patterns started showing up! Zip has been working with relocated charts since 1958.

Jim Lewis was the first person in the United States to show on a map the relationship between one's place on the Earth and aspects to the angles. His well-known system of Astro*Carto*Graphy created a map of the world on which the "lines" of the various planets were plotted. This provided the user with a quick, one-page picture of where on Earth each of the planets would be rising (near the Ascendant), culminating (near the Midheaven), setting (near the Descendant) and at lower culmination (near the IC).

Jim Lewis' original formulation used right ascension, the coordinate system based on the celestial equator which is used by astronomers. This does not yield exactly the same results as zodiacal longitude which is based on the ecliptic and used by astrologers. The system of right ascension will be closer to what we see when physically observing the planets. Early work with Astro*Carto*Graphy maps revealed some striking correlations between planetary lines and various earthly happenings. Jim Lewis' writings discuss much of this and are particularly rich in examples from mundane astrology (focusing on countries and major economic, political developments).

One current theory about relocating charts suggests that using right ascension is more appropriate for charts of countries and mundane or cycle work, while zodiacal longitude is more appropriate for charts of individuals. As always, the reader should test theories for him/herself.

Many astrologers working with personal clients did want something which provided an easy graphic picture, but included the traditional astrological aspects. That is the rationale behind the Astrolocality Maps developed by Astro Communications Services (then Astro Computing). Each Astrolocality Map is limited to a given "continental" area (*e.g.*, U.S.; South America; Australia, Europe, Far East, Africa, etc.). Each map includes the major

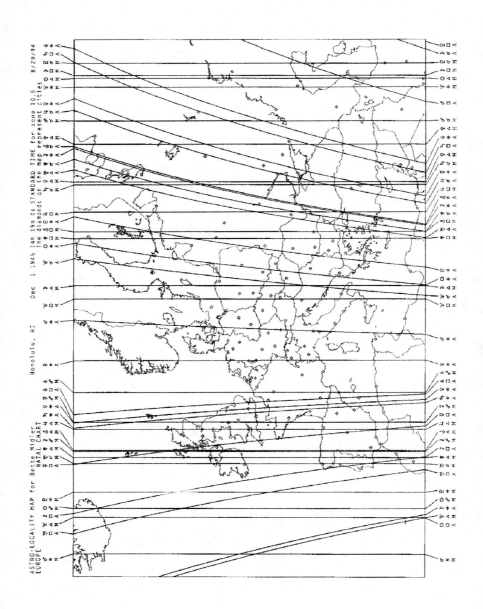

aspects (conjunction, opposition, sextile, trine and square). People could quickly and easily see which aspects to the angles they had in different parts of the U.S. (or other continents).

As wonderful as these maps were, however, they did not reveal the whole picture. They showed **only** aspects to the angles of the horoscope. The maps do not reveal changes in the house positions of the planets nor the changes in rulership. (For example, Saturn may rule a client's 2nd house natally and be trine the MC, but Uranus rules the 2nd in the relocation and is square the relocated MC.) Nor do the maps reveal changes of sign on any of the houses (including the Ascendant and Descendant). For fullest information, one had to return to the actual relocated charts (for each particular city)—which predate the maps.

The Meaning of a Relocated Chart

We never lose our natal charts; they are ours for a lifetime. The **relocated horoscope gives additional themes and issues** (like an overlay on the natal chart for your birthplace) which are particularly **relevant for that area**. A relocation chart is relevant while you are residing in that area, or doing business in that area, or involved with people living there. For example, if you do a lot of business with a company whose corporate headquarters are in Albany, New York, it is worth examining your Relocation Chart for Albany. If your mother lives in another city, your horoscope relocated to that city could give clues to your interactions with her. Anyone having important dealings with the federal government could examine his/her chart relocated to Washington, D.C. And so on.

If you move again (or stop interacting with people in that city), you would look at the relocated chart for the new city.

Kinds of Relocated Charts

You can relocate a natal chart—or progressions, solar arc directions and most major forms of current patterns. You can examine synastry in terms of relocation. (For example, one couple has her Juno [the marriage asteroid] conjunct his natal Ascendant and her Ascendant conjunct his relocated [for where they live] Descendant.) Some astrologers regularly choose the sites for their Solar Returns based on relocation principles. They will go to a particular city in order to have a Solar Return whose patterns they feel are more promising for the year ahead.

Factors Affected by Relocation

A Relocation Chart can change any of the following:

    (1)   aspects to the angles (Ascendant/Descendant axis; Midheaven/IC axis and—if you use them—Vertex/Antivertex axis and East Point/West Point axis)

    (2)   aspects to rulers of the different houses from the angles

    (3)   house placements of rulers of the angles

    (4)   house placements of planets (and stellia)

    (5)   signs on the angles

This book has five chapters (Three through Seven) which discuss the above five ways in which your horoscope can change when relocated. These five are in order of approximate importance. (For example, give more weight to aspects to the angles and the placement of angle rulers than to changes of sign on the angles.) Each chapter provides basic principles and possibilities in "cookbook" form (that is, an explanation for every possible shift). You can look up the possibilities for your own chart (or charts of friends or clients)—or read all the alternatives as a professional seeking more stimulation and insight. In addition, a number of examples are discussed (in Chapter Two) to help "bring to life" relocation issues.

The final chapter (Eight) offers suggestions for what astrological placements to seek for specific goals (*e.g.* career success, marriage, etc.) Chapter Eight can operate as a quick guide for working with Astrolocality Maps.

CHAPTER TWO
CASE STUDIES IN RELOCATION

New Tools and Techniques Support Symbolic Nature of Astrology

Astrology today is in an exciting state of flux as new tools and techniques are made available with the help of computers. As the new methods are discovered to be of value, many of them call into question the assumptions of materialism which looks for forces in the sky that supposedly "influence" or even "create" the conditions on Earth. For example, increasing numbers of astrologers are discovering the value of **heliocentric astrology** which uses the positions of the planets as they would appear if we were residing on the Sun. But if there are radiations or forces coming from the planets, obviously their heliocentric positions would show the times when they are impacting the Sun, not the Earth.

The **angles of a horoscope** such as the Ascendant-Descendant axis, the Midheaven-IC axis, etc. are formed by projecting great circles against infinity and noting where they would intersect the zodiac. Normally, there are no physical bodies at those intersections, but experience shows that these intersections of imaginary circles are at least as important as the planets.

The **nodes of the Moon and planets** are similarly located at the intersections of the orbit of the Moon or planet with the extended plane of the Earth's orbit. Usually, there is nothing "physical" at such intersection points but they are meaningful in a horoscope.

An incredible variety of systems exist which offer information on current issues and which allow us to look into the future. We can use the actual, current positions of the planets, or look at the sky **one day after birth for each year** of life, or look at it **one day after birth for each lunar month** of life, or look at it **one lunar month after birth for each year** of life, or move everything in the birth sky (as pictured in the natal horoscope) a set amount such as a degree per year, etc. In one system, a "Mars" issue may be shown by the planet Mars; in another system by a planet in the sign of Aries; in still another system, a planet in or ruling the first house of the horoscope may provide the information. When the issue can be accurately communicated by a variety of factors which share the same meaning, we are looking at a symbol system, a language, not a set of "forces."

The technique described in this book also supports the **symbolic nature of astrology**. Though some people continue to spend their whole lives in their place of birth, they are probably a minority of Earth's inhabitants. Certainly, U.S. citizens are noted for their frequent changes of residences. The houses in a natal horoscope are based on the latitude and longitude of an individual's location on Earth as well as on the date and the time of the birth. **These houses are a lifetime key to the basic nature of the individual**. But when people change their residences, they get a "new" set of houses which are calculated for the new place, and which are added to the primary chart. The Greenwich time is kept constant, so there is no change in the sign positions of the planets or in their aspects with each other. But as the house cusps change, the planets can be moved into new houses. Even a small move can change the angles of the chart so that natal aspects to the Ascendant, MC, etc. can be moved in or out of orb while current aspects to angles will either last longer or be repeated at a different time.

Astrology has a long history, and part of its excitement is the way in which it continues to evolve. Archaeology suggests that as long as twenty to thirty thousand years ago, the sky was being used by humans as a map and compass and as a clock and calendar. Scratches on bones and horns show that neolithic hunters were recording the phases of the Moon. In addition to humans, some species of migratory insects, birds, and animals continue to use the sky to orient themselves in space and time.

Earth and sky share the same time/space order which provides the framework within which our form of consciousness normally operates. Astrology goes beyond materialistic science in its recognition that **Earth and sky also share a common meaning**. Materialistic science denies that there is any inherent meaning in the cosmos, maintaining instead a basic belief in the rule of chance. Modern western science replaced the living, creative, conscious Absolute (which most people call God) with a nonliving, noncreative, nonconscious set of "natural laws" which permit complex evolution through chance mutations (genetic changes) and the survival of the fittest.

But the more one works with astrology, the more one explores the escalating numbers of tools and techniques becoming available with the help of computers, the less one believes in chance. In fact, the world may not just **include** meaning as an inherent part of it; it may literally **be** meaning. What we experience as consciousness (including the vastly larger part of it in this world which is not self-conscious) may literally **be the nature of reality**.

We can define "meaning" as knowledge or information acquired and used by consciousness. Meaning provides answers to a collection of words which, in English, begin with "wh": what, where, when, why. We can also add some words not currently used as often: whence, whither, wherefore, plus one word without the leading "w," how. Science is increasingly realizing that **information is part of basic reality** but most scientists are still trying to reduce it to subnuclear energy/particles, to nonconscious, chemical/electrical forces which are controlled by the laws of probability, that is, meaningless, random chance.

Our beliefs totally shape our lives. If we believe that something is impossible, it is - for us. Our goals are set and our choices made on the basis of what we believe is true, real, possible, desirable, morally right, etc. We interpret all of our experiences in terms of our beliefs. A great many astrologers have absorbed the materialistic beliefs of western science. They assume, not always consciously, that at birth we are created by and we continue to be influenced by, some kind of physical forces or radiations which emanate from the planets. It is hard to break out of a pervasive, cultural belief system; to consider the possibility that we (and everything else) are Mind and that the **planets**

symbolize the psychological principles which are functioning in any specific time-space framework. We can think of the psychological principles as life issues which must be faced and handled in that particular time-space location. In this theory, we are attracted to the particular time-space location which **fits** our basic nature and our current state of mind. By seeing ourselves in the mirror of our world, we learn to understand ourselves and to evolve. We learn to change our habits which are inviting or producing painful results and to expand our habits which are getting desired results.

If this belief-system is true, if the Absolute (ultimate reality) is Mind-Life-Spirit, omnipresent and eternal, and we are an individualized manifestation of that Absolute, we might be able to become conscious that we are part of the larger Whole and begin to manifest vastly more of its potentials. Beliefs are based on faith. We can't prove the nature of reality in a laboratory. But we can test our beliefs by acting on them and observing the results. Small tests are wise. If we think we have mastered the art of levitation, we can test it by stepping off of the bottom stair step, not the roof of the house. We learn about ourselves, about life, and about astrology by experience. We consider a new idea, reach out in a new effort, and see whether it "works" for us. If you have not explored the houses of your chart when they are calculated for your own changed residences, for the location of important people in your life, for the headquarters of employers, for the sites of major events which happened when you were traveling, you have an exciting new world waiting for you.

Astrology's Coordinate Systems

The primary tool of astrology is a map of the sky using the ecliptic coordinate system. To map a sphere, one measures around a circle as well as up and down from the circle. A point on the map can then be located by specifying a distance around the circle from an agreed-upon starting point, and a distance up or down from the circle. The ecliptic system measures around the **celestial ecliptic**, a projection against infinity of the Earth's path around the sun. The ecliptic is divided into the twelve zodiacal signs, starting with 0 Aries where the ecliptic crosses the equator in the spring in the northern hemisphere. The measurement around this circle is called **zodiacal longitude** and the measurement up and down is **zodiacal latitude**.

Astronomy also maps the sky with several other coordinate systems, each using a "great circle" which is defined as a circle which goes through the center of the Earth. Measurements around the **celestial equator**, a projection of Earth's equator against infinity, are called **right ascension**. Measurements up and down from the equator are called **declination**. Both systems begin their measurements around their circle from 0 Aries. Few astrologers use zodiacal latitude because most of the planets are close to the ecliptic, so their zodiacal latitudes will differ very little. Many astrologers do use declination in addition to zodiacal longitude. Aspects called **parallels** and **contraparallels** are formed when two factors in a horoscope are the same distance above or below the equator. Astronomers tend to be annoyed at this use of figures from two different coordinate systems in a single map of the sky, but astrologers simply respond that they use what works.

A third coordinate system in astronomy uses the **horizon**. Measurements around the horizon are called **azimuth**. Measurements up and down from the horizon are called **altitude**. The horizon system is the one normally used for visual observation of objects in the sky. Astronomers start their measurements from the northern point on the horizon and go clockwise. In recent years, astrologers have started using the horizon coordinate system and have renamed it "local space." Matrix does a local space map starting at the east point of the horizon and going counterclockwise. Both ACS and Mark Pottenger's CCRS astrology program offer the options of the normal astronomical approach (clockwise from the north) and the Matrix version (counterclockwise from the east). It is important not to confuse this system which is being called "local space" with the technique being described in this book which calculates horoscopes using the normal coordinate system which measures around the ecliptic, but which relocates the horoscope houses to an individual's local residence in addition to calculating them for the place of birth.

Birth Charts and Relocated Charts

As was indicated above, our birth horoscope — the map of the sky at our date, time and place of birth — is a lifetime map of our potentials. Even if a mother went to a hospital to have her child and left immediately afterwards so the child never lived in that city, the child would retain the horoscope drawn for that birthplace. But the horoscope for our place of residence is also meaningful. To repeat again, only the houses of the chart change as we move about on the earth. The Greenwich time of birth remains the same when the new, local chart is calculated, so the zodiacal positions of the planets and their aspects are identical in the two charts. **When we travel, we have temporary local charts** wherever we are. We can also have meaningful local charts for places which influence our lives. For example, individuals with parents or children who are still part of their lives but who live in other areas, will receive meaningful information from their own charts calculated for the locations of the relatives. People working for companies with headquarters in different areas will get useful information from their own charts calculated for the company headquarters.

Astrology's 12-Letter Alphabet

The basic interpretations of astrology are the same in any of these different charts. Different geographical areas will not "make" us different people, but horoscopes calculated for the new areas will help us to understand the opportunities and challenges which we will face in the alternate place. No factor in astrology is automatically "good" or "bad," pleasant or painful. **Astrology describes (symbolizes) a model of human nature with twelve basic desires or drives, twelve sides of life**. Everyone has the potential for all twelve since there is a planet, a sign, and a house (as well as many less-used variables) for each of them. Each chart is a unique combination of the same twelve psychological principles. Each of the twelve desires can be manifested in many different details, depending on one's previously developed habits. Our habits can be modified to produce different details (pleasant or painful), but habits are not easy to change. Sometimes, we wait until pain drives us into change. Self-awareness and self-mastery can help us to change before life becomes painful. Our horoscopes hold up a mirror to help us see what emotional and often subconscious habits inside of us are driving us. Then it is up to us to change the habits which are producing painful results.

Conflict is a normal, inherent part of life since we can't satisfy all twelve basic desires to their fullest extent at the same time. For example, we cannot be **totally** independent, dependent, in a committed peer relationship, and in control at the same time.

Any one of these **cardinal** sides of life, when carried to its fullest potential, will diminish the degree to which we can manifest the others. We can either satisfy these normal desires alternately if we want to go "all the way" with any of them, or we can compromise and have a little of each of them more or less simultaneously. If we choose compromise, we can have some independence to pursue our own interests, some dependence on others, some equalitarian "give-and-take" relationships, and some power and achievement in our lives. We can have our own hobbies, a home and family, a mate, and a career. When we say it that way, the **cardinal grand cross** does not sound so threatening. But it does take compromise.

The **fixed grand cross**, like the cardinal one, calls for learning to relate to other people, learning to balance their needs and desires against our own so that everyone involved can enjoy life. Power is an issue in both the cardinal and the fixed sides of life. The cardinal tendency is to change the overt framework when life becomes painful, when the conflicts are not integrated to make room for all the different, contradictory desires. So people change their personal actions, their home-family situations, their mates, and their careers. The fixed tendency is to keep on going to the "end." Individuals with a strong, fixed emphasis in their horoscopes may stay in a state of impasse and have periodic explosions, but when the dust clears, the same impasse is still there.

The **mutable grand cross involves mental issues**. We may feel pulled between interest in everything as a superficial spectator versus the urge to do something very well and get tangible results. We may consciously search for **truth,** for a belief system which gives us a clear value hierarchy, choices, and goals, or we may feel that we don't have to do anything because either we are already "there" or God (or someone else) should take care of it to give us a properly perfect world. Most commonly with the mutable dilemma, we are pulled between our ideals and the limits of what is possible in this world.

I call these life challenges, which are symbolized by the astrological crosses, the dilemmas. They are natural, inherent in life, so everyone has a little of all of these "dilemmas." Individual horoscopes are unique combinations of the same issues. **Our local houses may change the emphasis on our different dilemmas**, but quite typically we will just get a variation of the same message that we were given in our original birthplace chart. For example, we may move from an area where we had Saturn in the first house to a place where we have Capricorn rising. We may move from Neptune in the seventh house or Venus in the twelfth house to Virgo rising which puts Pisces on the seventh house cusp.

Relocation Shows Issues in High Focus

Wherever we go, we take ourselves with us, but the **local houses, especially planetary aspects to the new angles, will highlight the issues we will need to face in the new area.** Since each principle in astrology can be manifested in pleasant or painful ways, we can't assume that putting Jupiter or Venus on one of our new angles will guarantee a happy life. In fact, my experience so far is that an exact conjunction of any planet to an angle is more apt to be a challenge than an aid. A sextile or trine from a planet to one of the new angles (Ascendant, MC, etc.) is normally easier to handle constructively than a conjunction.

Wherever we have **Jupiter**, we are looking for some type of **ultimate value,** faith, and meaning. Putting Jupiter on a local angle could invite us to overemphasize that part of life. We are looking for pleasure wherever we have Venus, so **Venus** on an angle can invite excessive **pleasure** seeking. Even more than Venus, **Pluto** on an angle can encourage excesses through an obsessive search for **insight and self-mastery** or (when negatively expressed) indulgence and **power** at the expense of others. The **Sun** symbolizes a desire to create something more than we have done in the past, to project something into the world out of our own center, and to **achieve recognition** of some kind which will hopefully feed our self-esteem. The **Moon** is a key to **dependency and emotional security,** to the baby-mother relationship, our capacity to nurture others and to accept nurturing. **Mars** shows where we want the right to **do what we please. Mercury** indicates a focus on the conscious side of the **mind** while **Neptune** marks our subconscious **hunger for infinite love and beauty,** for oneness with the Whole. **Uranus represents the urge to resist any limits** while **Saturn** tells us about the **necessary limits,** the **rules** of the game, and it signals the **consequences** of how we have been playing the game. Once you are clear about the 12 basic principles, astrology is logical and there are always choices in the details we manifest with each of the principles.

PRESIDENT WILLIAM CLINTON IN THE WORLD

The president of the United States is one of the most powerful individuals in the world, and in that office, he can be involved in events almost anywhere in the world. Fortunately, in contrast to our last two presidents, we have a recorded birth time for Bill Clinton and the birth certificate time does seem to be accurate, based on the events in his life. He was born on August 19, 1946 at 8:51 AM CST, in Hope, Arkansas (Figure 1).

His natal chart has **Mars within one degree of the Ascendant, Neptune within one degree of Mars**, and **both planets within one degree of the East Point** which is like an auxiliary Ascendant. This combination indicates an intense, idealistic drive including a perhaps partially subconscious identification with God with the potential of playing the role of artist, or savior, or victim (or all of the above). In the sign of Libra, the combination also shows an identification with other people which often implies reluctance to be alone. **Libra can be either cooperative or competitive, and is often prominent in politicians**.

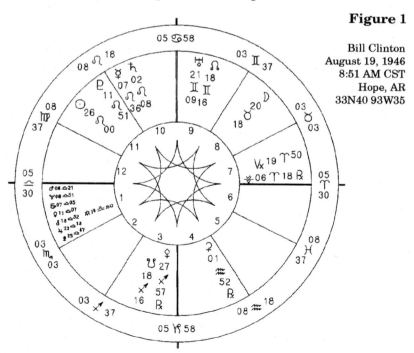

Figure 1

Bill Clinton
August 19, 1946
8:51 AM CST
Hope, AR
33N40 93W35

In addition to the Libra factors already mentioned, Clinton has Venus, Chiron, the Antivertex (another auxiliary Ascendant), Jupiter and Juno in the first house in Libra. The **overloaded first house intensifies the personal drive** since the first house caries the same meaning as the first sign, Aries. The combination suggests a **major issue around our personal right to do what we please versus the desire to please other people**. Putting Jupiter and Chiron (which I think is similar to Jupiter) in the first house adds to the **idealism** and the potential challenge. Either of two extremes is possible, both of them leading to difficulties. The individual can feel "I am God. I can do anything I want." Even when the desires are altruistic and noble, this grandiosity almost inevitably leads to periodic crashes.

Alternately, the individual may feel "I ought to be God, perfect, never making a mistake." Since we remain human, an individual seeking perfection will almost inevitably feel inadequate. "I'm never good enough."

The compromise feeling between these extremes calls for accepting our humanness, maintaining our goals of becoming more perfect, but realizing that we are on a long journey and can enjoy the process of moving toward perfection, not kicking ourselves because we have not yet arrived.

Both Venus and Juno are associated with a desire for close relationships, for a partner, so their presence in the first house strengthens the natural tendency of the Libra. They can also be a sign of **artistic talent or appreciation**. Conjunctions, when two or more factors are within a few degrees of each other, are the strongest aspects. Studies of famous people show that they tend to have more conjunctions than average people, and Bill Clinton's chart fits that observation.

A prominent Vesta is a frequent key to a person who is devoted to his or her work and likely to have an above-average impact on the world. This asteroid, or minor planet, can mark the ultimate Virgo workaholic; someone driven to do something worth doing and to do it well. A factor can be considered prominent when it has close conjunctions, including conjunctions with an angle. Bill Clinton has Vesta within one degree of his Descendant. Its placement in the seventh house also connects his Vesta to his choice of partners where it fits his very competent and independent wife, Hillary. The close oppositions of Vesta to

Clinton's Ascendant, Mars, Neptune, and East Point can also be a sign of **tension in close relationships**, often some form of the freedom-closeness issue. Compromise is needed to integrate one's own needs and desires with the needs and desires of others.

Clinton's chart is largely what I call a **"reverse zodiac"** with all but three of his standard factors in signs which are in houses that are opposite their position in the natural zodiac. Libra is in the Aries house, Sagittarius in the Gemini house, etc. The few exceptions include Ceres in Aquarius in the Cancer house and Saturn and Mercury in Leo in the Capricorn house. **This major emphasis on the natural polarities of astrology shows a need to integrate those parts of life**. Oppositions can manifest as partnerships. Each represents the opposite end of a polar principle. Each provides what the other needs in order to avoid destructive excesses. But if the individual fails to integrate the polarity, to find a compromise which allows some expression of both ends, a variety of uncomfortable consequences can follow.

Some individuals just alternate between the two ends and feel frustrated all the time, always focused on the end they lack. Using the "freedom-closeness" example, when such individuals are involved in a relationship, they feel trapped, and when they are free to do what they please, they feel lonely.

If we repress one of the conflicting desires, the blocked emotion remains in the subconscious and eventually it is likely to produce illness. Body symptoms are produced by, and body repairs are directed by, the subconscious side of the mind which manages the body. Symptoms are designed to "get our conscious attention." Our subconscious is saying, "Do something! I'm not happy." If the body problem is due to such factors as inadequate food, rest, exercise, shelter, or exposure to harmful chemicals, pollution, etc., we need to take practical action to rectify the situation. (This will be very difficult to do if we are jobless and homeless). If the problem in body functioning is due to blocked emotions, we can try to become aware of the anger, fear, guilt, resentment or whatever is being buried, and deal with it to help the body recover.

Projection is a common manifestation of an opposition if the individual fails to integrate the principles. **In projection, the person consciously identifies with one side of the polarity and is attracted to other people who are identified with**

and will express the opposite side. The danger with projection is that each of the individuals will tend to overdo his or her conscious drive and blame the other for not satisfying personal desires. For example, the person who consciously wants freedom attracts a possessive mate and vice versa. As long as each person thinks that the problem is the other person's fault, there is no solution. When each person realizes that the problem is inside, when they are conscious of their own ambivalence, they can work out a compromise.

The dominance of **air and fire** in Clinton's chart points to an exceptionally creative, versatile mind and verbal fluency. He has the lunar nodes across the third-ninth houses in Gemini-Sagittarius, so both signs and houses show a **perpetual student, natural teacher, writer, and traveler**. Air and fire combinations are usually confident, optimistic, outgoing, sociable, talkative, with a strong sense of humor. Individuals with this emphasis may be super-salesmen or just the "life of the party," sliding through life on wits and charm. But Bill Clinton's chart shows the potential for **serious ambition with Saturn in its own house in Leo**. Saturn and its house symbolize the executive principle. Leo marks the King, and the instinct is strengthened by the presence of Mercury, Pluto and the Sun which are also placed in Leo, the latter representing a double statement when a "planet" is in the sign or house it rules.

The **drive to do something worth doing and to do it well** (letters six and ten in our astrological alphabet) are further strengthened by **Saturn's trine to Vesta**, our Virgo asteroid. **The trine is especially emphasized since it remains exact within one-degree for many years in secondary progressions**. Aspects between earth factors (Saturn and Vesta), show the desire and the capacity to cope with the material world. This capacity is strengthened in Clinton's chart because natal Saturn is in its own earth house and progressed Vesta retrograded back into its own earth house, Remember, the horoscope houses carry the same meanings as the zodiac signs: the first house is like Aries, the sixth house like Virgo, the tenth house like Capricorn. In my experience, the **houses are more important than the signs**. The individual will manifest the principle of the planet through the principle of the house somewhat colored by the principle of the sign.

The fact that Clinton's **earth planets are in earth houses but also in fire signs creates a steamroller combination**. Fire shows the confidence to start while earth shows the willingness to keep going until something is accomplished. Clinton's Moon in Taurus adds a little more earth to his chart, but its position in the eighth house and natal Vesta in the seventh house show the potential for projecting some of his earth into partners. He does have a wife who is financially very successful. It is primarily the Vesta-Saturn trine with natal Saturn and progressed Vesta in their own houses which show Clinton's willingness to work really hard while the Leo planets in the tenth house show his drive to reach the top.

Fire represents our desire for something new or for more which stimulates us to act. We may want to do or to get something we want, or to escape something aversive. We may act on any level; physical, emotional, mental or spiritual. **Earth represents the physical level of manifestation.** Both fire and water are emotional, with **water symbolizing the subconscious or unself-conscious side of the mind** including the habits which largely direct our lives. **Air indicates the cognitive, conscious side of the mind.** As indicated above with the earth factors, the element of a planet's own nature is even more important than its house or sign position. Clinton's water potential is especially indicated by the **tight conjunctions of Neptune, a water planet, with his Ascendant, Mars, and the East Point.** All three of the factors which are closely conjunct Neptune are keys to personal identity, to what we do instinctively from the beginning of life, so **Clinton instinctively does Neptunian things.** The Moon, another water factor, is in the eighth house which carries the water meaning of Scorpio. Ceres is in another water house, the fourth. Pluto, our third water factor in planetary form, is conjunct Mercury. So, despite the preponderance of air and fire in Clinton's chart, he also has the capacity to work hard and to be realistic (earth) and to be sensitive and empathic (water).

When we recalculate Clinton's chart for places other than his birthplace in Hope, Arkansas, we can see some of the potential opportunities and challenges he might face there. His education took him to Yale in New Haven, Connecticut, to Oxford, England, and to Harvard in Cambridge, Massachusetts. He was elected and served repeatedly as governor of Arkansas in Little Rock. As Pres-

ident of the United States, he is living in Washington, D.C. He
not only has to deal with issues in our own country, especially
involving jobs and the economy; he faces challenges and decisions
in the former Yugoslavia, the former Soviet Union, the Near East
(including Iraq, Iran, Israel, Saudi Arabia, Kuwait, Syria, Leba-
non, Jordan, etc.), Europe, Canada, Asia (including North Korea,
Japan, China, India, Pakistan, Viet Nam, etc.), Somalia and the
rest of Africa, Mexico (NAFTA) and the rest of Latin America,
etc., etc. It really boggles the mind to think of the state of the
world, the degree to which the U.S. is considered the uniquely
powerful leader, and the degree to which our deficit limits our
options.

When we evaluate the relationship of a leader with another
country, we calculate the leader's chart for the capital of the country, so we will look at Clinton's horoscope in Baghdad, Belgrade,
Moscow, Mogadishu, Tokyo, Peking, Mexico City, etc.

New Haven, Connecticut (Figure 2)
Starting with New Haven, Connecticut where Bill Clinton met
his future wife, Hillary, we find that his local Ascendant there is
on the midpoint of Chiron/Jupiter, closely conjunct both of them.
It would be hard to imagine a more appropriate combination for a
law education. Letter nine of our astrological alphabet (Jupiter,
Chiron, Sagittarius and the ninth house), represents our search
for a belief system to guide our lives. Based on what we think is
real, true, morally right, and ultimately valuable, we set our goals
and make our choices. In our pursuit of this knowledge, we deal
with institutions of higher education, books, churches, and law
courts. The principle also covers the individuals who function in
these areas; teachers, preachers, writers, lawyers, etc. We may
travel long distances searching for ultimate value, so foreign countries are included in this principle.

The presence of Clinton's Jupiter and Chiron in Libra fits both
his reason for studying law, his political goals, and the fact that
he met his future wife at Yale. Even more precisely, the New Haven
angles include Juno, the marriage asteroid, on the midpoint of
Ascendant/East Point. Juno also squares Clinton's local MC, and
there have been power issues throughout their relationship. Yale
provided a good beginning for Clinton's higher education with his
ninth house Uranus trine his local Ascendant, but he left the school

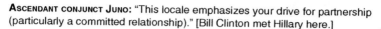

Ascendant conjunct Juno: "This locale emphasizes your drive for partnership (particularly a committed relationship)." [Bill Clinton met Hillary here.]

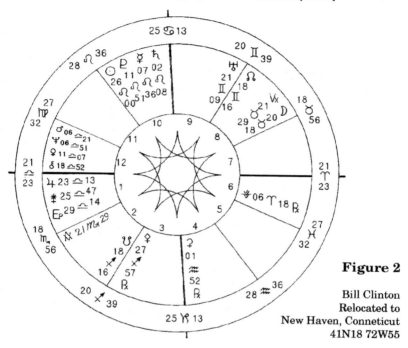

Figure 2

Bill Clinton
Relocated to
New Haven, Conneticut
41N18 72W55

to expand his options. The aspects most often associated with separation are the opposition and the quincunx and Clinton's New Haven Ascendant is quincunx his Moon while his local Antivertex is opposite the Moon and quincunx Uranus.

Oxford, England (Figure 3)

Thanks to a Rhodes scholarship, Bill Clinton was able to attend the world-renowned Oxford University in England. Living in England and visiting the continent offered Clinton both new knowledge and contacts with people who would influence his later life. Appropriately, he has Sagittarius rising in Oxford, the sign of higher education and foreign countries. His Libra Venus is just over one degree from his Oxford MC, and Clinton's P Sun was conjunct Venus when he was elected President. His choice of members to serve in his new Cabinet drew on the friends (professional contacts) he had made in Oxford. However, Clinton's

P Neptune was also square his Oxford East Point and he was disturbed to learn that during the campaign, high officials in the British government had tried to help his opponent for the Presidency, George Bush. Oxford is a relatively short distance from London, the seat of the British government, so the London angles are almost identical. Men working for Bush had been allowed to go through Clinton's records, looking for information which could be used to attack Clinton. When they did not find any negative information, they fabricated rumors that Clinton had secretly dealt with the Communists during a brief sight-seeing trip to Russia which he made while he was in Europe. Britain's

VENUS CONJUNCT MIDHEAVEN: "Professional contacts are accented....Being graceful, charming, pleasant, or practical could be a professional asset."

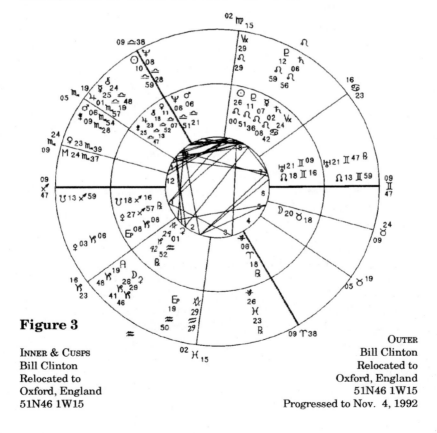

Figure 3

INNER & CUSPS
Bill Clinton
Relocated to
Oxford, England
51N46 1W15

OUTER
Bill Clinton
Relocated to
Oxford, England
51N46 1W15
Progressed to Nov. 4, 1992

Prime Minister, John Major, was not aware of the efforts of some of his fellow officials to influence the U.S. election. He apologized to Clinton and they appear to have achieved a reasonably good relationship.

Little Rock, Arkansas (Figure 4)

Clinton served several terms as governor of Arkansas in the state capital of Little Rock. His local angles there were only shifted one to two degrees from the angles in his birthplace of Hope, Arkansas. However, even a small change can be important if an angle is moved into a one-degree orb aspect to a slow-moving planet. In Clinton's case, his Little Rock Ascendant is even more closely conjunct his natal Mars-Neptune, and his local East Point was shifted about one and a half degrees so P Neptune holds a very long conjunction to it. As what looked like a minor business failure (Whitewater) has escalated in importance enough to produce the

ASCENDANT (OR EAST POINT) CONJUNCT NEPTUNE: "Lack of clarity could lead to fantasies, scandals, or secrets."

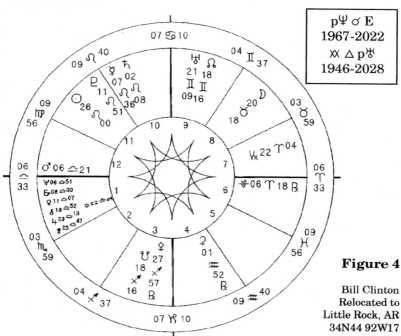

Figure 4

Bill Clinton
Relocated to
Little Rock, AR
34N44 92W17

appointment of a special investigator, as state troopers sell stories of Clinton's Little Rock "affairs" to the highest bidder in the tabloid media, and Clinton is sued by one alleged former mistresses, we are seeing manifestations of that increased prominence of Neptune. Neptune symbolizes our search for infinite love and beauty. We may empathize with others and try to heal the misery of the world, and/or we may seek personal emotional satisfaction through actions that are contrary to the morals of society and/or our own principles.

In astrology, water represents the subconscious side of the mind, the instinct to protect and preserve, to absorb or to be absorbed. Individuals functioning in the water side of life may be focused on self-preservation or on the needs and feelings of others, depending on the individual's faith. Water is the element of psychic ability. At the subconscious level, there is no separation — we are connected and open and therefore vulnerable if we lack faith in the ultimate goodness of the Whole. During the periods (which we all have) when our faith and sense of connectedness is shaky, the normal tendency of water is to focus on personal needs and to seek to satisfy them in secretive or manipulative ways. With faith, in ourselves and/or in the Absolute, we can act openly and we can empathize with others, considering their needs as well as our own.

Our first two fire letters, the Sun and Mars (including the Ascendant, East Point, and Antivertex which carry the same meaning as Mars), show our capacity to have faith in ourselves. Jupiter shows where we seek faith in something beyond our personal power, whether in the Absolute or in a fraction of life such as money, fame, power, pleasure, relationships etc. Turning a small part of life into an ultimate value is a kind of idolatry. We often lose our ideal and are forced to find a "bigger" God. (In ancient astrology, Jupiter ruled both of the signs of faith: Sagittarius as our more conscious belief system and Pisces as our subconscious faith. We now have Neptune as primary key to the Pisces principle, but Jupiter remains a co-ruler). Air represents the conscious side of the mind including the open, verbal expression of information.

Clinton's East Point (fire) in Libra (air) on Neptune (water) shows the challenge, the struggle of personal needs versus concern for the needs of others, and the issue of faith and morality which are based on beliefs. As is usually the case when air and fire are connected to the water, the hidden water is eventually brought into the open and communicated. Clinton is just too much a fire-air person to keep very much hidden for long. Plus, the likelihood that Clinton's personal actions (shown by anything in or ruling the first house) would be brought into the open is supported by another local angle. Clinton's Little Rock Antivertex was shifted enough from its Hope position to produce a very long trine to P Uranus in Gemini in the ninth house. The pattern fits the intense media attention on Clinton, his continuing intellectual brilliance, his learning/teaching seminars which have been devoted to a variety of problem areas including the economy, etc. Reporters continue to be amazed at Clinton's ability to speak without notes or prompts, at his verbal skills, his capacity for learning quickly, his broad grasp of many areas of human concerns.

Washington, D.C. (Figure 5)

As President of the United States functioning in Washington, D.C., Clinton certainly needs his intelligence (air) and his confidence/ faith (fire) to face the challenges in the current world. Most people associate the word "confidence" with Mars and the Sun which indicate one's personal self-confidence while "faith" is reserved for trust in something bigger than individual humans, the Source of everything which most people call God. When all three planetary keys to that traditional concept of faith (Jupiter, Chiron, and Neptune) are in the first house (a basic key to self-confidence) the individual may have supreme faith in himself: "my will is God and I can do anything I want." Alternately, he can feel "I must totally subordinate my own will to God and carry out His Will." When the planets are in Libra, the individual can put his faith in other people and try to please them. Since life is an "and" rather than "either-or," most people with a similar mixture will alternate between the options and/or do a mixture which may seem baffling and incomprehensible to observers. Astrology shows the issues. Individual humans struggle to integrate the often conflicting desires.

Clinton's chart angles in Washington reinforce the importance of faith in his life (which was shown by his natal angles) and highlight the keys to conscious faith. Neptune is moved away from the Ascendant and Chiron is shifted from a one-degree conjunction with the Antivertex to a conjunction with the Washington DC

Ascendant which is exact within 17 minutes of longitude. Jupiter is within two degrees of a conjunction with the local East Point and a square to the local MC. The local Antivertex moves into Scorpio where it opposes the Moon within a little more than two degrees. It is also exactly quincunx the ninth house north lunar node and semisextile Chiron, again connecting the local angles to issues involving faith. Our value hierarchy, our ethics, our judgments are based on our faith. Obviously, Clinton's beliefs and values are playing a major role in history today.

As carriers of the same meaning as Sagittarius, Chiron and Jupiter also point to the increased importance of foreign countries in Clinton's life. From his entry into national politics, Clinton made it clear that he felt his primary responsibility was to solve the U.S. problems at home rather than to try to "fix" the world. Yet, whether or not the charge is fair, he is being blamed for the world's failure to solve the civil war in the former Yugoslavia, the military take-over of Haiti, the challenges of warlords in

Ascendant conjunct Chiron: "Your expectations may be inhumanly high."

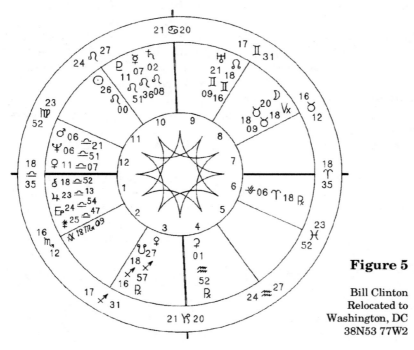

Figure 5

Bill Clinton
Relocated to
Washington, DC
38N53 77W2

Somalia, etc. Clinton's confidence in himself and his own destiny (along with his criticism of Bush's failure to solve the listed world problems) helped to elect him and now they backfire when he is not able to wave a magic wand and resolve insoluble world crises. When his chart is calculated for the capitals of these troubled regions, we can see the tensions though we may not be able to guess the details to come.

Brussels, Belgium (Figure 6)

Many areas will be mentioned only briefly. Brussels, Belgium is an important center for the European Community which some Americans have feared might in time try to limit imports from the U.S. Clinton's first visit to Europe as President when he met with NATO allies was considered a reasonable success despite the tension over Bosnia. In Brussels, Clinton's P south lunar node is exactly on the Ascendant. The south node is first a lesson, usually learned through relationships, and then it points to an area of life where we have an obligation to give something. Many political leaders approved Clinton's formulation of the Partnership for

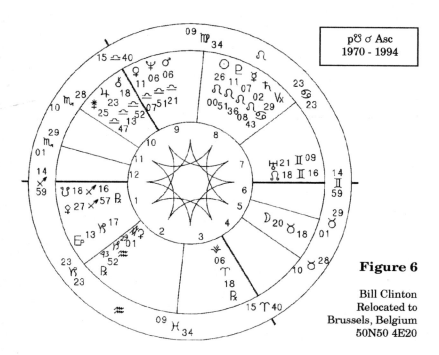

p℧ ♂ Asc
1970 - 1994

Figure 6

Bill Clinton
Relocated to
Brussels, Belgium
50N50 4E20

Peace as a way to gradually integrate the formerly Communist countries of eastern Europe into closer cooperation with western Europe.

Moscow, Russia (Figure 7)

In Moscow, the former center for the USSR and now the capital of Russia which remains an important country, Clinton's Moon is exactly on the IC. He is clearly concerned about the people of Russia who have recently voted against the economic chaos and hardships which have followed the collapse of the former Communist regime. Also, Clinton's Moscow Ascendant in just under 8 Capricorn is square his Vesta, Mars, and Neptune, and quincunx Mercury and P Saturn in Leo. The patterns clearly show tensions involving power and finances. Clinton's planets in Aries-Libra fall in the second and eighth (money) houses in Moscow. His local MC is also octile-trioctile his Mars-Neptune opposition to Vesta. There

Moon conjunct IC: "In this locale, nurturing could become a central focus. Children, pets, plants, or anyone and anything you can take care of may become more important."

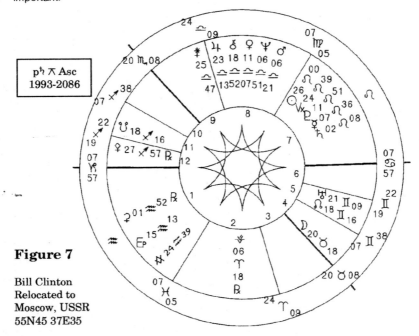

Figure 7

Bill Clinton
Relocated to
Moscow, USSR
55N45 37E35

are no easy solutions in Moscow. As our country struggles to deal with a ballooning deficit and our own financial problems including unemployment, we lack the money to provide the help that Russia needs.

Belgrade, Serbia (Figure 8)

In Belgrade, Serbia, the source of the weapons and nationalism which continue to fuel the war in Bosnia, Clinton's MC is exactly square his natal Saturn in his local seventh house and Ceres in his local first house. The fixed T-square in cardinal houses is a classic portrait of persisting power struggles. A greater emphasis on the cardinal quality (present in this case through the angular houses and Saturn's own nature) will tend to change the outer situation while a greater emphasis on the fixed quality will tend to stay in a state of impasse with periodic explosions.

JUPITER CONJUNCT MIDHEAVEN: "You are working on the balance between your ideals and material reality; optimism and pessimism; faith and fear."

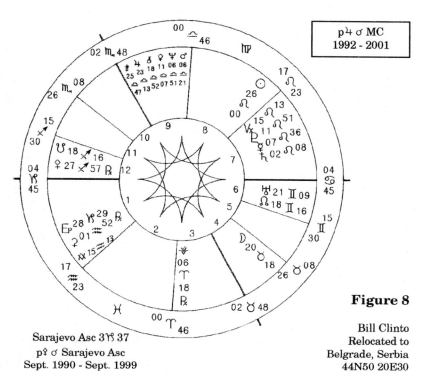

p♃ ♂ MC
1992 - 2001

Figure 8

Bill Clinto
Relocated to
Belgrade, Serbia
44N50 20E30

Sarajevo Asc 3♑ 37
p♀ ♂ Sarajevo Asc
Sept. 1990 - Sept. 1999

Clinton's Libra stellium moves into the ninth house in his Serbian-Bosnian charts, which could mean strong idealism but more talk than action. P Jupiter is also dominant in the charts, exactly conjunct his Belgrade MC and also square Saturn and Ceres. He would like to "save" the people but no country, including ours, wants to send their young men to die in the mountains of Bosnia.

Clinton's Belgrade Ascendant is a few degrees earlier than the angle in Moscow so it holds more widely the squares to Vesta, Mars, and Neptune and the quincunxes to Mercury and P Saturn. It is also exactly trioctile the natal Moon. In Sarajevo, the capital of Bosnia, where Serbian artillery continued daily for months to kill civilians including children, Clinton's P Pallas is exactly on his local Ascendant. Pallas is associated with fair play and social justice. Clinton feels keenly the anguish of the suffering people and he initiated air drops of food to the starving Bosnians and "safe zones" for refugees including air strikes against Serbian planes which attacked such zones, but the war continues to haunt the conscience of the world.

Jerusalem, Israel (Figure 9)
For a while, the Near East looked like one bright spot in a warring world as Israel and the Palestinian Liberation Organization (PLO) negotiated and some self-rule was offered to Palestinians in a limited area. But though a majority of the people involved probably do want peace, a militant minority on both sides continues to attack and counterattack their ancient opponents. Clinton's chart in Jerusalem certainly pinpoints the issue but leaves the outcome in real doubt. When he was inaugurated as President, Clinton's P Moon was conjunct P Ceres and both were on his Jerusalem Ascendant within one degree. The combination is a strongly nurturing one, and it was at Clinton's invitation that Yasser Arafat and Yitzhak Rabin shook hands in front of the White House and the cameras of the world. But continuing tensions are also shown with P Pluto holding an opposition to Clinton's Jerusalem East Point for years and his local P Ascendant in 1994 conjunct Vesta and opposite Mars. The latter aspects could show a real shift in the level of cooperation versus violence, but the shift could go in either direction. Horoscopes show issues. The details depend on the actions of individuals.

Baghdad, Iraq (Figure 10)

Iraq is still being held under quarantine by the United Nations, so the United States does not have primary responsibility for preventing Saddam Hussein from rebuilding his armaments. That should be one less headache for Clinton, and his chart in Baghdad suggests that Iraq would be a headache if he had to add it to his responsibilities. Clinton's natal Sun is exactly square his Baghdad MC and his Ascendant there is opposite the midpoint of his P Saturn/P Pluto. Clinton's Baghdad Antivertex quincunx his Mars-Neptune is also not very reassuring, nor was his P Mars approaching a square to his natal Baghdad Ascendant when he became

DESCENDANT (OR WEST POINT) CONJUNCT PLUTO: "You may draw in power trippers, manipulators, vengeful people, addicts, or the chronically abused."

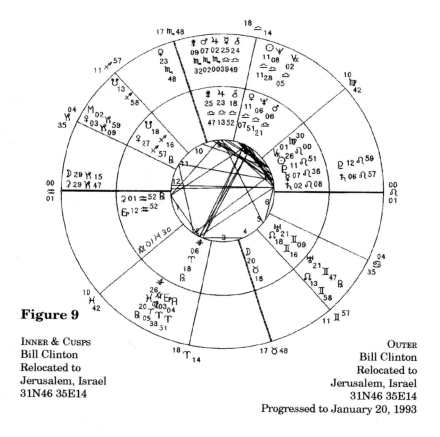

Figure 9

INNER & CUSPS
Bill Clinton
Relocated to
Jerusalem, Israel
31N46 35E14

OUTER
Bill Clinton
Relocated to
Jerusalem, Israel
31N46 35E14
Progressed to January 20, 1993

President. P Juno was already holding a square to this local Ascendant when Clinton was elected. Juno, like Pluto, can be a partner or an enemy if we cannot work out a compromise that shares power and pleasure. We do seem to need the U.N. in our combative world, but U.S. forces are still very involved in Iraq. As Clinton's P Mars moved closer to the square to his Baghdad Ascendant, our own military planes mistakenly shot down a plane full of U.N. personal, including several Americans.

ASCENDANT CONFLICT SATURN: "This region highlights your personal confrontation with power...Clashes with authorities are possible."

ASCENDANT CONFLICT PLUTO: "In this area, power struggle potentials are highlighted....Anger, resentment, violence..."

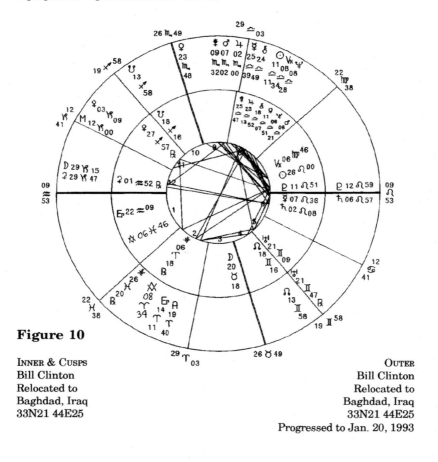

Figure 10

INNER & CUSPS
Bill Clinton
Relocated to
Baghdad, Iraq
33N21 44E25

OUTER
Bill Clinton
Relocated to
Baghdad, Iraq
33N21 44E25
Progressed to Jan. 20, 1993

Mogadishu, Somalia (Figure 11)

The U.N. is also about to take over full responsibility for the relief and peace-making efforts in Mogadishu, Somalia, and prospects in that suffering country look increasingly troubled after the U.S. pulls out. Clinton's natal Sun also squares his MC in Mogadishu, though not as closely as his Baghdad MC. On the positive side, his Mogadishu Ascendant forms a grand air trine to Uranus in Gemini and several planets in late Libra. Clinton's local P MC quincunx P Pluto and P north lunar node (to form a yod) plus P

PLUTO [PROGRESSED] CONFLICT MIDHEAVEN [PROGRESSED]: "Power struggles with authorities or business partners. ...Thoroughness (too much or too little) could become an issue....Know when to release and move on."

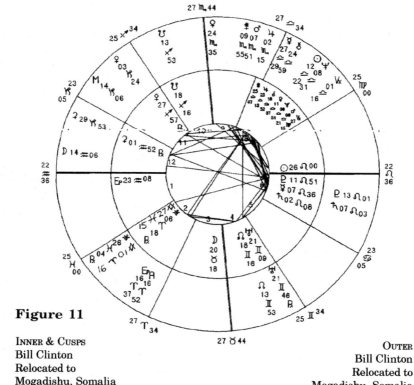

Figure 11

INNER & CUSPS
Bill Clinton
Relocated to
Mogadishu, Somalia
2N04 45E22

OUTER
Bill Clinton
Relocated to
Mogadishu, Somalia
2N04 45E22
Progressed to March 31, 1994

Mercury quincunx his P Vesta which is conjunct his local Anti-vertex, would fit a separation from the scene, or at least a major change in the details of handling it. There are enough stress aspects, including Clinton's natal Venus and P Sun octile his Mog-adishu MC and P Venus square the local Ascendant and East Point when he was elected, to throw doubt on the harmony suggested by the air trines. The mixed aspects suggest a lot of talk (air) but continuing dissatisfaction with the outcome of the effort.

Kabul, Afghanistan (Figure 12)

Moving on toward the east with Clinton's chart, we find his Uranus exactly on the IC in Kabul, Afghanistan. P Pluto is in and P Sun is moving into quincunxes to his Ascendant there, forming a yod to signal probable policy changes. I suspect that these aspects mark the residual results of the Reagan policy of arming and training the Afghan rebels. Some of these arms and the train-

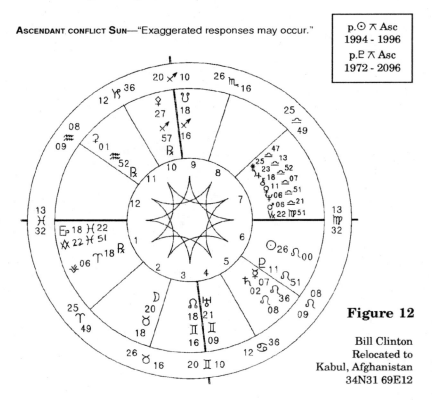

ASCENDANT CONFLICT SUN—"Exaggerated responses may occur."

p.☉ ⊼ Asc
1994 - 1996
p.♇ ⊼ Asc
1972 - 2096

Figure 12

Bill Clinton
Relocated to
Kabul, Afghanistan
34N31 69E12

ing by our CIA have come back to haunt the U.S. during Clinton's term, as in the New York bombing of the World Trade Center.

Saigon, Viet Nam (Figure 13)

Still further to the east, the U.S. is currently returning to normal diplomatic relations with Viet Nam. Other countries, especially western Europe and Japan, have been moving in to take advantage of new business opportunities and U.S. business leaders are eager to join the party, but the relatives of servicemen still "missing in action," (MIAs), are not happy. The former capitals of North and South Viet Nam are Hanoi and Saigon. Clinton's natal Saturn squares his Ascendant in both cities within one degree, Ceres squares and P Jupiter opposes Clinton's Ascendant in Saigon within one degree and the aspects are present for his Hanoi Ascendant within two degrees. He is in a double-bind between

ASCENDANT CONFLICT JUPITER: "This region may lead you to question your ideals, goals, philosophies, moral principles, or world view."

ASCENDANT CONFLICT NEPTUNE: "This region may emphasize challenges regarding your idealistic images."

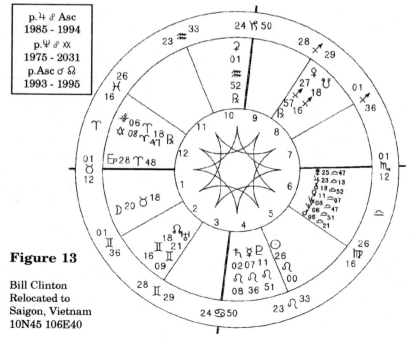

Figure 13

Bill Clinton
Relocated to
Saigon, Vietnam
10N45 106E40

the people (Ceres), the powerful business leaders (Saturn), and moral issues dealing with joint resources including investment (progressed Jupiter in Scorpio). Clinton's P Jupiter is exactly on his Saigon Descendant, P Neptune is opposite his Saigon Antivertex, P Hanoi Ascendant is on his Uranus, and P Saigon Ascendant is on his north lunar node. Despite the fixed cross which can lead to an impasse, there is enough fire in these aspects to point to change and we are already doing business in Viet Nam.

Beijing, China (Figure 14)
We have been doing business with China since Nixon opened the door to renewed relationships, but with a Democratic President in the White House, the U.S. is more serious about China's abysmal record of abuse of human rights. Much of China's growing prosperity is based on its exports to the U.S. and these are being threatened if China continues its harsh treatment of political dissidents. In Beijing, Clinton's IC is on the midpoint of his natal and progressed Saturn, conjunct both of them within three degrees. Ceres conjuncts and P Jupiter squares his Beijing MC within three degrees. His natal Sun squares his Beijing Ascendant within one degree. P Neptune is quincunx his local East Point within one degree and his local East Point squares Clinton's Mercury and P Saturn within two degrees. His Beijing P MC moved into a square to Clinton's Uranus within his first year in office. On the positive side, Clinton's natal Sun trines his Beijing Antivertex, his local MC is trine his natal Mars and Neptune and sextile his Vesta, and his P Venus reached his Beijing Descendant in 1994. Conjunctions are the strongest aspects in astrology so Venus conjunct the Descendant is especially important. Money is power. U.S. big businesses such as Boeing do not want to lose the Chinese market. Just about the time that Clinton's P Venus reached his Beijing Descendant, pressure from big business led to Clinton extending the favorable tariff regulations to China, keeping it in the class called MFN or "most favored nation." However, China's denial of human rights is likely to continue to be a problem.

Tokyo, Japan (Figure 15)
The U.S. is also engaged in negotiations with Japan over exports. The major issue in Japan involves the struggle to open their markets to foreign companies in order to cut our huge trade deficit. Clinton's natal Sun opposes his Tokyo MC within two degrees

and his lunar nodes fall on his local Ascendant/Descendant. He also has trines to both of these major angles from some of his Libra planets, so we can be sure of much continued talk whether or not there are any real changes of action. At least there is some potential for progress with Clinton's Tokyo East Point trine Ceres, sextile Saturn, and quincunx P Jupiter, and his Tokyo Antivertex quincunx Venus though it squares Pluto. His P Tokyo East Point

DESCENDANT CONJUNCT [PROGRESSED] VENUS: "Beauty, sensuality, or money could become more central in your relationships."

[PROGRESSED] JUPITER CONFLICT MIDHEAVEN: "Authorities may challenges your ideals and goals in this region."

CERES CONJUNCT MIDHEAVEN: "...ways of blending caretaking [human rights] and professional achievements" [U.S. businesses making money]

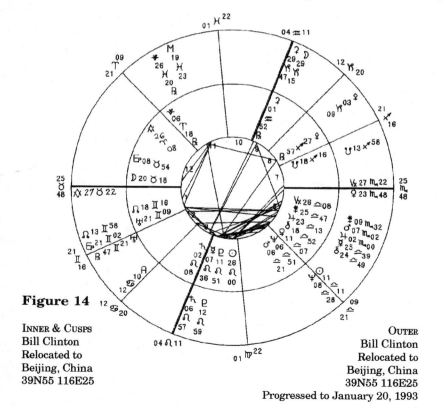

Figure 14

INNER & CUSPS
Bill Clinton
Relocated to
Beijing, China
39N55 116E25

OUTER
Bill Clinton
Relocated to
Beijing, China
39N55 116E25
Progressed to January 20, 1993

also squared Venus and P Sun when Clinton became President, and his P Tokyo Ascendant squared Juno and P Mercury. These squares are between the signs of Cancer and Libra which suggest a continuing relationship that is struggling with issues of personal security (a water principle) versus equality/fair play (an air principle).

Pyongyang, North Korea (Figure 16)

Korea may represent the most serious challenge facing Clinton in Asia. North Korea is suspected of having developed at least one atom bomb and it poses a real threat to South Korea where U.S.

SUN CONJUNCT IC: "Public recognition is possible. You may feel more ego-invested in...patriotism."

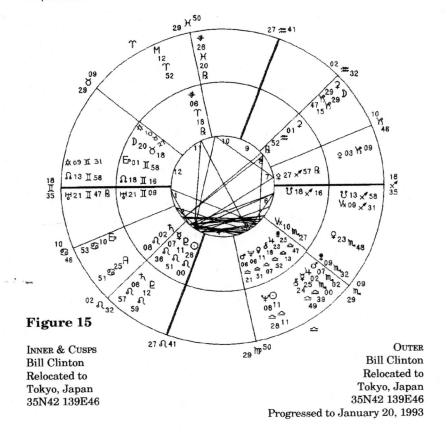

Figure 15

INNER & CUSPS
Bill Clinton
Relocated to
Tokyo, Japan
35N42 139E46

OUTER
Bill Clinton
Relocated to
Tokyo, Japan
35N42 139E46
Progressed to January 20, 1993

troops remain as protectors of freedom. Clinton's Ascendants in the capitals of the two countries are almost identical with both in six Gemini forming trines to Mars and Neptune and sextiles to Vesta, Mercury, and P Saturn. These aspects suggest that the situation will be resolved peacefully, though a P Mars quincunx to both Ascendants is less reassuring.

The latter aspect is a good illustration of the fact that an aspect can be expressed in more than one way. If the U.S. were pulled into another Korean war, we would be defending one of these capitals against the aggression of the other. The Mars aspect would fit both potentials.

PLUTO CONJUNCT IC: "You may have the opportunity to come to terms with manipulation, power plays, passive-aggressive behavior....as public agendas."

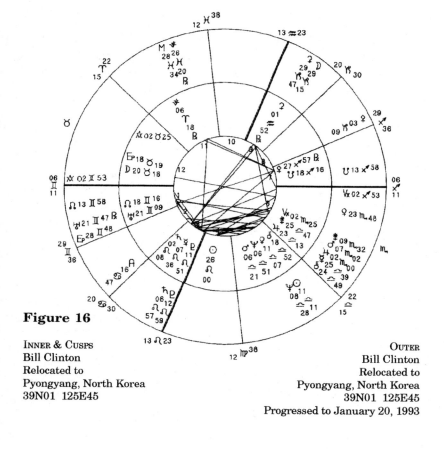

Figure 16

INNER & CUSPS
Bill Clinton
Relocated to
Pyongyang, North Korea
39N01 125E45

OUTER
Bill Clinton
Relocated to
Pyongyang, North Korea
39N01 125E45
Progressed to January 20, 1993

Clinton's MCs in the two cities are just over one degree apart, but it a crucial difference. Clinton's P Pluto is exactly opposite his MC in Pyongyang, North Korea, and not within the one-degree orb required for progressions to his MC in Seoul, South Korea. If our military power is engaged, the "smart" bombs the U.S. plans to send to South Korea will land on North Korea. But Clinton's progressed angles look more like continued talk than violent action. When he was elected, his Pyongyang MC and the East Points in both capitals were forming a T-square to his natal Pallas. These aspects have ended and Clinton's P Sun started a trine to his Pyongyang MC in the spring of 1994. On the conflict side, the Vertex axis in both Korean capitals completes a grand cross with Clinton's long T-square of P Jupiter to Saturn and Ceres. There is always the danger that Jupiter could be manifested as overconfidence and poor judgment which can meet a rude awakening from Saturn consequences. North Korea's power-driven dictator may be gradually shifting power to his son and, unfortunately, the son is said to be more reckless than the father. The recent visit of former President Jimmy Carter to North Korea and subsequent peace talks between the two Koreas has temporarily defused the escalating talk of war.

Port-au-Prince, Haiti (Figure 17)

Much closer to home, another Clinton headache involves the military rulers of Haiti who continue in major abuses of the human rights of their citizens. The economic sanctions imposed by many countries mostly hurt the poor people of Haiti, but U.S. citizens are no more eager to die for them than they are to die to save the Moslems in Bosnia. We keep saying that despite our military power, we are not the policemen of the world; that we have enough problems at home with unemployment and crime and the budget deficit. Clinton's chart in Port-au-Prince, Haiti puts natal Juno and P Mercury and P Chiron on the Ascendant and square the MC. The combination has so far manifested as a troubled conscience, tighter sanctions, and more talk than action. I suspect that most Americans prefer it that way. But Juno is too much like Pluto to rule out war and death. As this book is in its final stages, the flood of refugees is escalating and the war drums are sounding louder. The one hopeful applying aspect is P Venus coming into a trine to Clinton's Port-au-Prince MC. There has been talk of "buying off" the military dictators of Haiti, to persuade them to leave peacefully. We probably couldn't match what they are making by running drugs into the U.S., but our massing war ships around the island might tip the balance.

The preceding examples demonstrate the way in which local angles can point to issues likely to be faced by an individual in a place other than the birth place. But it is obvious that the aspects point to a range of potentials. Clinton met his future wife where Juno was on the midpoint of two angles which symbolize personal identity in action. As has been said before, Juno can be expressed in an intense love relationship. But passionate love also common-

JUNO CONFLICT MIDHEAVEN: "Power struggles (at work and home) and competition could emerge over issues of shared resources, pleasures, possessions, and finances."

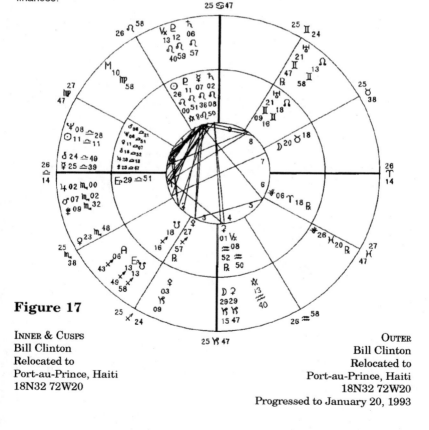

Figure 17

<table>
<tr><td>INNER & CUSPS
Bill Clinton
Relocated to
Port-au-Prince, Haiti
18N32 72W20</td><td>OUTER
Bill Clinton
Relocated to
Port-au-Prince, Haiti
18N32 72W20
Progressed to January 20, 1993</td></tr>
</table>

ly includes the need to face issues of power and pleasure. In Haiti, where Clinton's Juno is on one of those angles, the Ascendant, the power-struggle side of Juno is being manifested. Clinton's chart has both harmonious and stress aspects to the local angles in most of the geographic areas which we have considered, and often both potentials are operating, simultaneously or at different times.

Dallas, Texas (Figure 18)
In Dallas, Texas, the headquarters of Perot, Clinton's Ascendant is sextile natal Saturn, trine Ceres, and semisextile P Jupiter. During 1992, Clinton's Dallas P MC was sextile Chiron and the

ASCENDANT [PROGRESSED ANTIVERTEX] CONJUNCT [PROGRESSED] PALLAS: "Competition—or teamwork—may move into high focus."

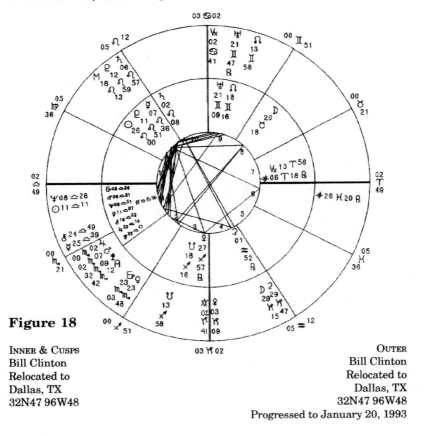

Figure 18

INNER & CUSPS
Bill Clinton
Relocated to
Dallas, TX
32N47 96W48

OUTER
Bill Clinton
Relocated to
Dallas, TX
32N47 96W48
Progressed to January 20, 1993

north lunar node. Most political commentators think that Perot helped Clinton win the Presidency. But most of the time since then, Perot has attacked Clinton's policies - especially during the battle over NAFTA (the North American Free Trade Agreement). Clinton's P Pallas, our most political asteroid, has been conjunct his Dallas P Antivertex and both have been square to his Dallas Ascendant and East Point and opposite his Dallas MC. Other current aspects include Clinton's local P Ascendant square his P Pluto for the personal battles. The helpful P MC aspects to the nodes ended early in 1994, and the sextile to Chiron is also separating while P Pallas and the Dallas and Little Rock P Antivertices are moving to square Clinton's natal Ascendant and later his natal Mars/Neptune/Vesta.

Mexico City, Mexico (Figure 19)
Clinton's Mexico City angles are only about two degrees from his angles in Dallas except for the Antivertex. In areas close to the equator, the Antivertex can make extreme shifts, at times to the right half of the horoscope in contrast to its normal range from the eleventh to the second house. Clinton's Antivertex in Mexico City is in his local sixth house in 25 Pisces. When NAFTA was signed and went into effect in the winter of 1993-4, P Vesta was conjunct that local Antivertex and formed a double quincunx (yod) to Clinton's natal Sun and his Juno and P Mercury. Both Vesta and the sixth house are keys to Virgo (work and workers), so the aspects fit the estrangement between Clinton and many U.S. workers. Time (and the future decisions of U.S. factory owners) will tell whether the anxiety and anger of many Democratic voters will be validated and be translated into political action. The Vesta message is repeated by the close quincunx of Clinton's Mexico City MC to both his natal and P Ceres. Ceres symbolizes the nurturing side of Virgo, including protection for workers as well as their services to others. Though the mainline economists deny it, NAFTA looks like a gift to the power elite which may prove to be at the expense of ordinary workers.

Transiting Pluto is nearing the end of its passage through its own sign. Obviously, we have not learned to express its positive potential. We have not learned to recognize when we have enough, when to compromise, or how to share resources, possessions, pleasure, and power. Individualism and competition are increasingly glorified at the expense of cooperation. The U.S. and the world are dealing with the issues of the cardinal and fixed dilemmas, trying to find a way to harmonize personal rights and needs with the rights and needs of others. Bill Clinton's chart fits the issues of our times. His life is a morality play being witnessed from Little Rock to the White House, to theaters worldwide.

Principles — Not Details
William Clinton has been in office as President of the U.S. for over a year as this book is being readied for the printer. We have

CERES CONFLICT MIDHEAVEN: "You may feel torn between ... humble service [workers] versus executive power." [the elite]

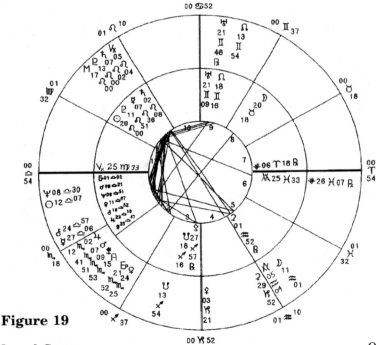

Figure 19

INNER & CUSPS
Bill Clinton
Relocated to
Mexico City, Mexico
19N24 99W 9

OUTER
Bill Clinton
Relocated to
Mexico City, Mexico
19N24 99W 9
Progressed to January 1, 1994

relocated his chart to countries where a variety of events have occurred and where future challenges are also likely. The balance of the examples offered here are from individuals who have had major events in regions other than their birth places.

When we discuss events, it is important to remind ourselves that astrology is a psychological system. This recognition is still spreading slowly through different astrological subspecialties. It is most widely accepted in the interpretation of natal charts where increasing numbers of astrologers are realizing that astrology deals with principles, each of which can be manifested in many different ways depending on our choices. Artistic talent can be directed into painting, poetry, music, dancing, gardening, photography, etc., depending on personal interests. However, practicing astrologers sometimes forget the "open-endedness" of the principles when they are projecting ahead. Partly, this is due to pressure from clients who are more likely to want to be told "what **events** are going to **happen** in the future" rather than "what **psychological issues** the client will face in the future."

Our topic in this book, the use of "local houses," is one of our "newer" subspecialties. As already noted, a chart is calculated for a residence (or even a temporary visit) in a location other than one's birth. Increasing numbers of astrologers are discovering the value of local houses, but the common interpretations of such a relocated chart still tend to use the ancient "good-bad" descriptions of the planets. Both natal and progressed planetary aspects to local house cusps are important, but the associated events in the life depend on individual choices, including the subconscious "choices" made by habits. Of course the consequences of past actions are also always part of the picture. Unfortunately, there are still astrologers who assume that a location which puts Jupiter conjunct a major angle is bound to bring fortunate conditions while putting Saturn on an angle is a guarantee of disaster. Some of the following charts were chosen to illustrate the inadequacy of such simple "good-bad" astrology.

Stormin' Norman (Figure 20)

We know that General Norman Schwarzkopf was born in Trenton, New Jersey on August 22, 1934 at 4:45 AM EDT, thanks to Lois Rodden who has his birth certificate. His horoscope illustrates the inaccuracy of the traditional belief that the twelfth house is always negative. The most strongly occupied house in Schwarzkopf's natal chart is the twelfth where he has the East Point, Mars, Pluto, Venus, and the mean position of the south lunar node. The nodes fall on the Ascendant-Descendant axis within one degree with the mean nodes on the cadent side and the true nodes on the angular side. As most citizens of the U.S. will remember, Schwarzkopf was a successful general throughout his life, but he is best known as the commander of the extremely successful Gulf War against Iraq in January-February 1991.

When Schwarzkopf's horoscope is calculated for Baghdad, Iraq (Figure 21), his twelfth house stellium is moved into the ninth house (with its association to foreign countries among many other meanings), and his Leo Mercury and Sun as well as Neptune in Virgo move from the natal first and second houses to his local tenth house. He was not only the supreme power in his role as

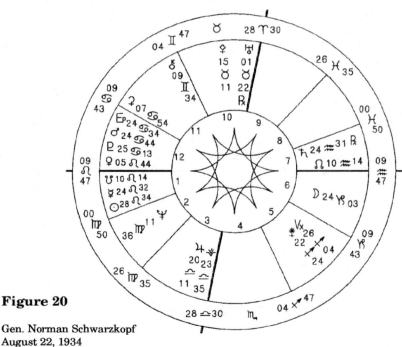

Figure 20

Gen. Norman Schwarzkopf
August 22, 1934
4:45AM EDT
Trenton, NJ
40N13 74W77

commanding general in the Near East; he was also a Leo show-man in his news conferences with media representatives from all over the world. Natal Mercury, the key to information carried by the media, is just over one degree from his Baghdad MC.

Exactly opposite his natal Mercury, Schwarzkopf's natal Saturn is conjunct his IC within just over a one degree orb. His local IC is within one degree of the midpoint of natal and progressed Saturn which is equivalent to an exact conjunction of all three

SATURN CONJUNCT IC: "You probably feel safest when in control. You may take on ...power...with the public, homeland. ...Adversarial relationships with authority figures..."

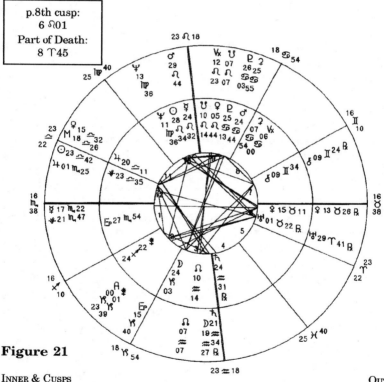

p.8th cusp:
6 ♌01
Part of Death:
8 ♈45

Figure 21

INNER & CUSPS
Gen. Norman Schwarzkopf
Relocated to
Baghdad, Iraq
33N21 44E25

OUTER
Gen. Norman Schwarzkopf
Relocated to
Baghdad, Iraq
33N21 44E25
Progressed to January 16, 1991

factors. The Baghdad IC and Saturn are both octile the local Part of Death within one degree using the Placidus house system. The "traditional" reading of those aspects would predict terrible disaster for Schwarzkopf in that area, very possibly his own death. Instead, the armed forces which he led inflicted that disaster on Baghdad and the citizens of Iraq. The principle of Saturn, the **law** and the karmic consequences of past actions, were clearly in effect, but Schwarzkopf was the instrument of the karmic law, not its victim. He came home hailed as a hero, retired with a comfortable pension, and continued to make money on a book and lectures. Can you imagine how he would react if he read an astrological pronouncement warning him to stay away from any area where he had Saturn on an angle?

During the last two months of the military build-up before the war, Schwarzkopf had his progressed Baghdad MC trine his P Moon in Aquarius in the local third house. His P Mercury was conjunct his natal local Ascendant throughout the preparation for and the conduct of the brief war. The progressed aspects repeat the message in the relocated natal chart, the enormous media attention focused on Schwarzkopf. Other aspects to local angles included P Ascendant sextile P Jupiter and trine Uranus, appropriate aspects for the much publicized high-tech equipment used in the war. P local East Point was sextile the local Ascendant and trine Pallas but square P Venus. Venus and Pallas were quincunx each other. These aspects suggest inner harmony in personal decisions and actions. The two angles are both keys to identity so they are similar to having Mars sextile Mars. However the aspects to Venus and Pallas indicate a mixture of tension and cooperation from partners.

Using the Placidus house system, Schwarzkopf's P eighth house cusp was conjunct the P south lunar node which represents a lesson. The eighth cusp, like Pluto, Juno, and Scorpio, includes an association with death among many other possible details. P Vesta, a key to job and/or health efficiency, (a physical body that functions effectively), was conjunct Schwarzkopf's Kuwait Ascendant as well as square P Saturn. P Moon moved into a conjunction with P Saturn and a square to Vesta and the Kuwait Ascendant during the war. Despite some harmonious aspects to his local angles, I suspect that many traditional astrologers would have advised Schwarzkopf to avoid any risks while he had P Moon on Saturn square Vesta, and not to go to the Near East.

Obviously, war is a stressful activity, even for the winners. We do have an aspect that fits the traditional association of Jupiter with success if we go to midpoints. The midpoint of the progressed MCs in Baghdad and Kuwait was on natal Jupiter.

Money Matters (Figure 22)

Turning to another power figure in the world, Michel Camdessus was born in Bayonne, France on May 1, 1933 at 1 AM. Camdessus is the head of the International Monetary Fund, (IMF) which is one of the most powerful international agencies in the world of finance along with the World Bank and the Bank of International Settlements (BIS). Traditionally, a European is chosen to be the head of the IMF while the World Bank is headed by an American, but both institutions have their headquarters in Washington DC.

In his natal chart, Camdessus has a grand trine in earth signs which includes his Jupiter in thirteen Virgo, his Ascendant in twelve Capricorn, and his Sun in ten and Venus in twelve Tau-

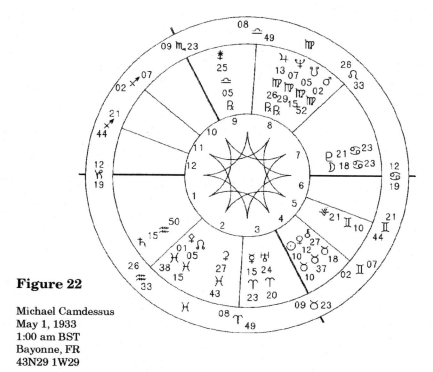

Figure 22

Michael Camdessus
May 1, 1933
1:00 am BST
Bayonne, FR
43N29 1W29

rus, both closely conjunct the IC in nine Taurus. Mars, south lunar node, and Neptune are more widely involved in the grand trine, placed in early Virgo in the eighth house with Jupiter. Letter eight of our alphabet of astrology is associated with all forms of joint resources, including debts, taxes, inheritance, return on investment, etc. Taurus is associated with personal pleasure in the physical world, including personal income and possessions. Capricorn is related to the law, bureaucratic systems, and authority figures. Earth trines point to an individual who has the ability to cope effectively with the physical world. In addition to his Capricorn Ascendant, Camdessus has Saturn in his first house to reinforce his identification with power. His natal chart clearly fits his position in the world.

DESCENDANT CONJUNCT VENUS: "...material resources are highlighted. ...money could become more central in your relationships."

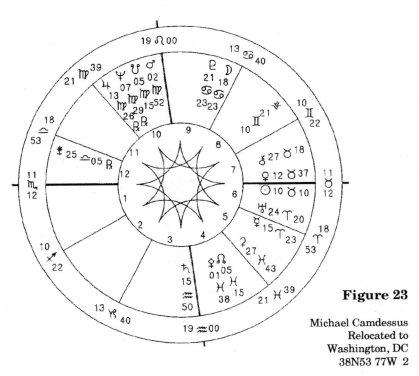

Figure 23

Michael Camdessus
Relocated to
Washington, DC
38N53 77W 2

When we calculate the Camdessus chart for the IMF headquarters in Washington DC (Figure 23), his eighth house Virgo stellium is moved into the local tenth house, an appropriate pattern for the power he acquired when his job took him to Washington. Camdessus' local Ascendant was changed to eleven Scorpio, putting his Sun-Venus on the Descendant. Saturn is on his local IC within just over three degrees, producing a grand cross in fixed signs with the MC at nineteen Leo. The pattern fits his challenging job in view of the financial tensions in the world during Camdessus' term of office. We have seen escalating debt and a critical recession while the rich have become richer and the poor more desperate. But Washington brought increased power to Camdessus, not personal disaster. How would he react if he were told by astrology that he should avoid the U.S. capitol?

The Divine Miss M (Figure 24)

Success with an angular Saturn is not limited to men. Bette Midler was born in Honolulu, Hawaii on December 1, 1945 at 14:19 HST. The data is from Lois Rodden. Midler's natal chart is strongly fire with Aries rising, Mars and Pluto in Leo, a stellium in Sagittarius including Sun, Ceres, Mercury, and Vesta, as well as Jupiter and Chiron, (planetary forms of letter nine), closely conjunct the Descendant. She is clearly a warm, dramatic, expressive individual. Her wide square from Saturn in Cancer to the Ascendant is a conflict aspect, but conflicts may be helpful in preventing problems stemming from excesses. The earth-water caution of Saturn (an earth planet in a water sign and house) represents common sense and security instincts which have probably helped to curb what could have been an overdose of fire.

Midler's initial fame began in 1966 in New York where she has Saturn conjunct her Ascendant within less than two degrees. Her local angles in New York also put Neptune, a potential key to creative imagination and artistic talent, just over one degree from her IC. Her Leo Mars and Pluto shifted to the first house where Pluto formed a trine to her local MC. Would a well-intentioned astrologer have been reassured by the Pluto trine or would Midler have been advised to stay away from New York where she had both Saturn and Neptune on angles, the two planets most feared by traditional astrology?

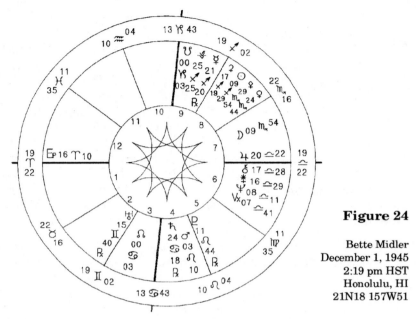

Figure 24

Bette Midler
December 1, 1945
2:19 pm HST
Honolulu, HI
21N18 157W51

ASCENDANT CONJUNCT SATURN: "Your career, status, power…could become a major focus."

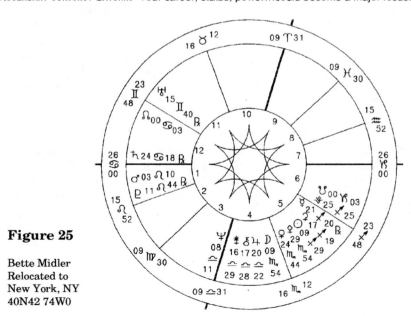

Figure 25

Bette Midler
Relocated to
New York, NY
40N42 74W0

A Fiery Armageddon (Figure 26)

We shift now from a successful general, financial executive, and Broadway star to a leader whose life fit the traditional doom which many astrologers still associate with an angular Saturn. The data for David Koresh comes from his mother, Bonnie Haldeman, who gave the birth time to Joyce Mason. Joyce passed the information on to Lois Rodden who printed it in her monthly publication, *Data News*. David's birth name was Vernon Howell and he was born on August 17, 1959 at 8:49 AM CST in Houston, TX. Natal Saturn was one degree and 13 minutes from his IC, the exact distance between Schwarzkopf's Saturn and his Baghdad IC though Koresh (to use the name he adopted for himself) had Saturn on the third house side of the angle.

SATURN CONJUNCT IC: "You may take on excessive burdens or power within the home, family." [cult members]

"Adversarial relationships with authority figures are possible."

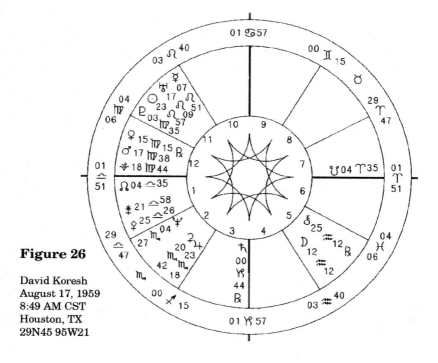

Figure 26

David Koresh
August 17, 1959
8:49 AM CST
Houston, TX
29N45 95W21

Since the MC carries the same meaning as Saturn and its sign, Capricorn, an MC opposite Saturn is like Saturn opposed to itself. Obviously, the aspect shows an issue involving power, the LAW, and the consequences of how we have been handling the laws of nature, society etc. But as we can see in just a few examples, an individual with this position may be wielding the law in an authority position (Schwarzkopf and Camdessus), or fighting it like Koresh, or trying vainly to run away from it. Escape is not possible. Eventually, the law brings the consequences of how we have handled it — Karma, to use an eastern term.

In the case of David Koresh, it is particularly significant that his move to the Waco area of Texas (Figure 27) made a relatively small change in his chart houses but one with momentous meaning. Saturn was retrograde when Koresh was born and it never left the first degree of its own sign, Capricorn. The move to Waco was just far enough to the west to move the IC back to zero Capricorn, so P Saturn remained exactly on the local IC, opposite the local MC, all of Koresh's life. He remained in a perpetual battle with the laws of the society and its authority figures at the same

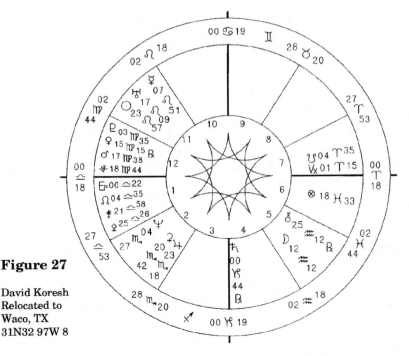

Figure 27

David Koresh
Relocated to
Waco, TX
31N32 97W 8

time that he maintained almost total power over his followers who shared his "home" in the cult compound. The male followers were not just kept in the position of subordinate children; they were humans while he was "God." The women, including girls as young as eleven years old, were his "wives" while the men in the group, including the former husbands of some of the "wives," were forced to remain celibate.

Secondary progressed aspects involving outer, slow-moving planets are often ignored by astrologers as if something which moves only a degree or so during one's life could not be important. If the astrologer is only interested in predicting events in the life, it is true that events involving the slow planets are most likely when faster-moving progressed planets or angles come into aspect with the slow ones. But if the slow planets at birth are aspecting other planets or angles within one degree, they will continue to hold those aspects for many years - sometimes, for the whole life - and that is vitally important information to anyone who wants to understand the individual. **Those long-term progressed aspects are basic keys to the foundation principles of the individual's character!** They are among the most useful items of information in a horoscope. Harmony aspects show natural talents, desires that are complementary and reinforce each other, while stress aspects show conflicting desires where we need to integrate, to find appropriate outlets for the contradictory desires. The progressions show the evolving stages of the character pictured in the natal chart. Long-lasting progressed aspects mark enduring character tendencies. We lose a lot if we ignore them.

The houses of a horoscope change as the earth rotates around its axis, so every day the houses turn past all of the planets and signs. Though most astrologers use only a single point for the MC which is unaffected by the latitude of birth, there are two possible auxiliary Ascendants which, like the Ascendant, are the intersections of "great circles" that go through the center of the earth. These additional Ascendants, the East Point and the Antivertex, can be in different signs from each other and from the "traditional" Ascendant. Twice each day, as the Ascendant moves into zero Aries and zero Libra, the three "Ascendants" merge so at zero Aries and zero Libra they are identical, regardless of birth latitude. The Waco houses for Koresh are shifted back enough so that his local Ascendant and East Point are both zero Libra and his local Antivertex is just over one degree of Libra. Therefore, his P Saturn not only had a lifetime opposition to the Waco MC; it had lifetime squares to all three Waco Ascendants. The Ascendant, like Mars and Aries, represents one's sense of personal identity; our right and power to do what we please. These aspects show Koresh's intractable struggle between personal will (letter one of our astrological alphabet) and the limits of personal will and power (letter ten).

The Branch Davidians are an offshoot of the Seventh Day Adventist church which was formerly noted for its belief in the

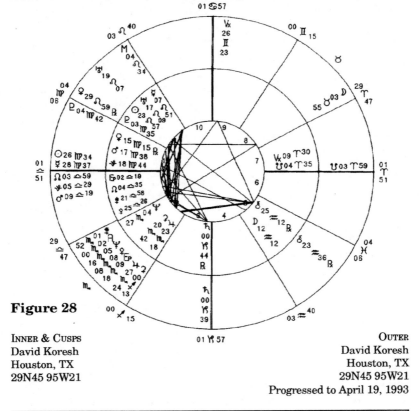

Figure 28

INNER & CUSPS		OUTER
David Koresh	01 ℞ 57	David Koresh
Houston, TX		Houston, TX
29N45 95W21		29N45 95W21
		Progressed to April 19, 1993

Waco Angles		
p.A 00♏08	Part of Death	Davida 08♏01
p.℞ 20✗01	Houston: 19✗26	p.Davida 16♏02
p.E 07♏35	Waco: 15✗59	
p.M 02♌56		

prophecies of Armageddon, a violent destruction of the earth described in the *Book of Revelation*. The Davidians were founded by a Bulgarian immigrant named Victor Houteff who broke off with the mother church over his interpretation of the books of *Ezekiel* and *Revelation*. In 1935, Houteff moved from Los Angeles to Waco, Texas where he established the world headquarters of the sect. David Koresh was raised as a Seventh Day Adventist in Tyler, Texas, but he was thrown out of the local church after a variety of episodes which included informing the pastor that God had told him to sleep with the pastor's young daughter. Koresh was torn between his desire to be a rock star guitarist and his obsessions with sex and violence, especially with Armageddon. Koresh combined these apparently incompatible desires by becoming the religious leader of the Branch Davidians, first seducing and then taking power from the 67-year-old widow of the previous leader. In 1984, Koresh is said to have taken 14-year-old Rachel Jones as the first of his many "wives."

In marathon daily sermons, Koresh taught his followers that the world would soon erupt into battles between the "elect" who were favored by God and the rest of the world who were described as the "Babylonians." The cult amassed an arsenal of weapons including many such as rockets and rocket launchers which were illegal for private individuals. U.S. authorities were alarmed over both the increasing store of armaments and the reports of child abuse and statutory rape; David's predilection for young girls. But the action by the ATF (the Bureau of Alcohol, Tobacco, and Firearms) was bungled from the beginning. Their raid to arrest Koresh and confiscate illegal weapons was supposed to be a surprise, but the Davidians were warned in advance. The ATF was told that the Davidians were warned, and the ATF chose to go ahead.

The importance of an accurate birth time and of both natal and local chart angles is shown by many of Koresh's progressed aspects during the initial battle and ensuing siege of the Branch Davidian compound and its final destruction by fire. The initial effort of the ATF agents to arrest Koresh occurred on the morning of February 28, 1993 between 9 and 10 AM. The agents were met by a barrage of gunfire which killed four of them and wounded twenty others. The ATF fired back, killing or wounding a number of cult members, and then began a siege of the cult compound.

The FBI (Federal Bureau of Investigation) soon took over the management of the siege. The end came near noon on April 19, 1993 (Figure 28) when the FBI sent tanks to break holes in some of the walls of the compound and inject tear gas, hoping the Davidians would run out. Instead, according to the official report, some of the Davidians set fire to the building and very few escaped. Some burned to death or died of smoke inhalation in the fire, and some were shot in the head at close range.

The battle began with Koresh's P Moon square his Waco P MC, trioctile natal Mars, quincunx his natal Houston Ascendant, and opposite his Houston P Ascendant and P Juno. The firestorm at the end which killed 85 of the cult members and children came with P Moon square his Houston P MC, quincunx his P north lunar node, and opposite Neptune. P Mars was conjunct natal Antivertex and P Antivertex squared P Sun. P Waco Antivertex was octile P Neptune. P Waco East Point was conjunct P Pallas, the asteroid associated with law, politics, social justice, etc. Both were also conjunct David's "name" asteroid, Davida. (Asteroids with "ordinary" orbits used to be given feminized names even when they were named for famous men. The policy changed after protests from feminists.) P Davida was conjunct P Themis (divine justice) with both trioctile the Waco MC and octile P Saturn. Both the natal and local Parts of Death were aspected, using the Placidus house system. The Waco P Ascendant was octile the Waco Part of Death and P Neptune was octile the Houston Part of Death.

In addition to aspects to the angles, of course many purely planetary aspects are relevant. These include a dramatic picture of conflicts over religious faith with P Chiron holding a long-term opposition to natal Sun and a square to natal Jupiter, all in fixed signs and houses for the intractable nature of Koresh's convictions and the potential of worshipping sensuality and power. P Mars had finished its octile to Jupiter but remained octile the Sun and trioctile P Chiron, so all of the planets just listed and the natal Antivertex were connected in the network of overlapping aspects. Where conflict aspects between Mars and Saturn point to conflict between personal will and the LAW in some form, conflict aspects between Mars and the keys to faith (Jupiter, Chiron and Neptune) indicate conflict between personal will and power versus one's faith, beliefs, goals, and values. The most common expression of this conflict is frustration or disappointment that we can't achieve our goals and ideals. David carried his efforts to force the world to conform to his personal beliefs and goals to the final end - to death. He said, "I am God and my will is God's will."

P Neptune in a lifetime quincunx to the south lunar node in the seventh house offered a related message. Reading the south node as a lesson, its position in the sign of Aries and the house of Libra pointed to lessons involving Koresh's personal will and action versus the rights of other people while Neptune connected this issue to Koresh's subconscious faith.

The charts of Schwarzkopf, Camdessus, Midler, and Koresh show the danger of assuming that Saturn on an angle will inevitably indicate either positive or painful details in the life of the individual. We shift now to a horoscope where the local Ascendant on Jupiter did not confer the "good luck" commonly associated with that position.

Looking for God in All the Wrong Places (Figure 29)

Frances McEvoy has provided the birth data for one of the children who died in the Waco disaster. According to her birth certificate, Rachel Esther Sylvia was born on June 9, 1979 at 11:20 AM EDT in New Bedford, MA. Her mother brought her to live in the Waco compound with David Koresh when Rachel was 4 years old. She was described as a bright and inquisitive child. Her older brother, Joshua, was released before the final tragedy, but Rachel's mother and two-year old sister died with her in the fire. Koresh was reportedly the father of the sister and had had sex with Rachel as well as with her mother. Apparently, most of the women and children who were kept in the compound and were killed in the final disaster, either by gun shots or the fire, were sex objects or offspring of Koresh.

Rachel's birthplace angles had appropriate aspects for her violent end (though we could not have predicted the details). P Mars was conjunct her natal MC. P MC was square the lunar nodes, connecting her fate to problematic relationships. P East Point was conjunct P Saturn. P Ascendant was square P Venus and trioctile P Vesta. Vesta is the ultimate Virgo: efficient functioning in one's job or body, so it is often an indication of health issues. It also can manifest as a kind of tunnel-vision focus on a limited area that reduces awareness of other important matters which can then be neglected and lead to problems. It is as if one's concentration on a "job" (defined as any immediate personal goal) leads to a lack of awareness of what is going on in other people, so conflict aspects to Vesta are often associated with difficulties in human relationships.

In contrast to her birthplace angles which had stress aspects to Mars, Saturn, and Vesta, representing three of our most challenging primary drives, Rachel's chart in Waco, Texas had P Jupiter exactly on the natal Ascendant and her natal East Point was sextile Venus and P Mars. P Pallas was sextile the local MC

VENUS CONJUNCT MIDHEAVEN: "This area highlights your seeking of pleasure, comfort stability. ... You may look for an easy job, enjoy high status, seek power through beauty or money."

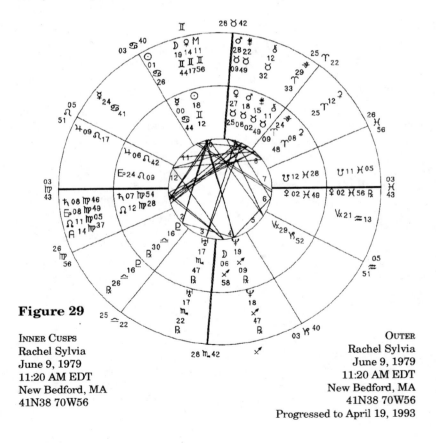

Figure 29

INNER CUSPS
Rachel Sylvia
June 9, 1979
11:20 AM EDT
New Bedford, MA
41N38 70W56

OUTER
Rachel Sylvia
June 9, 1979
11:20 AM EDT
New Bedford, MA
41N38 70W56
Progressed to April 19, 1993

from one side and P Sun was just coming to a sextile to it from the other side. P MC was conjunct Juno, the Plutonian asteroid I have found associated with both marriage and death. In Rachel's case, Juno signaled both. Her role as sex object for David was undoubtedly the reason she was not sent out with her brother. Rachel's P Ascendant in Waco was sextile P Moon and trine Neptune. Her P Antivertex was semisextile P Mars on one side and the natal Waco East Point on the other side. These local angle aspects are considered harmonious. Venus, Juno, and Pallas are all associated with

ASCENDANT CONJUNCT JUPITER: "This area reinforces your enthusiasm, ideals, goals, values, beliefs. ... You could go 'where angels fear to tread' ...carrying what you idolize to an extreme."

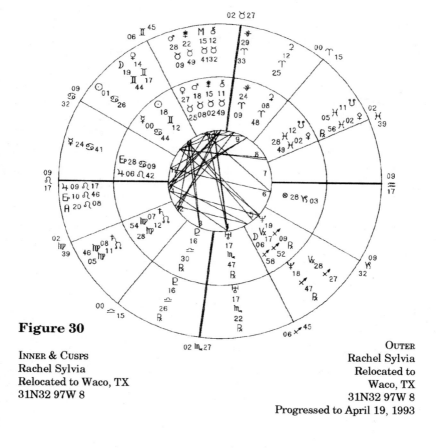

Figure 30

INNER & CUSPS
Rachel Sylvia
Relocated to Waco, TX
31N32 97W 8

OUTER
Rachel Sylvia
Relocated to
Waco, TX
31N32 97W 8
Progressed to April 19, 1993

peer relationships which can include marriage though at 13 years of age, Rachel was legally off-limits.

If we assume that a prominent Jupiter always represents "luck," or no more than mildly excessive acquisitive behavior, while harmony aspects to Venus, Juno, and Pallas mean "happy" relationships with happy outcomes, Rachel's local angles do not "make sense." But if we interpret the relationship aspects as a mutual attraction between Rachel and someone else which might lead to lasting happiness or might lead to temporary emotional or sensual excesses and resulting problems, then the aspects make sense. Also, when we know that Jupiter symbolizes our search for the Absolute more consciously and Neptune a similar search more subconsciously, then the high focus on those planets (and on Chiron which is similar to Jupiter) is highly appropriate.

Koresh was the head of a religious cult, so we expect a Jupiter-Chiron-Neptune emphasis in the charts of his followers. When Rachel's mother brought her to the compound of the Branch Davidians, Rachel's P Jupiter approaching her local Ascendant fit her personal exposure to religion. Rachel also had P Neptune in a very long-term opposition to her natal Sun and, during the siege by the ATF and FBI forces, Rachel's P Moon was crossing her natal Sun and opposing Neptune. As already mentioned, the religious emphasis was also shown by the Waco P Ascendant trine Neptune. P East Point had been moving over P Jupiter for two years but had ended the aspect about four and a half months before the beginning of the siege. Instead of the Jupiter aspect, P East Point had moved into a quincunx to P true south lunar node in the eighth house. Additional emphasis on faith was shown by the Waco P Antivertex which was about to end a three-year octile to Chiron.

Jupiter, Neptune and Chiron symbolize our need for something we can trust, something to give meaning to our lives, for a belief system with which to determine our value hierarchy, the basis for our choices, for our long-range goals. Rachel's chart mixes this search for the Absolute with her desire for love and a mate which are symbolized in astrology by Venus, Pluto, Juno, Pallas, and the planets in or ruling the seventh and eighth houses. Pallas is in Pisces and Pisces is in the eighth house in Waco, on the seventh house cusp in Massachusetts. Remember that both the seventh and eighth houses are part of our ability to be a partner.

Juno, the asteroid most associated with marriage, is conjunct Chiron. Their tenth house position in Waco adds the idea of a mate who would be a "father-figure." Venus is also in the tenth house in Waco, supporting an attraction to a father-figure or one's father as a role model for a choice of mate. (Role models can be either positive or negative. We may seek someone like or the opposite of the role model). Jupiter in Leo and Neptune in the Leo house could manifest by idealizing love or worshipping a lover, or being attracted by a lover who thought he was god, etc.

The shifts in house positions from Massachusetts to Texas include the natal ninth house stellium in Taurus moving into the tenth house in Texas. Rachel's search for God (ninth house) was directed toward Koresh who filled the roles of "father" (tenth house), "lover" (Venus and Juno), and "god" (Chiron and the natal ninth house). The harmonious aspects suggest that Rachel was a willing target of Koresh's attention. Her faith may have been sufficiently vested in him to convince her that if anything happened, they would immediately go to heaven together. Faith can be an unbelievably powerful force. The spiritual drive is grossly underrated if we write it off as a genial "sugar-daddy" or "fairy godmother" or as a tendency toward harmless excesses. Our beliefs truly rule our lives, and we need to become conscious of them.

Assassination (Figures 31 and 32)

Luis Donaldo Colosio provides an even more recent example of the need to remember that astrology deals with principles, each of which can be manifested in many different details. Jupiter conjunct a local angle is not a guarantee of "luck" in that area and neither is Venus, the other so-called "benefic" in astrology. Colosio was expected to win the August 1994 election to become President of Mexico. He was generally popular in the country, and was the candidate of the political party, the PRI, which has never lost a national election since their founding in 1929. His birth data comes from a Mexican astrologer who has obtained birth information on the political leaders in his country. Colosio was born on February 10, 1950 at 11:45 PM MST in Magdalena de Kino, Mexico. He was shot and killed in Tijuana, Mexico on March 23, 1994.

Natal Venus is just over two degrees from Colosio's IC when his chart is calculated for Tijuana and it rules his local Ascendant. He wanted to reach poor people with his message that he would try to improve their lives if he were elected President. To speak to such people in person, he rejected police security and went into one of the neighborhoods of Tijuana where people live as squatters in makeshift shacks without water or power. As Rachel's faith in Koresh probably contributed to her early death, Colosio's basic friendliness, shown by his stellia in Libra and Aquarius, added to his idealism shown by a stellium in Sagittarius, led him to assume that ordinary people would respond to his genuine desire to help them. The basic optimism of strong air and fire could have contributed to his premature death.

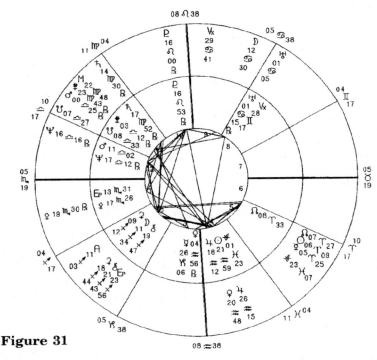

Figure 31

INNER & CUSPS
Louis Donaldo Colosio
February 10, 1950
11:45PM MST
Magdalena de Kino, Mexico
30N38 110W57

OUTER
Louis Donaldo Colosio
February 10, 1950
11:45PM MST
Magdalena de Kino, Mexico
30N38 110W57
Progressed to March 23, 1994

Obviously, one cannot simply look at a single factor such as a planet conjunct an angle. The potential for conflict is clearly indicated in Colosio's chart by P Jupiter trioctile natal Mars and P Mars trioctile natal Jupiter as well as square Uranus. P Uranus held a trioctile to natal Jupiter and an octile to Pluto while P Pluto remained opposite natal Jupiter throughout Colosio's life. These conflict patterns of fire planets in air signs plus Uranus, an air planet and Pluto in a fire sign, fit both the possibility of over-

VENUS CONJUNCT IC: "Feeling good and making affirming connections with other people becomes more important. Accepting, trusting, accommodating, or getting comfortable could be overdone."

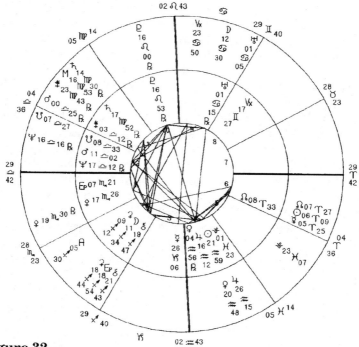

Figure 32

INNER & CUSPS
Louis Donaldo Colosio
Relocated to
Tijuana, Mexico
32N32 117W 1

OUTER
Louis Donaldo Colosio
Relocated to
Tijuana, Mexico
32N32 117W 1
Progressed to March 23, 1994

confidence and the fact that Colosio was engaged in a political contest for the votes of his country men and women. The PRI has been accused of widespread fraud in past elections, and there was great pressure on the Party to risk defeat by conducting a "clean" election. Colosio was trying to reach the ordinary people, using his air-fire eloquence to persuade them to vote for his Party.

The combination of conflict aspects involving Mars, Uranus, Jupiter in Aquarius, and Pluto in the house of Saturn could also picture potential revolution. Mars symbolizes the willingness to fight to assert oneself, to defend what are considered to be one's rights. Uranus reinforces the Mars' demand for freedom, the urge to resist limits. The Jupiter principle includes the desire for freedom in order to pursue whatever has been defined as an ultimate value and goal. Aspects which connect Jupiter, Mars, and Uranus are likely to intensify the drive for freedom. Saturn and its sign and house show the limits; laws and the bureaucracy, the authority figures who enforce the laws, and the conscience, our inner law.

The MC represents the same principle as Saturn while the Ascendant, East Point, and Antivertex are equivalent to Mars: personal will in action, the basic life force. Colosio's P MC in Tijuana had just reached a conjunction with natal Saturn when he was killed, and it squared his Tijuana natal Antivertex. His birthplace P Antivertex squared his Tijuana natal Ascendant. His P Tijuana East Point was just two minutes of longitude past the square to Saturn so the aspect would have been in effect when the assassination was planned and the gun purchased. P local East Point was also conjunct Chiron (little brother to Jupiter) and P Ceres which, like Vesta, can be associated with health.

TABLE OF QUOTIDIAN ANGLE POSITIONS
For Luis Donaldo Colosio,
Relocated to Tijuana, March 23, 1994

QMC	01 ♏ 05
QA	12 ♑ 16
QE	26 ♑ 54
QXX	20 ♒ 40

Quotidian angles move around the whole zodiac circle plus one degree in a year, so they move approximately one degree a day. Colosio's quotidian (Q) angles for Tijuana also had appropriate aspects.

Q Ascendant squared Mars during the day of the death as last minute plans would have been finalized. Q East Point was conjunct Mercury in the third house for the media coverage which actually included a video of the killer while he was in the act of shooting Colosio. Q Antivertex was conjunct P Venus, reminding us that nothing in astrology is automatically "good" or "bad." Q MC was in a grand trine to Uranus and Vesta and octile Colosio's local P MC. The combination reminds us that adding a grand trine to a conflict configuration will not necessarily defuse the conflict. In this case, it added more power to the long-term progressed conflict aspects described above involving Uranus, Mars, Pluto, and Jupiter.

Of course, all aspects are part of the picture and have meaning. The trines can suggest both the unrealistic faith and idealism of Colosio. They may also represent the immunity of the people behind the assassination. Rumors in Mexico suggest that wealthy, ultra-conservative members of Colosio's own Party might have planned the action, to remove someone regarded as too liberal, too concerned with the deteriorating condition of the poor in Mexico. Many other aspects could be described. Colosio's progressed birthplace angles were also appropriate, including P MC conjunct P Juno (like Pluto) and quincunx natal Sun. P Ascendant was conjunct natal Moon and the progressed Part of Death (11 ♐ 11) for Colosio's birthplace! Colosio's chart provides strong evidence for the importance of local angles and for the reliability of Placidus house cusps which were used to calculate the Part of Death.

Though Rachel's Jupiter on her local Ascendant and Colosio's Venus on his local IC did not protect them from an early death in those areas, obviously there are other individuals with "benefics" on an angle who have been more successful. Like Schwarzkopf, Camdessus, and Midler, Ross Perot is a successful person with Saturn closely conjunct an angle, but in his case it is on his birthplace Descendant. Of course, the house cusps of one's birthplace are always present, no matter where we move. Perot also has his Sun and Jupiter more widely conjunct his natal Ascendant. He became a billionaire by developing computer software to manage government records. More recently, he has played a prominent role in United States' politics through 1992-3.

Entrepreneurial Enterprise (Figure 33)

Perot's birth data is provided in the *Gauquelin Book of American Charts*, and, like all of their data, it is from his birth certificate. Perot was born on June 27, 1930 at 5:34 AM CST in Texarkana, TX. He has a massive stellium in Cancer which is partly in the twelfth and partly in the first house. (Are there any astrologers who still believe that a strongly occupied twelfth house has to be negative?) Jupiter is conjunct the Sun within five degrees in early Cancer in the twelfth house, so it would be on his Ascendant in areas a few degrees west of his birthplace. His Sun on the midpoint of Jupiter/Ascendant is similar to a triple conjunction of the three factors. Saturn was on Perot's Descendant within one degree at his birth, an appropriate position for a power-struggle life.

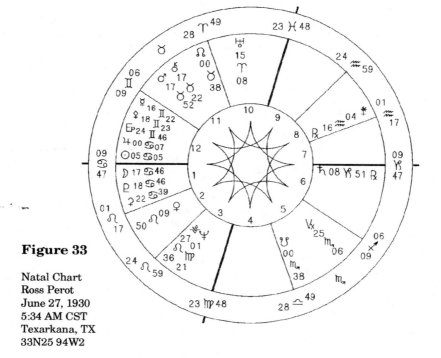

Figure 33

Natal Chart
Ross Perot
June 27, 1930
5:34 AM CST
Texarkana, TX
33N25 94W2

Remember, we can have healthy, game-playing competition in sports, business, politics, etc. or we can have life-and-death struggles which may be destructive for everyone involved. Healthy competition includes playing fairly, "by the rules," being able to win sometimes and lose sometimes while remembering that it is a "game."

Perot's life has seen major action in many different places. He was briefly in the navy and admires the military, is sometimes accused of running his business like a regiment, and often hires retired military people. Aries in the tenth house may be manifested as: "My will is law. I know what I want and I will make the world that way." Mars on Chiron can idealize personal power and courage and/or identify with presenting one's personal "truth" to the world.

Ross Perot's life was in danger in Tehran, Iran (Figure 34) where employees of his company were in jail and the authorities had threatened him. His natal Mars-Chiron formed an exact square to his Tehran MC at 17 Leo, showing the potential for a power struggle with authorities. However, Perot also had helpful aspects to the local MC from Uranus, Mercury, Pallas, Moon and Pluto. Native employees were successful in starting a riot on February 11, 1979 which allowed Perot's U.S. employees to escape from the jail. At the time, Perot's progressed local Ascendant at 17 Sagittarius was opposite his Mercury, quincunx Mars-Chiron and Moon to form a yod, and trine his natal local MC. Oppositions and especially quincunxes show a tendency to separate, to move in new directions, and the U.S. employees escaped from Iran. Harmonious aspects to Perot's local cusps fit both his earlier financial success in Iran and the successful escape after the change in Iran's government had put his people in jeopardy. Progressed Jupiter trined Perot's local Ascendant and his progressed East Point trined progressed Neptune. But there were also many stress aspects to show the tension. Progressed East Point was tri-octile natal Mars-Chiron and local MC. Progressed MC was tri-octile progressed Chiron though also trine Juno. Progressed Antivertex squared the lunar nodes, was tri-octile both natal and progressed Mercury and octile progressed local Ascendant. Progressed Mars was quincunx the local natal East Point while the progressed Sun squared that same point. It was certainly a tense place and time for Perot.

Another challenging chapter in Perot's life was played out periodically in **Viet Nam** where Perot tried to uncover information on MIAs, U.S. armed services personnel who were "missing in action." Perot confronted both the authorities in Viet Nam and in the U.S. as he followed up rumors that some U.S. servicemen remained imprisoned in Viet Nam or more likely in Laos. In Saigon, the capital of the former South Viet Nam, Perot has Saturn exactly on the local Ascendant. As far as I know, Perot was not personally threatened in Saigon, but he was not successful in rescuing any MIAs. His natal Uranus is just over one degree from

MARS CONFLICT MIDHEAVEN: "This location could bring potential clashes with authorities or males. ... You may resist limits, rules, or the need for cautious planning. ... Impatience, anger, rashness, self-centeredness, or 'macho' tendencies could present challenges."

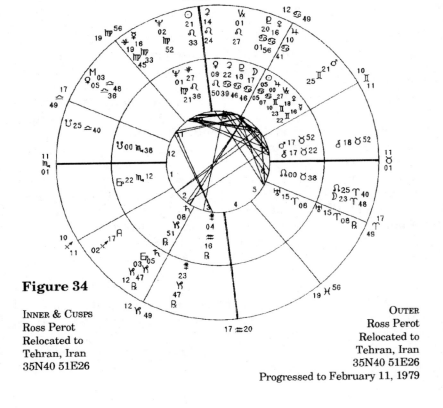

Figure 34

INNER & CUSPS
Ross Perot
Relocated to
Tehran, Iran
35N40 51E26

OUTER
Ross Perot
Relocated to
Tehran, Iran
35N40 51E26
Progressed to February 11, 1979

his local IC, opposing the MC; Mars-Chiron are quincunx the MC, and Neptune is octile the MC, the latter three within one degree. At the time that we supposedly pulled the last of our troops out of the country, Perot's P Jupiter was on the local Descendant, opposing Saturn, P Pallas opposed his local East Point, P Mercury opposed his local Antivertex, P local Ascendant was quincunx Pluto, and P MC was square natal Vesta in the local eighth house. Separations occur often when there are oppositions and quincunxes. They suggest the need to change tactics, to try a new direction. Though Perot invested considerable money and personal

ASCENDANT CONJUNCT SATURN: "This area may reinforce your sense of responsibility" [to U.S. servicemen]

"You might battle authorities."

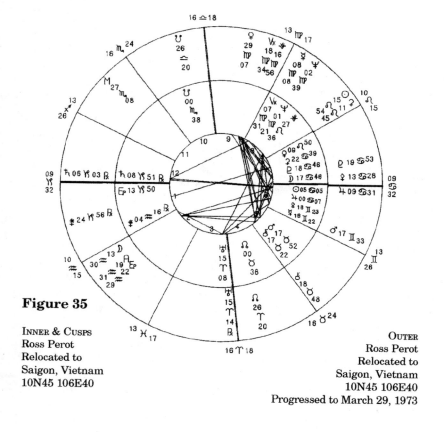

Figure 35

INNER & CUSPS
Ross Perot
Relocated to
Saigon, Vietnam
10N45 106E40

OUTER
Ross Perot
Relocated to
Saigon, Vietnam
10N45 106E40
Progressed to March 29, 1973

effort in the attempt to locate abandoned prisoners, no one was rescued and the U.S. government is still denying any culpability.

Many locations have played a role in Perot's business career. Perot made his start in the computer business at the IBM headquarters in **Armonk, New York**. At the GM headquarters in **Detroit, Michigan**, he tried to change the giant automobile business. In New York, he took over a failing brokerage business and tried — but failed — to change the stock market. **Dallas, Texas** is the headquarters for his major current business. In **Washington D.C.**, the Federal Government provided the Medicare accounts which jump-started his initial success and immense wealth. He has also had some business success in the tough market of **Tokyo, Japan**.

In his **Dallas** headquarters where Perot runs his successful business and his more unevenly successful political campaign, his local Ascendant is conjunct his natal Sun and opposite his natal Saturn within two degrees. His natal Sun\Saturn midpoint is square his Dallas Ascendant within two minutes of longitude and his Dallas Descendant was just six minutes from the midpoint of natal and P Saturn at the beginning of 1993 with the aspect becoming more exact as Saturn retrogrades. These challenging aspects have certainly not prevented Perot from immense success. He has proved that he can be a tough competitor, but he has also pulled out and cut his losses on more than one occasion, including pulling out of the race for the U.S. Presidency when he thought his family was threatened. As would be expected with his Cancer stellium, Perot is devoted to his family and his homeland.

Calculating Perot's chart for **Armonk, New York** (Figure 36) puts his Ascendant in 0 Leo with exact squares to the true lunar nodes and a wider opposition to Juno to form a grand cross in fixed signs. His local Antivertex in Armonk is in Gemini exactly conjunct Mercury and sextile the local MC, while Uranus in Aries is exactly on his local MC. Mercury and Uranus on angles are appropriate keys to the knowledge he acquired at IBM which became the source of his fortune when he started his own computer business.

However, these aspects did not guarantee Perot's success! His chart in Manhattan only differs from Armonk by a fraction of a degree on the angles and he was not able to rescue a failing brokerage business or to shake up the system in the New York stock market. Nor, of course, was he able to change IBM. In both New York and Armonk, in addition to his local Ascendant exactly square the true lunar nodes and Uranus conjunct the MC, Perot's local MC squared his Moon-Pluto conjunction, adding a cardinal T-square to the fixed cross. These patterns certainly fit Perot's struggle against entrenched bureaucracies and rigid traditions. Character creates destiny. Perot has battled his way through life in many situations.

As indicated above, Perot's major financial success began with contracts with the U.S. government in **Washington, DC** (Figure 37). Our capital is only a few degrees west of New York and Armonk but it shifts his Ascendant back to late Cancer and moves his MC over two degrees from Uranus. At first glance, the planetary aspects to local angles look mostly negative. Vesta is exactly

URANUS CONJUNCT MIDHEAVEN: "This location highlights your need for freedom, variety, openness, or unconventionality in regard to your career. ... future orientation or new technology and ideas."

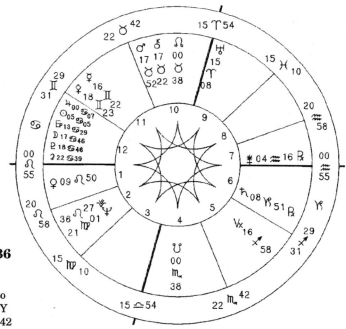

Figure 36

Ross Perot
Relocated to
Armonk, NY
41N 7 73W42

trioctile the Washington MC though it is also semisextile the Ascendant. The progressed lunar nodes held squares to the local Ascendant for many years. Venus is widely trine the Washington MC but we have to go to midpoints to find much harmonious strength involving the local angles. Perot's Washington DC Antivertex is sextile his Venus and Uranus and the aspects are strengthened because the local Antivertex is exactly conjunct their midpoint which fits making money with computers. Perot also has his Sun (ruling 2nd) conjunct the local East Point/Jupiter midpoint. He undoubtedly got a good deal from the government which paid a high price for his services, but he had to work for it.

Detroit, Michigan (Figure 38) put Perot's natal Sun exactly on his local East Point and moved his local MC into an exact square to the Sun-East Point and to P Saturn. The cardinal T-square accurately pictures another battle against a bureaucratic establishment. Perot does have his local Antivertex sextile natal Venus for possible financial gain. His Ascendant in Detroit is conjunct "parental" Ceres in Cancer within two degrees. Perot had

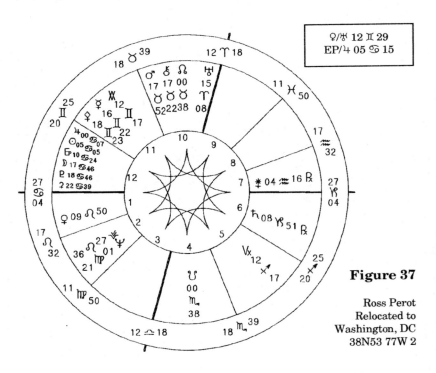

Figure 37

Ross Perot
Relocated to
Washington, DC
38N53 77W 2

sold the profitable company which he had founded, his "baby," to General Motors. He ended up with a lot of money but was unable to change the power hierarchy at GM which was losing market share to other automobile companies. After intense friction, the GM executives paid him to depart, and Perot promptly started a rival computer-management company in violation of his contract.

Tokyo (Figure 39) flipped Perot's Ascendant from its position in New York to the same degree in the opposite sign as Saigon's Ascendant had flipped to the same degree and opposite sign from his Ascendant in Texarkana. However, the Tokyo MC-IC axis was quite different from New York. Perot has P Chiron in a lifetime conjunction with natal Mars as one of the keys to his intellectual brilliance but sometimes less rational idealism. It also holds a lifetime sextile to natal Pluto. In Tokyo, P Chiron is on the IC within two degrees. Perot's Tokyo MC trines his natal Moon-Pluto-Ceres in the sixth house which shows the capacity to function effectively in a job. P Pluto holds a lifetime trine to his Tokyo MC,

ASCENDANT [OR EAST POINT] CONJUNCT SUN: "In this area, you may want more recognition and pursue leadership roles."

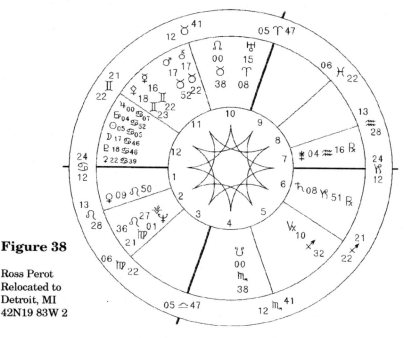

Figure 38

Ross Perot
Relocated to
Detroit, MI
42N19 83W 2

while Uranus holds a lifetime sextile to his Tokyo East Point. The chart does imply that Perot has what it takes to make a dent in a very tough market.

The preceding locations have provided both successes and challenges to Perot, but none of them put Jupiter on Perot's Ascendant. In fact, it is in the city where he is mostly seen as an enemy that Jupiter is closest to Perot's local Ascendant. In **Mexico City** (Figure 40), Jupiter conjuncts the Ascendant within two degrees. Perot's vigorous fight against NAFTA (the North American Free Trade Agreement) was featured in the media in both the United States and Mexico. Mexico's government, located in Mexico City, wanted NAFTA. The Indian revolution in Chiapas which started at the end of 1993 demonstrated that many poor people knew that the agreement would only help the wealthy and would probably make their lives even more desperate. How could an astrologer interpret such a complicated outcome? After the fact, we can say that Perot had good will for ordinary people in both the U.S.

PLUTO HARMONY MIDHEAVEN:"This area highlights skills for the business world and research."

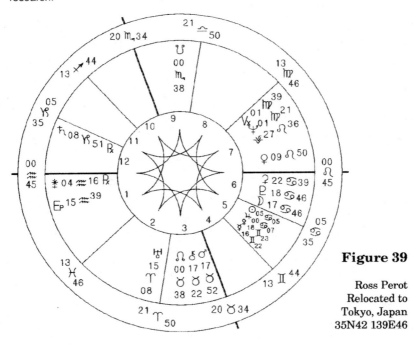

Figure 39

Ross Perot
Relocated to
Tokyo, Japan
35N42 139E46

and in Mexico; that he just opposed the power elite. Remember, his Saturn in Capricorn opposes his natal Sun and Jupiter in Cancer. Such an interpretation would also fit the square of Perot's Mexico City MC to Pallas, the asteroid which is connected to politics and social justice among other meanings. The Mexico MC also squares Mercury in Gemini within two degrees which fits the media coverage that became increasingly negative in the course of the contest. Perot's Mexico MC was also more widely octile-trioctile his T-square of Juno square the lunar nodes. At the same time, the MC is sextile Mars-Chiron in Taurus and trine his Moon-Pluto-Ceres in Cancer. Perot is likely to benefit financially from the passage of NAFTA. Clearly, the principles work but predicting details is a risky (or impossible) effort.

ASCENDANT CONJUNCT JUPITER: "You may experience more exaggeration, excesses, restlessness."

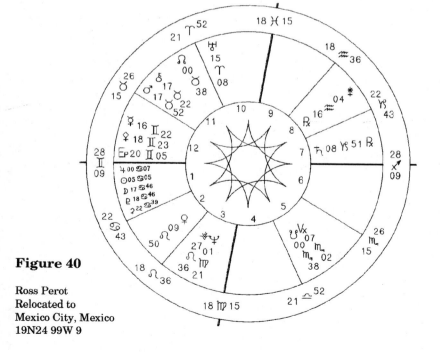

Figure 40

Ross Perot
Relocated to
Mexico City, Mexico
19N24 99W 9

Junk Bond King (Figure 41)

Michael Milken was a financial leader in the go-go 1980s, credited as a primary originator of so-called "junk" bonds. He helped companies in need of money to bypass banks by selling bonds issued by their companies directly to investors. Companies which lacked sufficient resources to satisfy bank requirements offered above average interest to make up for the higher risk. As long as the world economy continued to expand, which it was doing mostly by going more deeply into debt, the "junk" bonds generally continued to make their interest payments. But in the late 1980s, the debt mountain began to take its toll and many players in the "junk" market were among the casualties. Eventually, Milken was indicted for securities fraud. On April 24, 1990, Milken pleaded guilty and agreed to pay 600 million dollars in fines and penalties. On November 21, 1990 he was sentenced to 10 years in jail.

Milken's data comes from Lois Rodden. He was born in Los Angeles, California on July 4, 1946 at 7:31 AM PST. Milken's natal

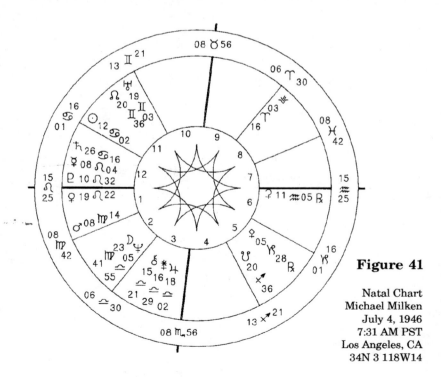

Figure 41

Natal Chart
Michael Milken
July 4, 1946
7:31 AM PST
Los Angeles, CA
34N 3 118W14

chart certainly shows the potential for making money. His birthplace Ascendant is on the midpoint of Pluto and Venus, the two primary keys to money, conjunct each of them within five degrees. The Ascendant is also closely sextile Juno which is like an alternate Pluto, and Juno is conjunct Jupiter and Chiron, keys to our search for the ultimate. Additional indications of his potential for success include Venus sextile-trine the lunar nodes and Mars in Virgo on the second house cusp in a grand trine to the MC and Pallas in Capricorn. Milken's Cancer Sun also sextiled the MC and Mars. However, he also had the potential to overreach with Mars in an octile to Saturn and a close Mercury-Pluto conjunction in Leo square his MC. Remember that Saturn and the MC represent the "rules of the game," what is possible and what is necessary if we are going to survive in this world. Conflict aspects to Saturn and/or the MC can mean trying to do more than is possible or trying to avoid doing what is necessary.

Ascendant conjunct Moon: "In this area, the following qualities tend to be highlighted: emotions, ... security needs, vulnerability, ...or involvement with the public."

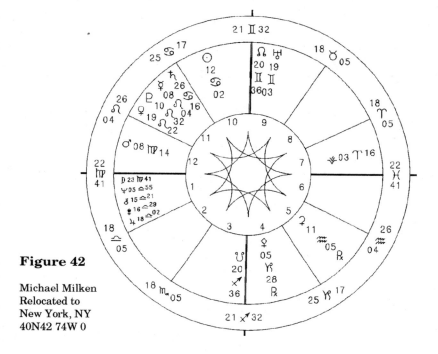

Figure 42

Michael Milken
Relocated to
New York, NY
40N42 74W 0

Milken maintained his office in his Los Angeles birthplace but his work had a major impact in New York which is the U.S. financial center and location of the primary U.S. stock market. When Milken's chart is calculated for New York (Fig. 42), the true lunar nodes are on the MC-IC within one degree and P Uranus remains conjunct the MC for many years. Uranus can symbolize both the innovations which Milken introduced into the bond market and the dramatic destruction of his career when he was indicted and convicted of fraud and conspiracy. In addition to the lunar nodes on one angle axis, Milken's New York Ascendant was

ASCENDANT [OR EAST POINT] CONFLICT SATURN: "Challenges may arise involving your sense of responsibility, drive for power, concept of reality, career goals, status ambitions and expertise. ... You are learning to balance confidence and caution, speed [junk bonds] and temperance, personal will and the 'rules of life.' "

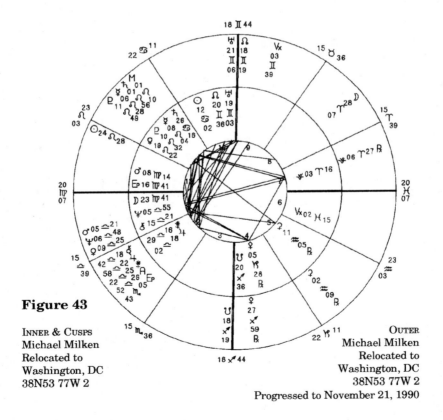

Figure 43

INNER & CUSPS
Michael Milken
Relocated to
Washington, DC
38N53 77W 2

OUTER
Michael Milken
Relocated to
Washington, DC
38N53 77W 2
Progressed to November 21, 1990

conjunct his natal Moon in Virgo within one degree. His work certainly affected huge numbers of people. Some people gained through the high interest of the "junk" bonds while those who invested in companies which failed ended up losing a great deal. The junk bonds were also widely used to buy companies, with or without their consent and often by paying exorbitant prices which helped to create the debt mountain that now afflicts the world.

Since the federal government prosecuted Milken, his chart in Washington, DC is also relevant (Fig. 43). His MC there is just enough earlier than New York to put his natal Uranus and P north node exactly on the MC. His Washington P MC was conjunct P Saturn when his jail sentence was handed down. P Saturn had held an octile to Milken's Washington East Point for years and his P Washington Ascendant was square natal Saturn.

The establishment (Saturn) ended Milken's career as a broker, but despite the huge fine, he still has a considerable fortune. He has already been released from prison but he is reportedly critically ill with cancer. Milken's east coast charts do reinforce his potential for financial success which was shown in his natal chart. Natal and progressed Jupiter are moved into his second house on the east coast. Jupiter and Juno trine Uranus, the north lunar node, and the local MCs, and Venus sextiles all of the preceding. But I think most people given a choice between millions of dollars earned with a high stress life and a healthy body maintained with a low stress life would choose the latter.

Pearl Bailey (Figures 44, 45, and 46)

Another famous person with Uranus on a local angle was able to manifest a more positive potential out of its many possibilities. Pearl Bailey's birth data also comes from Lois Rodden's data collection. Bailey was born in Newport News, Virginia on March 29, 1918 at 7 AM EST. She was a successful singer in both New York and Hollywood, making her stage debut in New York in *St. Louis Woman* in 1946. The move from Virginia to New York changed her Ascendant from the midpoint of Mercury/Vesta to an exact conjunction with Vesta, square to Saturn, semisextile to Jupiter and a semisextile to the Sun which was just over one degree. Her New York Ascendant was therefore on the midpoint of Sun/Jupiter, considered by most astrologers to be a really auspicious position. A planet or angle on the midpoint of two other factors (plan-

ets and/or angles) provides the same meaning as a conjunction
with both of the two factors. Bailey's birthplace and New York
charts are similar to being born with Sun, Mercury, Vesta, and
Jupiter on the Ascendant. The fire emphasis includes Sun and
Jupiter by their own nature, factors in Aries, Leo and Sagittarius, plus the strongly aspected Ascendant which carries the meaning of Mars. What a dynamo!

Bailey's Vesta is in Taurus and it carries the meaning of Virgo while Jupiter is in the Taurus house, Mars is in Virgo, and
Ceres is in Capricorn so we have added earth to the fire to make a
potential steam roller. But Bailey has strong water houses and
the Moon close to the Descendant, showing enough water to have
empathy and compassion. She also has a grand trine in air signs
with Venus and Uranus also in an air house, so the chart indicates high level ability to learn and to communicate, to win friends
and influence people.

In Hollywood (Figure 46), Bailey's close Venus-Uranus conjunction moved to the Ascendant adding an important angle to

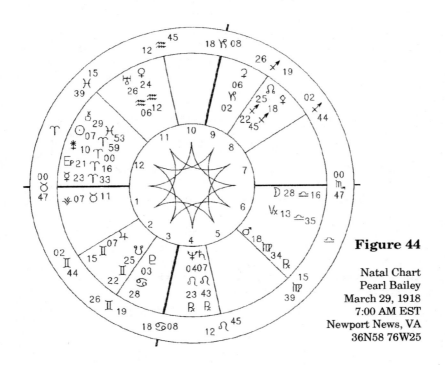

Figure 44

Natal Chart
Pearl Bailey
March 29, 1918
7:00 AM EST
Newport News, VA
36N58 76W25

ASCENDANT CONJUNCT VESTA: "This area provides the opportunity for you to increase your efficiency, concentration....Doing your work your own way becomes more and moral vital."

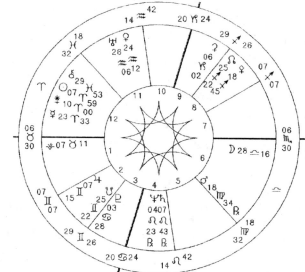

Figure 45

Pearl Bailey
Relocated to
New York, NY
40N42 74W 0

SUN HARMONY MIDHEAVEN: "This region highlights creative, promotional, sales, speculative, risk-taking skills which could advance your career."

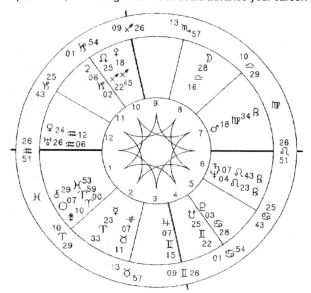

Figure 46

Pearl Bailey
Relocated to
Hollywood, CA
34N 5 118W19

the grand air trine. Also in Hollywood, Jupiter was conjunct the IC and the MC filled in the missing Sagittarius corner to form a grand fire trine with Saturn and the Sun. I suspect that all astrologers would have encouraged Pearl Bailey to head for Hollywood.

Patricide and Matricide

Another "famous" relocated inhabitant of the Los Angeles area was less successful in handling Uranus on an angle. Erik Menendez was born in Livingston, New Jersey on November 27, 1970 at 23:23 EST. The Menendez family hit the headlines when Erik and his brother Lyle reported the murder of their parents in Beverly Hills shortly before midnight on August 21, 1989. In late October and in December 1989 the brothers began confessing to their psychiatrist that they had shot their parents. The psychiatrist, Dr. Oziel, tape recorded some of their sessions, and invited his girl friend, Judalon Smyth, to listen from an adjoining room. March 6, 1990, Judalon went to the police who arrested Eric and Lyle two days later. Simultaneous but separate trials of the brothers began on July 20, 1993. On January 13, 1994, Erik's jury reported to the judge that they were hopelessly deadlocked and could not reach a decision. Lyle's jury reached the same impasse a few days later.

The murdered parents were Jose Menendez, born on May 6, 1944 in Havana, Cuba, and Kitty Menendez, born on October 14, 1941 in Oak Lawn, Illinois. Lyle Menendez was born on January 10, 1968 in New York City. So far, we only have a birth time for Erik whose birth certificate has been obtained by Lois Rodden. Erik has Neptune exactly on his IC in his natal chart (Fig. 47), connecting his search for the "emotional absolute" to his home, parents, and basic security needs. The possibilities are endless with this mixture of principles. Erik could have had a parent who was religious, perfectionistic, artistic, a victim or a victimizer in many different ways. When the details are known, as is usually the case, we find that many of the alternatives were manifested. Erik's father was in the music business and his mother was a model and would-be actress, expressing the artistic potential of Neptune connected to the home and parents. Jose, and possibly Kitty were born into Catholic families but the family apparently had little active religious involvement. The brothers testified that they were sexually abused as children by Jose and that their mother offered no help and contributed to the psychological abuse. Certainly, the parents were also victims, killed in their home by their own children.

Erik's Neptune was also on the midpoint of his Sun and Moon, within a five degree conjunction to both of the lights. Many astrologers consider the Sun/Moon midpoint to be one of the most important. As has been indicated, aspects to a midpoint are read as equivalent in meaning to aspects to both of the planets (or angles) which form the midpoint, so Erik's Neptune (and the IC which conjuncts it) are interpreted as forming exact conjunctions with both the Sun and Moon. The Sun is also exactly square Erik's Ascendant. The patterns fit Erik's intense emotional security issues and also the immense publicity which followed the crime and trial.

When Erik's chart is calculated for Beverly Hills where the murders occurred (Figure 48), the IC is moved into a conjunction with Uranus. Though the aspect is not as close as Neptune in the

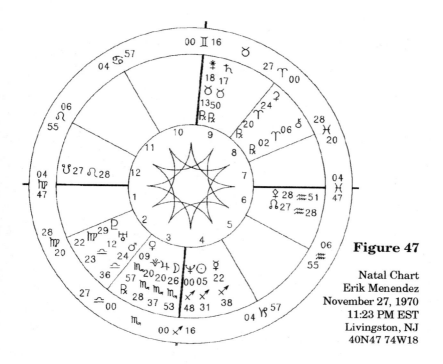

Figure 47

Natal Chart
Erik Menendez
November 27, 1970
11:23 PM EST
Livingston, NJ
40N47 74W18

birthplace chart, it is within three degrees of the IC as well as square the local East point within one degree. Erik's local Antivertex is exactly trioctile Mars and quincunx Venus, with both planets in his local fourth house. In addition to its square to Uranus, the local East Point is trioctile Erik's Moon. His local Ascendant trines his Moon but it squares Ceres (a key to one's mother along with the Moon). It is also sextile Pluto with both factors quincunx the north lunar node in the local eighth house to form a yod. The double quincunx or yod is typically associated with major changes, often involving separations. In this collection of Ascendant aspects the trine to the Moon is harmonious but we have to remember that the natal Moon squares Pallas and its own nodes

URANUS CONJUNCT IC: "In this area, freedom, innovation, and change are highlighted within the family matrix. ... Protection could be erratic."

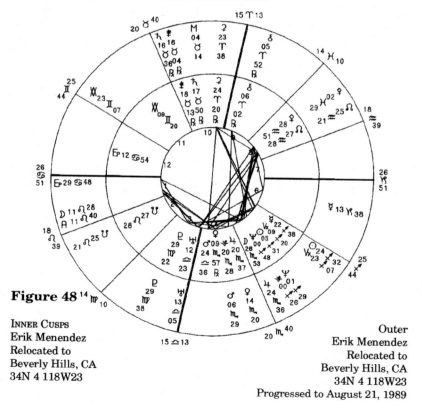

Figure 48

INNER CUSPS
Erik Menendez
Relocated to
Beverly Hills, CA
34N 4 118W23

Outer
Erik Menendez
Relocated to
Beverly Hills, CA
34N 4 118W23
Progressed to August 21, 1989

(which I interpret as carrying the same meaning as the Moon) and it is quincunx Ceres. Conflict aspects between different keys to Erik's mother (Moon, Ceres, Nodes) show that she experienced inner conflict. According to testimony in the trial, Kitty was in conflict within herself over the role of motherhood. She told the brothers repeatedly that their births had prevented her from pursuing a successful career as an actress.

Both the birthplace and local natal charts have appropriate aspects but an equally or more dramatic picture emerges when we look at the progressed factors on the date of the murders. As has been indicated previously, the progressed Placidus eighth house cusps are normally aspected in events which involve death. When he helped to kill his parents, Erik's California P eighth house cusp was exactly opposite his New Jersey Ascendant and his New Jersey P eighth house cusp was exactly conjunct his California MC. Cardinal factors are almost always involved at the time of events which change one's outer circumstances while fixed and mutable factors may mark emotional or mental activity without major overt changes in the life. Major events are likely when any progressed factor, planet or house cusp, crosses the major angles, the Ascendant and/or the MC.

Many other relevant aspects could be mentioned including angle crossings which often signal overt events, changes in life circumstances. P Vesta conjunct Erik's natal IC-Neptune fits the total alienation between the son and his parents and, of course, we could say that changes in his life included the state of his parents' health and work, his own status since he became an orphan, his home situation including the move to jail within a few months, his public reputation and his relationship to the law, etc. The P Antivertex was conjunct the natal Ascendant and the P local Ascendant was conjunct the P Moon and sextile Uranus. P local Antivertex opposed Mercury, another aspect which fit a change connected to home and/or parents or other authorities. P local East Point was quincunx Pallas and activating a yod with Pluto. P Venus quincunx Erik's local MC repeated the potential for changes connected to authority figures and/or the law. Erik started his confession two months after the murder when his P MC reached a quincunx to natal Vesta which is closely conjunct Jupiter. The

P MC quincunx to Jupiter and P local East Point conjunction with the natal Antivertex were exact by the time Erik was arrested.

In the end, perhaps the mutable dilemma is the most crucial of the three major crosses in astrology. Our beliefs determine our values, our ethics, and our ultimate destination since they produce the acts which shape our lives. Erik's future is in limbo as this book is being put together. The state has announced that the brothers will face a new trial. Bill Clinton is not alone in living out a morality play. He is just doing it more publicly than most people, in more regions of the world.

Domestic Violence

We will close with another dramatic morality play which just hit the headlines of the world. O.J. Simpson, a football star and later sports broadcaster who added to his fame with movies and commercial advertising, has been accused of murdering his ex-wife and a male acquaintance. The major TV networks interrupted their scheduled programming to follow the drama as O.J. rode slowly up the L.A. freeways, followed by a half dozen police cars, in a car driven by a friend while O.J. held a gun to his own head. His former wife, Nicole Brown Simpson, and a waiter from a restaurant where Nicole ate often, were found slashed to death on the sidewalk in front of Nicole's home in Brentwood, California. The waiter, Ronald Goldman, had brought Nicole's prescription sunglasses to her, at her request, after she had lost them at the restaurant earlier in the evening. O.J. has hired Robert Shapiro, one of the top criminal lawyers in the U.S. along with two other top lawyers as advisors. TV continues to follow the preliminary hearings, watched by many citizens who are shocked by what is happening to their hero.

According to the *Gauquelin Book of American Horoscopes*, O.J. was born in San Francisco, CA on July 9, 1947 at 8:08 AM PST. Whether or not he is guilty as charged, there have to be major conflict aspects in his chart for him to be in jail with a double murder charge hanging over his head. O.J.'s P Sun was octile his natal Sun so, using the system to progress the angles which I prefer, his P MC was also octile natal MC and still just within orb of a trioctile to natal Jupiter which is conjunct his IC. His P Ascendant was octile Jupiter. Since Jupiter symbolizes our faith and consequent judgment and morality, the conflict aspects show a challenge in that area. (See Fig. 49.)

However, O.J.'s local angles in Brentwood are more dramatic and give a clearer picture of the issues (Fig. 50). His local P MC was conjunct P Mars, P Vesta, and the midpoint of Mars/Saturn. P Mars was still in orb of a conjunction with the midpoint of Ascendant/MC. The combination presents a repeated theme; a confrontation between personal will and action (Mars and Ascendant) and the limits of personal will (Saturn and MC). Vesta shows a one-pointed focus that can lead to great success but sometimes at the cost of alienation from one's fellow humans as the immediate purpose overrides attention to anything else.

O.J.'s P Ascendant in Brentwood was conjunct natal Neptune and within a one-degree square to the whole stellium listed above:

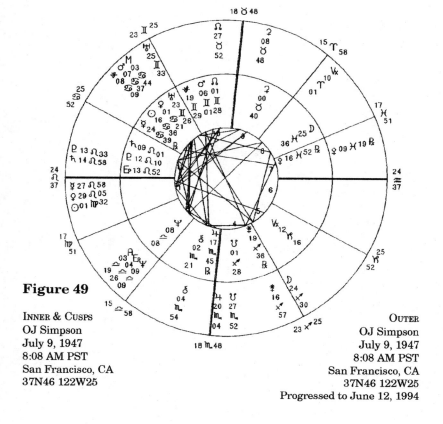

Figure 49

INNER & CUSPS
OJ Simpson
July 9, 1947
8:08 AM PST
San Francisco, CA
37N46 122W25

OUTER
OJ Simpson
July 9, 1947
8:08 AM PST
San Francisco, CA
37N46 122W25
Progressed to June 12, 1994

Ascendant/MC, Mars/Saturn, P Mars, P Vesta, and P local MC. His local P East Point was conjunct P Neptune and square three more natal midpoints: local Ascendant/local MC, Mars/Pluto, and East Point/Mars. His P Antivertex was also conjunct P Neptune and his local P Antivertex was square natal Mercury. The combination reinforces the message of personal action (Ascendant, East Point, Antivertex) driven by subconscious emotions (Neptune) and problems with rational objectivity (Mercury). P local Antivertex was also quincunx natal Moon in Pisces in the eighth house so it participated in the T-square of Moon, P Moon in Sagittarius, and

[PROGRESSED] MARS CONJUNCT [PROGRESSED] MIDHEAVEN: "You may confront, challenge, and fight authorities or limits of any kind. Anger, impatience, freedom, rashness… could arise… in respect to societal structures and expectations."

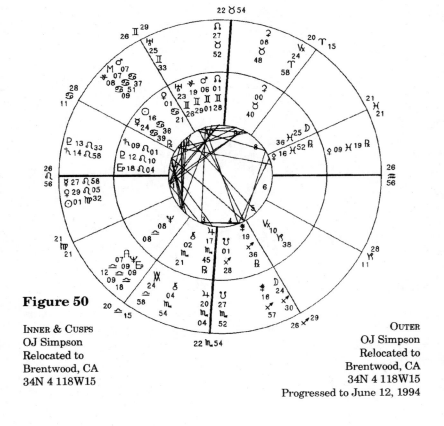

Figure 50

INNER & CUSPS
OJ Simpson
Relocated to
Brentwood, CA
34N 4 118W15

22 ♏ 54

OUTER
OJ Simpson
Relocated to
Brentwood, CA
34N 4 118W15
Progressed to June 12, 1994

Uranus in Gemini. The mutable signs of the T-square repeat the issue of faith/ideals versus rational objectivity. Their placement in (natal) fixed houses brings in issues of power and pleasure; our own versus our ability to share them with others.

One other important midpoint was featured by angle aspects in O.J.'s chart. Saturn marks an area of life where we learn the "rules of the game" in this particular world. The south lunar node is also a lesson area, usually one learned through close relationships where we seek to satisfy our dependency needs. The midpoint of Saturn/south lunar node can mark a key area for personal growth. I first noticed the potential importance of this midpoint in the chart of a man whose P Ascendant was on Saturn/south node when he killed his wife and her lover and then committed suicide. None of these points in a chart have to be negative. If we learn voluntarily, we then have something positive to give the world at these points. However, if we fail to learn voluntarily, we are pressured in some way by the world. O.J.'s P East Point from his birthplace was on his natal Saturn/south node and his P Ascendant will reach it by the fall of 1994. His local P Ascendant was conjunct P Saturn/P south node.

Of course, many additional aspects could be cited from O.J.'s chart, but the focus in this book is on the importance of the local angles. Studying our experiences in the light of our horoscopes calculated for the locations of the experiences can enhance our self-knowledge. Understanding our drives and our conflicts, understanding what **inside** of us permitted or produced what happened **to** us, can be a major step on the path to producing a more satisfying life.

CHAPTER THREE
ASPECTS TO ANGLES

This chapter summarizes major issues in focus when planets (or the "big four" asteroids and Chiron) aspect the angles by relocation. Aspects are discussed only in terms of conjunction, harmony (which would include sextile and trine) and conflict (which would include square, opposition and quincunx). It is our experience that trying to discriminate further just creates artificial distinctions. Remember that **every aspect has an "up" side and a "down" side**. Conflict aspects require more attention and effort to express positively, but can point to valuable assets once we integrate the drives symbolized. Harmony aspects show a likely sense of ease, but can point to excesses and overdoing unless we maintain moderation.

The first section discusses aspects to the Ascendant and, of course, to the Descendant as well. Harmony to the Ascendant means harmony to the Descendant. Conflict to the Ascendant means conflict to the Descendant as well. The exception is conjunctions. (Conjunctions to one end of an angle axis equal oppositions to the other.) Conjunctions to the Descendant are discussed following those to the Ascendant. Since we tend to experience the issues of planets conjunct the Descendent through our relationships, those qualities are susceptible to projection: where we disown the characteristics involved and unconsciously attract other people who overdo them. Both personal expression and projection will be discussed with Descendant conjunctions.

The later section of this chapter discusses aspects to the Midheaven/IC axis.

This chapter can supply a quick reference for identifying themes likely to arise in those places where these aspects exist in your chart. These are the aspects which would be easily revealed by an Astrolocality Map. For many people, their first step in considering relocation is to peruse the Astrolocality Map for likely areas. Once a possible area has been spotted, they go to the actual Relocation Chart for more details. Happy hunting!

Ascendant/Descendant Aspects

ASCENDANT CONJUNCT SUN

In this area, you may want more recognition and pursue leadership roles, magnetism, charisma, excitement, or take risks for greater gain. Ego issues could surface, with you feeling too proud (or too ashamed) of yourself. Your inner child, vitality, life force, creativity, fun-loving spirit, enthusiasm, and spontaneity may be encouraged here.

ASCENDANT CONJUNCT MOON

In this area, the following qualities tend to be highlighted: emotions, moodiness, food issues, security needs, vulnerability, receptivity, habit patterns, your home and family or involvement with the public. You might end up feeling torn between independence and closeness or needing to nurture in your own way. Your body may be more sensitive or reactive. Emotional attachments may increase in importance. Issues around nuturing, protection, and safety may arise.

ASCENDANT CONJUNCT MERCURY

This location emphasizes communication. Verbal (or listening) skills, logic, flexibility, learning, gathering information, perceptiveness, curiosity and restlessness may be further developed. You may become more observant or find your mind (and tongue) work more quickly—leading to biting, ironic, sarcastic, satirical wit, leaping to conclusions, or being able to reason well under pressure.

ASCENDANT CONJUNCT VENUS

In this location, you are likely to face issues involving: pleasure, money, possessions (what you own and earn), sensuality, comfort, ease, affection, self-indulgence, stability and predictability. Sweetness, accommodation, and relationships might be over emphasized. Sharing equally may present challenges. You might become personally involved with beauty (including physical grace).

Example: Pearl Bailey's chart, relocated to Hollywood, California, puts Venus (and Uranus) conjunct her Ascendant.

ASCENDANT CONJUNCT MARS

This locale would support your tendencies toward: assertion, personal expression, spontaneity, independence, doing your own thing, being physically active, feeling your anger, and pursuing your personal power. Immediate gratification may seem more compelling and your energy level or sex drive could go up. You might become quite a pioneer and ground breaker here.

Example: In Little Rock, Arkansas, Clinton's relocated Ascendant closely conjuncts his Mars.

ASCENDANT CONJUNCT JUPITER

This area reinforces your enthusiasm, ideals, goals, values, beliefs, and urge to seek expanded horizons. You may experience more exaggeration, excesses, restlessness, recklessness, honesty, education, travel, generosity, and faith. You could go "where angles fear to tread" and over promise or overreach, carrying what you idolize to an extreme. Your confidence, optimism, belief in self, and recognition of opportunities may increase.

Example: Rachel Sylvia (who died with Koresh) had Jupiter conjunct her relocated Waco Ascendant.

ASCENDANT CONJUNCT SATURN

This area may reinforce your sense of responsibility, realism, ambition, career goals, desire to achieve tangible results, self-criticism, discipline, and ability to learn through experience. You might battle authorities until firm in your own power or feel pulled between inhibition and action. Your career, status, power or parental issues, or tendency to overdo or underdo limits, could become a major focus. Your dedication and willingness to work hard may increase.

Examples: Bette Midler's chart relocated to New York features Saturn conjunct the Ascendant. So does Ross Perot's chart relocated to Saigon, Vietnam.

ASCENDANT CONJUNCT URANUS
This location may highlight your individuality, eccentricity, run-away tendencies, frustration at limits, need for freedom, inventiveness, originality, detachment, or humanitarian instincts. You could fight for justice and fair play, become quite involved with astrology, new age activities or groups, or be more of a rebel and risk-taker (perhaps even rash or foolhardy). You may be able to go "where no one has gone before" with your mind and actions.

Example: Pearl Bailey's relocated chart for Hollywood puts Uranus (and Venus) conjunct her Ascendant.

ASCENDANT CONJUNCT NEPTUNE
In this area, you could become more idealistic, empathic, compassionate (perhaps self-sacrificing), romantic, physically graceful, mystically inclined, or spontaneously psychic (instinctively doing the "right" thing). You may fall into savior/victim relationships or fight for the underdog. Lack of clarity could lead to fantasies, scandals, or secrets. You may exhibit grace or beauty through your body, physical movement, or personal action. You could become more sensitive (to drugs, allergies, etc.), escapist, spiritual, religious, or artistic.

Example: Bill Clinton's relocated Ascendant in Little Rock conjuncts his Neptune very closely (0°18')!

ASCENDANT CONJUNCT PLUTO
This locale highlights your intensity, concentration, endurance, drive for self-mastery, urge to transform yourself and others. Sexual needs or intimacy issues may become central. Courage and cruelty may surface, so learning to release, let go, forgive and forget may be challenging. With insight, you can share the sensual, material and financial world with another—for mutual pleasure. You need to explore your inner depths (and Shadow side) here, to deepen your understanding of life's underlying causes and patterns.

ASCENDANT CONJUNCT CERES
While in this area, you may find yourself falling into an "earth mother" role: supportive, competent, productive, work-oriented, analytical, instinctively taking care of others. You may pioneer or break new ground with family members. You could get more personally involved with pursuing health. You will probably try to do

your work more quickly or seek a field which is more self-directed. A protective, caretaking attitude is likely.

ASCENDANT CONJUNCT VESTA

This area provides the opportunity for you to increase your efficiency, concentration, ability to find the flaws, tunnel vision, pragmatism, self-criticism and organizational skills. Health or work could become quite a significant focus in your life. Your single-mindedness (along with occasional alienation from people or areas relegated to lesser importance) and "fix-it" skills may increase. Doing your work your way becomes more and more vital.

ASCENDANT CONJUNCT PALLAS

This area highlights your potential for dealing with polarities, comparisons, and contrasts; seeking equality; pursuing the artistic or aesthetic. Competition—or teamwork— may move into high focus. Justice, fair play, taking turns, evenhandedness and similar concerns may arise. Relationships could become more important as you are likely to define yourself partly in comparison to those around you.

ASCENDANT CONJUNCT JUNO

This locale emphasizes your drive for partnership (particularly a committed relationship)—learning through interacting with someone else. Sharing, beauty, grace, control issues, or intimacy may increase. Competition, justice, and the balancing act between personal power and shared power (your desires and your partner's desires) and the handling of possessions, pleasures, and resources are apt to become quite significant. You will probably want to put more of yourself in your associations.

Example: Bill Clinton met Hillary at Yale. His relocated chart (for New Haven) puts Juno conjunct the midpoint of his Ascendant and East Point (an auxiliary Ascendant): 4°24' from his Ascendant and 3°27' from his East Point.

ASCENDANT CONJUNCT CHIRON

In this region, you have opportunities to develop more optimism, experimentation, freedom, faith (beliefs), seeking and searching behaviors, eager, restless urge for **more** in life. You could become personally involved in a quest for perfection or knowledge, wanting to travel beyond known boundaries. Your expectations may be inhumanly high. Finding your own answers (particularly in regard to moral/ethical issues) is probably vital; your mind could be quite sharp and quick here.

DESCENDANT CONJUNCT SUN

This area highlights issues of love, passion, ego, admiration and attention through relationships. If projected, one person may play the perpetual "Star"—always on stage, self-centered, magnetic and exciting—while another person plays the role of audience. If shared, you and a partner are each other's best fans, looking up to one another, and spurring each other on to greater, larger efforts. Intense love bonds are possible here, or increased leadership, recognition.

DESCENDANT CONJUNCT MOON

This locale highlights issues of dependency, nurturance, vulnerability, and emotional security in relationships. If projected, you may attract people trying to mother you ("for your own good") or people expecting you to be all-nourishing, all-protecting, all-supportive to them. If shared, you take turns in relationships caring and being cared for, leaning and being leaned upon. A strong family focus with much warmth is possible.

DESCENDANT CONJUNCT MERCURY

This region emphasizes themes of thinking, communication, objectivity, and detachment in relationships. If projected, you may draw in scattered, superficial, cool, talkative, or youthful types. If shared, communication may increase in relationships. You may become more involved with people through mental pursuits, enjoy laughing together, become a bit more lighthearted, casual, and able to relate easily to others.

DESCENDANT CONJUNCT VENUS

In this place, comfort, sensuality, pleasure, indulgence, and material resources are highlighted in relationships. If projected, you may become involved with stodgy, materialistic, hedonistic, or lazy individuals. If shared, beauty, sensuality, or money could become more central in your relationships. You and a partner may enjoy pampering one another. A focus on love increases.

Example: Michael Camdessus (head of the International Monetary Fund) increases his financial focus with Venus conjunct his relocated Washington Descendant (in Taurus).

DESCENDANT CONJUNCT MARS

This locale puts assertion, independence, action, adventure, and personal will in high focus. If projected, you may unconsciously attract selfish, highly physical, impulsive, unavailable, excessively independent, or even violent people. If shared, you are likely to seek more space in relationships, to enjoy some separate time, to pursue active pastimes, and to gain a firmer sense of who you are and what you want through your associations.

DESCENDANT CONJUNCT JUPITER

Issues of ultimate Truth, seeking, questing, expansion, and faith are emphasized in this area. If projected, you may draw in self-righteous, arrogant, foolhardy, humorous, restless individuals— or people who expect you to make their lives perfect, to give them meaning. If shared, the search for final answers becomes more central: through books, travel, education, spiritual quests, or anything which expands physical, mental, spiritual horizons.

DESCENDANT CONJUNCT SATURN

In this locale, authority issues figure largely in relationships. If projected, you may draw in controlling, dictatorial, restrictive, critical, workaholic, demanding people — or people who expect you to do all the work, carry the load, take on all responsibilities. If shared, you may work hard on building good, solid, enduring relationships. You might work with a partner, establish business connections, or increase your practical perspective on relationships.

DESCENDANT CONJUNCT URANUS

In this place, issues of freedom, innovation, change, and openness become central in your relationships. If projected, you may draw in erratic, undependable, impersonal, detached, excessively independent people. If shared, tolerance and friendship increase. Your associations may be a bit unusual or feature people with a unique twist. Individuality for everyone is apt to be strengthened.

DESCENDANT CONJUNCT NEPTUNE

This region highlights themes of beauty, grace, imagination, fantasy, rose-colored glasses, and transcendence. If projected, you may draw in artistic types, helpers and healers, or victims of all sorts (ill, alcoholic, chronically unfortunate, unable to cope with life). If shared, you and others bring illumination, touch the Infinite, increase beauty or goodness in the world.

DESCENDANT CONJUNCT PLUTO

In this location, shared resources, sexuality, intensity, confrontation, and unconscious, Shadow issues move into central focus in relationships. If projected, you may draw in power trippers, manipulators, vengeful people, addicts, or the chronically abused. If shared, you learn more about your depths through others; you own your own power through face-to-face encounters with others. You can deepen your inner understanding and self-mastery.

DESCENDANT CONJUNCT CERES

In this area, themes of practical nurturing, work, health, and sensible caretaking become paramount in relationships. If projected, you or a partner may fall into Earth Mother roles: too willing to serve, to look after, to clean up other people's messes. If shared, working partnerships are possible, or relationships which heighten your efficiency, health habits, concern for the Earth, or desire to be efficient and helpful.

DESCENDANT CONJUNCT VESTA

In this place, themes of flaw-finding, nit-picking, pragmatism, discrimination, and realism loom large in relationships. If projected, you may draw in people who are endlessly critical—or consistently elicit criticism from you. Work could compete with relationships. Alienation from emotional matters is possible. If shared, you may create practical associations, establish a working relationships, and/or be dedicated to building the most efficient partnership possible.

DESCENDANT CONJUNCT PALLAS

In this location, justice, equality, fair play, balance, and aesthetics are more central in relationships. You may increase your aesthetic involvements. If projected, you may draw in competitive, righteous, "score-keeping" individuals. If shared, you increase your teamwork activities and work to create a more and more level playing field for everyone in your relationships.

Example: General Schwarzkopf's Pallas conjuncts his relocated Descendant in Baghdad.

DESCENDANT CONJUNCT JUNO

In this region, themes of intimacy, power, commitment, intensity and appearances could increase in significance. You may unconsciously attract people who want more commitment than you do—or who are excessively demanding in terms of closeness. Power struggles could develop. If shared, you learn much about yourself through the mirror of "the other." You may do much inner work and increase your sense of personal power and mastery.

DESCENDANT CONJUNCT CHIRON
In this area, idealism, mental stimulation, restlessness, and freedom are highlighted. If projected, you might draw in people who want more than is possible, can't settle down, or never stop learning. If shared, your associations with others encourage you to study, travel, seek Higher Truth, create the best, and look on the bright side of life.

ASCENDANT/DESCENDANT HARMONY SUN
This area encourages your urge to shine, to be creative, to lead, to seek excitement, recognition, and admiration. Your vitality, ego focus, and childlike enthusiasm may increase. An emphasis on recreation, speculation, loving and being loved, or having fun may emerge. You're eager to do more than you've done before and have others notice and applaud.

ASCENDANT/DESCENDANT HARMONY MOON
This location supports your drive to seek security, to build a nest, to look after others. An emotional focus is likely and you may increase your nurturing and/or dependency needs, receptivity, moodiness. Home, family, and/or children could become more central in your life. Opportunities to balance assertion and assistance are likely here.

ASCENDANT/DESCENDANT HARMONY MERCURY
This locale encourages your communication skills, adaptability, dexterity, rationality, detachment, and perceptiveness. You may learn more, teach, gather much information, increase your awareness and both listen and talk more. An urge toward new experiences and more variety could emerge. Objectivity may be enhanced.

ASCENDANT/DESCENDANT HARMONY VENUS
This area encourages you to seek pleasure, sensuality, material comfort, an easy, predictable flow. Tangible beauty may become more of a focus. You may increase your physical gratifications, possessions, and earning power (along with self-indulgence, weight, and hedonism). You probably find it easier to be kind and affectionate. Love may become a central focus.

ASCENDANT/DESCENDANT HARMONY MARS

This location tends to reinforce your: assertiveness, quick reactions, physical energy, self-expression and independence. Anger may flow more rapidly or impulsivity increase. Your desire nature will be more in focus, so personal power could become an issue. Being yourself and doing what you want may feel easier here — or just more important.

ASCENDANT/DESCENDANT HARMONY JUPITER

This region reinforces your ideals, goals, quests, and search for meaning. Your faith, optimism, ethical concerns, moral judgments, confidence, and extroversion may increase. Over extension, rashness, arrogance, or righteousness are also possible. Your good judgment, a love of travel, or a yen for further education and expanded (physical, mental, spiritual) horizons may be fed here.

ASCENDANT/DESCENDANT HARMONY SATURN

This area supports your sense of realism, responsibility, and ambition. Power is highlighted here; you may face and handle issues around limits (too many or too few). Career may move more center stage for you. The wisdom of experience will be significant here; authorities can be helpful if you are open. You can develop more discipline, practicality, success, and achievements.

ASCENDANT/DESCENDANT HARMONY URANUS

This locale tends to encourage your individuality, originality, inventiveness, spontaneity, humanitarian instincts, intellect, and detachment. You may discover more alternatives, options, choices and openness; the future could exert a strong pull for you here. You may encourage experimentation and a broad perspective.

ASCENDANT/DESCENDANT HARMONY NEPTUNE

This locale may encourage your urges toward idealism, seeking beauty, grace, compassion, and intuition. You may carry your quest for Oneness or Union further, put energy into helping and healing, or fall into rescuer/enabler entanglements. Dreams or visions could inspire your actions, feed your courage, further your freedom to move toward self-actualization.

ASCENDANT/DESCENDANT HARMONY PLUTO

In this region, you may appreciate intensity, enjoy intimacy, easily focus on self-mastery. Sexual drives may increase. Issues of resentment, forgiveness, sharing money and resources may move toward center stage. Sharing could flow more easily. Here you may face your Shadow (dark side) and transform negatives into positives. You can courageously probe hidden areas and topics.

ASCENDANT/DESCENDANT HARMONY MIDHEAVEN
In this locale, you may find it easier to develop a sense of authority, career aspirations, status, and power drives. Realism may feel more natural; you can blend initiative and cautious planning. Mentors might assist you here. Your energy, vitality, and pioneering instincts are apt to flow toward vocational ambitions. You can become comfortable in the role of expert.

ASCENDANT/DESCENDANT HARMONY CERES
In this location, you feel energized when furthering competence, health, productivity, efficiency, and analysis. You may support nurturing on a practical level. Here, you are learning to care for others and still maintain personal freedom. Doing things "right" feels natural. Parental figures may lend assistance or you may find yourself more involved with children or protective endeavors. Tangible accomplishments help you feel good.

ASCENDANT/DESCENDANT HARMONY VESTA
In this region, self-improvement may become a constant focus. You may work hard at efficient functioning on the job and in your body. You might further develop concentration, tunnel vision, pragmatism, organizational skills, flaw-finding instincts or critical judgment, or your ability to repair things and situations. You can appreciate a "fix-it" approach. Self-criticism is possible, but less likely to be excessive and destructive with harmony aspects. It can be used for self-improvement.

ASCENDANT/DESCENDANT HARMONY PALLAS
In this area, you may gravitate more toward equality, competition, justice, balance, teamwork, or partnership. You could become more graceful, artistically pioneering, or aesthetically open. Here, you are learning to blend independence and sharing, your needs and those of others. A partner may assist you.

ASCENDANT/DESCENDANT HARMONY JUNO
In this area, your personal expression could be assisted through a partner or partnership. You may develop more grace, charm, intimate interactions, or artistic connections. You could help support a partner, or find a spouse (or partner) furthers your personal

development, or helps out materially or financially. You may find that courage or assertion contributes to your relationships and deep sharing revitalizes you.

ASCENDANT/DESCENDANT HARMONY CHIRON

This area accentuates your quest to know **more** and your urge to go beyond known boundaries in search of perfection. Experimenting, risk-taking, independence, optimism, faith, teaching, learning, interest in healing, or travel could increase. Restlessness, a need for variety, and taking on too much may also grow in this area. Intellectual curiosity, progressive ideas, and a quest for ultimate meaning are highlighted here.

ASCENDANT/DESCENDANT CONFLICT SUN

This area could present challenges (too much or too little) to your self-esteem, your need to shine, your inner child, creativity, or need for excitement. Ego and leadership issues could arise. Exaggerated responses may occur. You may find you are playing excessively or not enough. It is important to maintain constructive outlets for your speculative, fun-loving, ambitious, and risk-taking sides.

ASCENDANT/DESCENDANT CONFLICT MOON

In this region, you may have to work to feel comfortable with your emotional side, security needs, caretaking instincts, vulnerabilities, and homing instincts. Conflicts with women, children, or family members are possible—until you reach a balance between emotional attachments and your personal freedom; activity and receptivity; dependency and independence.

ASCENDANT/DESCENDANT CONFLICT MERCURY

This region may highlight challenges around clear communication, logic, detachment, and objectivity. Thinking may be out of balance with action; or talking with listening. Impulsivity or anger could affect your communications (quick-tongued? sharp-tongued?). Personal desires may sidetrack adaptability (or vice versa); you are learning to be flexible, but get your own needs met!

ASCENDANT/DESCENDANT CONFLICT VENUS

This region may highlight personal challenges around pleasure-seeking (too much or too little), sensual needs, or your desire for possessions, ease, and stability. Financial conflicts may arise until you feel comfortable about what you earn and own. Relationship conflicts are possible as you work on compromises between personal and interpersonal needs. You will be balancing competition and sweetness; assertion and accommodation.

ASCENDANT/DESCENDANT CONFLICT MARS
This locale could highlight tension between different ways of expressing yourself, assertion (too much/too little), independence (when, where, and how), or issues around anger (overdone, repressed?). At times, you may fight yourself–or others–while developing a healthy sense of personal power. Constructive excitement and activity are vital here.

Example: Bill Clinton's Mars quincunxes his relocated Baghdad Antivertex (an auxiliary Ascendant).

ASCENDANT/DESCENDANT CONFLICT JUPITER
This region may lead you to question your ideals, goals, philosophies, moral principles, or world view. You may feel torn regarding what you trust and value. Impulsivity could lead to sometimes acting against your better judgment or seeking the "impossible dream." You may confront expectations which are too high or too low, or strive for balance between rashness (excessive faith) versus being too cautious (lacking faith). A quest for the truth is vital and expanded horizons can help.

ASCENDANT/DESCENDANT CONFLICT SATURN
This region highlights your personal confrontation with power. Challenges may arise involving your sense of responsibility, drive for power, concept of reality, career goals, status ambitions, and expertise. Clashes with authorities are possible; self-criticism might be overdone. You may feel torn between spontaneity and the wisdom of experience (immediate impulses and disciplined effort). You are learning to balance confidence and caution, speed and temperance, personal will and the "rules of life."

Example: Progressed Saturn holds a quincunx to Clinton's Moscow Ascendant for many years.

ASCENDANT/DESCENDANT CONFLICT URANUS
This location could accentuate challenges regarding your personal independence, humanitarian instincts, intellectual distance, or fascination with the future. Clashes with friends, groups, or networks are possible as you strive to balance intellect and action. Eccentricity and a willingness to be different may be overdone (or

underdone). A constructive outlet for your restless, runaway, rebellious side is essential.

ASCENDANT/DESCENDANT CONFLICT NEPTUNE

This region may emphasize challenges regarding your idealistic images, quest for infinite love and beauty, intuition, rescuing instincts, compassion, or mystical yearnings. Faith and aspirations could affect your energy level; keep a balance between self-assertion and self-sacrifice; between personal needs and universal needs. A lack of groundedness can attract deception, secrecy or succumb to escapism. Your physical body may become more sensitive to drugs. In this area you are learning to integrate dreaming and doing.

ASCENDANT/DESCENDANT CONFLICT PLUTO

In this area, power struggle potentials are highlighted. You could feel torn between personal power and shared power; between self-expression and self-control; between independence and intimacy; between outer action and inner understanding. Anger, resentment, violence, and forgiveness (including of self) might be important issues to face. Power struggles with mates may emerge over sexuality or shared finances and resources. You are learning to be strong and forceful in constructive ways.

ASCENDANT/DESCENDANT CONFLICT MIDHEAVEN

This locale may highlight your inner tension between independent action and status drives; immediate impulses and reality constraints; personal power and societal power (including that vested in authority figures); between speed and caution. You may find yourself taking on too much (or resisting) responsibility; fighting the limits (or giving up too soon). You are learning to do as much as you can of what you want within the realistic limits of the way the world works.

ASCENDANT/DESCENDANT CONFLICT CERES

This region may highlight challenges around your nurturing instincts, competence urges, health habits, work routines, or analytical capacity. Impatience may arise on the job or with family members until you can balance caring for others and caring for yourself. Duties, practicalities, and the desire to do things **right** may exhaust you until you learn pacing and moderation. Your challenge is to direct your pragmatism into healthy, sensible accomplishments.

ASCENDANT/DESCENDANT CONFLICT VESTA

This area may encourage your self-critical side; be sure to count assets as well as flaws. You could face challenges in regard to efficiency, health habits, your ability to see shortcomings, and your need for exactness. An imbalance around work (too much or too little) may require attention. You could slip into tunnel vision (obsessive about certain details) or alienation from associates unless you practice tolerance and a wider scope. Enhanced "fix-it" and organizational skills can be a boon if directed toward the tangible world rather than your own personality (or that of other people). You can achieve a great deal.

ASCENDANT/DESCENDANT CONFLICT PALLAS

This region highlights the balancing act between self and other. Independence may compete with equality and sharing; being yourself with maintaining a relationship. You might fight with a partner, find your perceptions challenged, or fall into competitive exchanges where teamwork is needed until you achieve a just, fair, even exchange. You may develop a passion for justice, balance, harmony or beauty.

ASCENDANT/DESCENDANT CONFLICT JUNO

This area emphasizes challenges in regard to committed relationships. You may have conflicts with a spouse or partner until you can share money, possessions, and pleasures equally for mutual gratification. Independence could vie with partnership instincts; personal desires compete with joint satisfaction. Grace, charm, or beauty may be questioned. You will have many opportunities to learn about and master yourself through relating to another person. Healthy competition offers a constructive outlet.

ASCENDANT/DESCENDANT CONFLICT CHIRON

In this area, you may experience conflicts in regard to your quest for answers and inspired knowledge. Your urge for **more** (answers, truth, fun, frolic, stimulation, excitement...) and seeking of perfection may lead to dissatisfaction or excessive restlessness. Risks, experiments, studies, travel, or a quest for "the truth" could be overdone (or underdone). Clashes over beliefs, values, and expectations are possible until you achieve a clear sense of life's meaning which still allows you to be human, fallible, and free to discover more.

Midheaven/IC Aspects

SUN CONJUNCT MIDHEAVEN
This area emphasizes your quest for power, authority, recognition, status, and leadership roles. You may seek more excitement, creativity, fun, risks, speculation, recreation, or positive feedback in your work. Issues revolving around charisma, pride, or egotism could arise with authority figures (including boss). You are likely to feel most vital, alive, and energetic when successfully in charge, handling responsibility, and gaining practical results.

MOON CONJUNCT MIDHEAVEN
In this region, you may seek security through being an authority, having power, status, or a safe professional role. Your career could come to involve emotions, women, the home, land, the public, commodities (food, shelter, clothing...), or nurturing or caretaking activities. You are likely to work on balancing home and family with career; dominance with dependency; pragmatism with compassion. Realism, roots, and responsibility tend to be highlighted here.

MERCURY CONJUNCT MIDHEAVEN
This region highlights the incorporation of listening skills, talking, dexterity, logic, relatives, thinking, communicating, learning, variety, commerce, media, business, paperwork, or mental stimulation in your career. You may succumb to too much criticism of your thinking and communicating abilities — or center your mind on professional and realistic matters, concepts which are useful, and becoming an authoritative communicator. Your perception of reality may become more adaptable, seeing multiple options. You can put your mind to work in the world.

Example: General Schwarzkopf's Mercury conjuncts his relocated Midheaven in Baghdad.

VENUS CONJUNCT MIDHEAVEN
This area highlights your seeking of pleasure, comfort, stability, and ease through your career, power role, structures, regulations, safety, and predictability. Professional contacts are accented.

Business partnerships could develop. You may look for an easy job; enjoy high status; seek power through beauty or money; work for pleasure; or bring more sensuality, finances, people or stability into your work. Being graceful, charming, pleasant, or practical could be a professional asset. You might become more pragmatic about monetary matters. The focus is more material, physical here.

MARS CONJUNCT MIDHEAVEN
This locale highlights your drive for power and independence in your work. You may confront, challenge, and fight authorities or limits of any kind. Anger, impatience, freedom, rashness, high energy, courage, and pioneering spirit could arise on the job or in respect to societal structures and expectations. You are likely to work on the integration of personal will (what you want) and the rules of the game (what is possible in the real world of other people, authority figures, and established conventions). You may find responsibility, power, authority, and achievements quite energizing. You need to be active in the world.

JUPITER CONJUNCT MIDHEAVEN
In this area, your contribution to society may involve beliefs, values, ethics, principles, optimism, expanded potentials, faith, idealism, philosophy, religion, the law, travel, or anything which broadens people's (physical, mental, emotional, spiritual) horizons. You might put your faith into status, authority, power, expertise, your career, or physical reality. You are working on the balance between your ideals and material reality; optimism and pessimism; faith and fear; expansion and contraction. An optimum blend leads to recognizing many opportunities and working hard to make them manifest.

SATURN CONJUNCT MIDHEAVEN
In this locale, you are likely to feel quite responsible, practical, realistic, and reliable. Power issues are highlighted and you may want more authority, status, and control in your career. The need for tangible results, discipline, thoroughness, dedication, and effort is emphasized. You may deal more with structure or the issue of limits and limitation. Much of your learning here comes through experience.

URANUS CONJUNCT MIDHEAVEN

This location highlights your need for freedom, variety, openness, or unconventionality in regard to your career and place in society. You may be drawn to a humanitarian or new-age profession, or something involving a future orientation or new technology and ideas. The authorities you meet may seem eccentric or erratic if you do not have a satisfactory outlet for your individualistic side. You might wield power in an unusual fashion and could become rather objective and detached (or erratic and careless) about responsibilities, limits, traditions, and control. You can find freedom in power and power in freedom.

Examples: Ross Perot's chart relocated to Armonk, NY (IBM and computers) features Uranus conjunct the Midheaven. The innovative junk bond dealer, Michael Milken, also gets Uranus conjunct his Midheaven [breaking traditions and rules] when his chart is relocated to New York or Washington, DC.

NEPTUNE CONJUNCT MIDHEAVEN

In this region, you may be drawn to fields involving art, compassion, or escapism. You could become a professional rescuer, artist or victim. You can put your imagination to work here. Your sense of reality has mystical or magical overtones. Authorities may appear idealistic, mystical, confused, compassionate, or escapist if you have no constructive outlet for your inspired side—or you could want more than is possible vocationally and job-hop or be chronically dissatisfied. Your status may be romanticized, idealized, hazy, or unclear. Constructively, you can blend the real and the ideal: bringing dreams to earth. You may inspire others, perhaps gaining power through transcendent experiences. Higher consciousness could be a major focus.

PLUTO CONJUNCT MIDHEAVEN

In this region, you are likely to experience an intense drive for power. Issues around self-discipline, self-control, addictions, and compulsions could arise. Practicality about joint finances and shared resources may be essential; a business partnership could develop. Power issues could affect sensual/sexual interactions. An urge to plumb the depths is probable. A need for control is highlighted, so learning to let go, to forgive and forget, may be a challenge. You might be drawn to experiences which are emotionally intense.

CERES CONJUNCT MIDHEAVEN

This area puts your efficiency, productivity, organizational skills, and practicality in high focus. You could be quite responsible and hardworking here. You may be drawn toward service, health, healing, or professional nurturing. The need to do things **right** is accented. You might end up carrying more than your fair share on the job, or getting involved with authorities who play the Earth Mother role. A family business connection is possible—or other ways of blending caretaking and professional achievement.

VESTA CONJUNCT MIDHEAVEN

A single-minded focus on accomplishment may come more easily in this region. Responsibility, hard work, tangible results, health and healing, efficiency, productivity, and organizational abilities are highlighted. You could develop skills in science, business, or any detail-oriented work. You may succumb to nit-picking or supercritical tendencies (toward yourself, others, or improving your job skills). If overdone, alienation from others is possible. You may carry more than your fair share of the load; be willing to delegate. Overwork could lead to stress on your body; stay moderate. You can get a lot done and be quite grounded here.

PALLAS CONJUNCT MIDHEAVEN

This area suggests you may bring to your work more beauty (design, fashion, decorating, etc.), harmony, relationships (counseling, consulting, personnel work, arbitration, politics), or teamwork. You might meet a partner through work, work with a partner, or establish a business relationship. Practicality about people is highlighted and your position in society may be affected by your close relationships. Your passion for justice, fair play, and equality may be highlighted.

JUNO CONJUNCT MIDHEAVEN

This area emphasizes a blending of intimacy, intensity, aesthetics, and shared resources with your quest for success and achievement. You might make a profession out of relating to people (including marriage, personnel, counseling, consulting) , bring an artistic element into your job, or be attracted to political power and action. You could meet a partner through work, work with a partner, or get involved with strong, responsible (perhaps dominating) individuals. Questions around giving, receiving, and sharing pleasures, possessions, and power may move into high focus.

Authority and career are likely to influence—and be influenced by—your significant partnership(s).

CHIRON CONJUNCT MIDHEAVEN
This location highlights issues of the free-ranging mind in your work. You may be drawn toward intellectual vocations (writing, teaching, computers), or into a healing profession, and are likely to seek variety. You might travel or broaden people's horizons. Vocational independence may become more important; you could take more risks for success. You might idealize power, authority, the work ethic, or competence. Grounding your goals and achieving practical results is likely to increase in importance.

SUN CONJUNCT IC
In this area, family and love relationships are probably more important. Attention, applause, and admiration may be sought through the home, roots, land, or providing basic resources. Public recognition is possible. You might feel more ego-invested in children, a "showplace" home, patriotism, or other forms of shining and being noticed through emotional attachments and root foundations. Emotions may be a bit more volatile with positive feedback vital.

MOON CONJUNCT IC
In this locale, nurturing could become a central focus. Children, pets, plants, or anyone and anything you can take care of may become more important. Warmth and closeness are sought. Home-centered activities may be given more attention. Food (and weight gain) could move up in significance. Old feelings about "Mom" could be revisited. Intuition may increase. Emotional security and safety are vital. You may place more priority on feelings, public involvements, your homeland, or matters promising protection or support.

MERCURY CONJUNCT IC
In this region, a light touch gains importance. You may leave home periodically, especially for short trips. You could bring in lots of neighbors, conversation, or mental stimulation. Involvement with the public through media is possible. Safety becomes tied to thinking, communicating, and (perhaps) being fast on your feet—moving, making a quick quip, or knowing when to change the subject. Variety in the home will probably appeal.

VENUS CONJUNCT IC

In this place, pleasure in and through the home become vital. Sensual indulgence (especially in food or drink) is possible. The comfort of touch can be very gratifying. Collecting and holding on to things may have more appeal. Security is apt to be sought on emotional and physical planes. Feeling good and making affirming connections with other people becomes more important. Accepting, trusting, accommodating, or getting comfortable could be overdone. You may enjoy your family, your home, or the public more—or get satisfaction through roots, antiques, history, or other connections to the past.

MARS CONJUNCT IC

In this area, personal needs and action are probably given priority in the home. You may assert yourself more with family or regarding domestic matters. (Fights with family members would be a less pleasant prospect.) You may be very active and energetic about the home. Ambivalence is likely between pleasing yourself and maintaining close, emotional ties. Some compromise will be essential. Old scripts and resentments about nurturing and anger can be faced, and an integrated approach— being yourself and still maintaining close ties— can be achieved. You probably feel safest when doing your own thing.

JUPITER CONJUNCT IC

In this locale, you are likely to bring the world into your home, or take your home into the world! High ideals are likely for the nest, but restlessness in regard to actually staying in one place. You might fill your home with books, philosophical discussions, intellectual stimulation, people of other cultures, and spiritual seeking. Or, you could take your home on the road (travel, trailer, living abroad part of the year, journalism, politics, etc.). You might influence people on a large scale. High expectations are likely in regard to nurturing, family members, and the physical home. Be reasonable! Keep a balance between roots and adventure.

Example: Pearl Bailey's chart, relocated to Hollywood puts Jupiter conjunct IC.

SATURN CONJUNCT IC

In this region, responsibility is strongly tied to your emotional foundation. You probably feel safest when in control. You may take on excessive burdens or power within the home, family, or with the public, homeland. Be clear about the limits and willing to let others do some of the work. Adversarial relationships with authority figures are possible unless power is wisely handled. A practical focus is essential in regard to emotional matters. You'll work on the balance between home/ family and career/ work in the world; between dominance and dependency; between pragmatism and emotional support. A reasonable compromise—the best of both—works well.

Examples: General Schwarzkopf's Saturn conjuncts his relocated IC in Baghdad. So does David Koresh's in Waco, Texas.

URANUS CONJUNCT IC

In this area, freedom, innovation, and change (or chaos and disruption) are highlighted within the family matrix. This might means periodic changes of residence, or alterations in domestic routines, or in the people living in your home. Safety might vie with unpredictability; protection could be erratic. Communal situations could arise, or you might just fill your home with astrology, friends, computers or other new technology. You may offer a unique perspective to the public. A resistance to routine is likely; don't force commitment where you do not feel it. Nurturing freedom and inventiveness works well.

Examples: Erik Menendez's chart relocated to Beverly Hills features Uranus conjunct IC. (So does Clinton's relocated chart for Kabul, Afghanistan.)

NEPTUNE CONJUNCT IC

In this location, empathy, imagination, and sensitivity (physical, emotional, psychic) are highlighted. You may understand many things on a non rational level. Rose-colored glasses regarding family, the home, and emotional matters are possible and negative options include escapism or victim behavior (drugs, alcohol, abuse, etc.). Be sure your idealism is constructively channeled. You may wish to create a more beautiful home. Co-dependent entanglements could develop. A better option is to share meditation, spiritual goals, compassion, philanthropy, or an artistic pursuit with the public or people in your domestic environment.

PLUTO CONJUNCT IC

In this locale, your connection to the unconscious is stronger. Psychic intuition could be developed. You may face the "Shadow"— the parts of yourself you've disowned in the past. Power struggles (especially with family members) are possible if intense emotional matters are not subject to constructive compromise. Beware of burying emotions too deeply. Dig inside and you will learn much. You may have the opportunity to come to terms with manipulation, power plays, passive-aggressive behavior, or addictions within the family circle or as public agendas. You'll need more privacy; be sure you get it. Great mastery of your inner life is possible.

Example: Bill Clinton's Pluto conjuncts his relocated IC in Pyongyang, North Korea.

CERES CONJUNCT IC
In this area, issues of practicality and caretaking move into high focus. Family could become more central. Domestic duties are likely to be significant; be sure they are sufficiently shared—lest one person end up "servant" to the others. Your connection to the land may deepen. Efficiency, practicality, and helping people to be more effective in their lives appeal very strongly here.

VESTA CONJUNCT IC
In this region, issues of work, health (or illness), focus, concentration, follow-through, and efficiency become central. You may be inclined to carry too many domestic burdens. Alienation could follow a sense of doing too much. Cleanliness or doing things "just so" could be carried to an extreme. Criticism—from you toward family and/or from family toward you—could become a problem. Keep a balance between unconditional support and the necessities of life which cannot be ignored or overlooked. You can accomplish a great deal.

PALLAS CONJUNCT IC
In this location, safety becomes melded with justice and fair play. Teamwork appeals. Shared family activities may gain more priority. Intellectual stimulation within the home will probably be more valued. Relationships may be given more attention, with a desire to share becoming paramount. Emotional connections matter.

JUNO CONJUNCT IC
In this area, intimacy gains priority. Marital and family commitments may move up in significance. Emotional ties become increasingly important, although jealousy, abuse of power, and pos-

sessiveness are also possible. Security feels connected to blood bonds. Sharing, particularly on a nonverbal level, could increase. Co-dependent associations could arise. Constructively, people tune deeply into each other's souls, understand each other's feelings and nurture self and other carefully.

CHIRON CONJUNCT IC

In this region, family ideals may move to center focus. Issues of trust, faith, and values emerge as significant. Restlessness regarding the physical home is likely, so travel is an option—as is lots of mental stimulation or visitors. Looking for the best in emotional matters is a worthy goal, but be sure expectations are reachable. Nurturing independence, understanding, and spiritual or educational quests makes the most of this combination.

SUN HARMONY MIDHEAVEN/IC

This region highlights creative, promotional, sales, speculative, risk-taking skills which could advance your career. Authority figures, loved ones, or your own expertise could assist your professional accomplishments (and status); your ambitions could amplify. Your handling of reality and responsibility may feed your power drives, need to shine, pride, ego, or drive for excitement. You can learn to balance self-confidence with cautious pragmatism here.

Example: Pearl Bailey's Sun trines her relocated Midheaven in Hollywood.

MOON HARMONY MIDHEAVEN/IC

In this locale, your caretaking instincts may further your career; family and professional matters can enhance each other. Women, emotions, family members, nurturing figures, a feeling for the public may contribute to your status and achievements. You can balance strength and gentleness; caring and capability; compassion and the bottom line; domestic desires and outer world achievements. Security needs are probably reinforced.

MERCURY HARMONY MIDHEAVEN/IC

In this area, your career, status ambitions, and authority may be advanced by social contacts, communication skills, dexterity, adaptability, flexibility, relatives, or your willingness to learn. Media, commerce, or skill with paperwork and gathering information could contribute to your success. You can become more objective and light-hearted about power issues, increasing your realism, logic, and problem-solving capabilities. Your mind, perceptiveness, and awareness can help you make a contribution to society.

VENUS HARMONY MIDHEAVEN/IC

This region suggests that beauty skills, women, love, sensuality, financial ability, groundedness, grace, or charm could contribute to your achievements. You may be inclined to go along with authorities, the status quo, what is comfortable, familiar, and stable. Your sensuality, material resources, indulgence, pleasures, or status may increase. Authorities could contribute to your material base.

MARS HARMONY MIDHEAVEN/IC

In this place, you may find it easier to direct your self-assertion, personal expression, spontaneity, and independence toward power, authority, achievement, career aspirations, and realistic accomplishments. You may get along better with authority figures. Men, doing your own thing, being first (a pioneer), active and energetic could contribute to your successes. You can balance spontaneity and control; speed and caution; impulses and planning; personal desires and pragmatic necessities.

JUPITER HARMONY MIDHEAVEN/IC

In this location, your ideals, optimism, enlarged perspective, optimism and values may further your career, status or power. Your philosophy, religion, or quest for truth may parallel those of authorities. A willingness to risk could enhance your position in society. You can bring your dreams and visions into material manifestation. You notice opportunities for advancement.

SATURN HARMONY MIDHEAVEN/IC

In this area, your sense of responsibility, practicality, discipline, and willingness to work can be significant vocational assets. Your willingness to learn through doing may assist your career. Your understanding of limits, drive for power and control, and executive instincts contribute to your success. Authority figures may assist your ambitions. You might have a good sense of when to consolidate your gains here. Tangible results and accomplishment are highlighted.

URANUS HARMONY MIDHEAVEN/IC

In this region, your individuality, inventiveness, objectivity, detachment, open mind, and independence may become vocational assets. The future and "cutting edge"—or sudden, unexpected changes— could contribute to you professionally or advance your status. You might seek power in order to gain more freedom. Humanitarian instincts or new-age principles may enhance your worldly accomplishments. You can blend the old and new; conventional and unconventional; traditional and original for best results.

NEPTUNE HARMONY MIDHEAVEN/IC

In this area, art, beauty, magic, inspiration, intuition, or imagination could assist you vocationally or enhance your status. You can harness compassion and responsible productivity. Authorities may be charmed by your artistic, compassionate, or inspiring qualities. You can bring together the mystical and the physical; the transcendent and the material. You may get a good sense of when to control and when to "go with the flow." You can blend inspiration and perspiration.

PLUTO HARMONY MIDHEAVEN/IC

This area highlights skills for the business world and research. Organizational abilities, endurance, follow-through, focus, concentration, discipline, self-control, and an urge to look beneath the surface are talents likely to be further used here. Loyalty could become a significant issue. Power struggles are possible. Constructively, you may gain more authority and control. A mate or partner may offer support to your vocational efforts. A stronger focus on endurance is probable. You may learn to work well with authorities.

CERES HARMONY MIDHEAVEN/IC

This location highlights potentials skills in regard to accuracy, organization, dedication, planning, and a willingness to work. Family members or nurturing figures could contribute to your success. Mentoring relationships might arise. You may find it easy to get along with colleagues here. Service instincts flow more naturally into your work; a feeling for plants, protection, sustenance or emotional support could contribute to your work. You can carry productivity and tangible accomplishments further. You may

increase your craftsmanship and dedication to getting it right.
You can balance caring and common sense.

VESTA HARMONY MIDHEAVEN/IC
You may find it easier to utilize your practicality, concentration,
flaw-finding instincts, flair for organization, dedication, and common sense in this region. Putting effort into your ambitions comes
more easily. You may be highly motivated to do things **right**, using analysis, planning, discriminating judgment. Skill with details could be further developed. You may become more interested in health and healing. Relationships with colleagues are likely
to go well. Craftsmanship is emphasized here.

PALLAS HARMONY MIDHEAVEN/IC
This location suggests social contacts, grace, harmonizing instincts, aesthetic ability, or political skills could enhance your
vocation. Other people (partners, friends) may contribute to your
success here. Comparing, contrasting, and competing may increase. Keeping up appearances becomes easier. You can probably balance love and work; equality and control; thinking (observing) and acting (accomplishing) more easily.

JUNO HARMONY MIDHEAVEN/IC
In this locale, your career may receive an assist from your emotional intensity, artistic ability, relationships, social contacts, or
skill with joint resources. Your ability to look beneath the surface, competitiveness, and understanding of power could enhance
your work. You might become more practical about relationships
and deal more sensibly with strong feelings. Work and love needs
may be integrated more easily here. You might learn to balance
your executive (in charge) and equalitarian instincts.

CHIRON HARMONY MIDHEAVEN/IC
In this area, your status or career might be enhanced through
travel, idealism, taking risks, broadening people's horizons, stimulating people's minds, or seeking more knowledge, truth, training, and understanding. Intellectual openness could be a source
of power; your pursuit of meaning strengthens your authority.
Mentoring figure(s) could contribute to your quest for higher understanding. In this region, you are working on the combination
of idealism and realism, of visions and pragmatism which can
heal and help the world.

SUN CONFLICT MIDHEAVEN/IC

In this location, your professional ambitions may clash with your drive for excitement, need to shine, your children or inner child, speculative instincts, or creative spirit. Reality (or authority figures) may seem at odds with your need for recognition, applause, and good self-esteem. Issues around pride, power, and positive regard could arise. Time and energy demands between love and work; recreation and discipline; realism and risk-taking; pride and pragmatism might require integration. With balance, you can shine professionally and also relax, play and love appropriately.

MOON CONFLICT MIDHEAVEN/IC

In this location, emotional and practical needs may seem at odds with each other: professional ambitions clash with commitment to home and family; power drives compete with dependency/nurturing; emotions war with pragmatism. Challenging issues may arise involving women, emotional matters, parenting, or the public until you can balance compassion and competence; feelings and tangible results; domestic duties (home and family) and outer-world (career) successes. You are learning to be highly effective in a warm, supportive context.

MERCURY CONFLICT MIDHEAVEN/IC

In this location, your vocational aspirations may clash with social needs; dedicated practicality with casual light-heartedness; curiosity and restlessness with the urge to achieve results; youthful attitudes with conventional wisdom and experience. Your thinking or communicating style may conflict with authorities, or power struggles with relatives might develop. Issues could arise involving logic, rationality, adaptability, flexibility. the media, or business. Discrimination about paperwork, commercial transactions, what knowledge to pursue, and the handling of information will be essential. Seek to balance theory and practice; thinking and doing; structure and flexibility.

VENUS CONFLICT MIDHEAVEN/IC

In this location, your power needs and career aspirations may compete with your drive for pleasure, sweetness, beauty, relaxation and ease. Women, financial matters, or relationship (love) needs may challenge you vocationally until you achieve balance. You are learning to integrate love and work; duty and pleasure; effort and ease; power and peer relationships. Security, sensual rewards, and some material gratification are essential for you.

MARS CONFLICT MIDHEAVEN/IC
This location could bring potential clashes with authorities or males or between your desires and your conscience. You may resist limits, rules, or the need for cautious planning. You could feel torn between seeking power or practical achievement versus going your own way. Impatience, anger, rashness, self-centeredness, or "macho" tendencies could present challenges to your success or your need to conform could inhibit your spontaneity and independence. You are learning to balance spontaneity and control; personal will and societal constraints; desire and practicalities. With integration, you can direct much energy into personal, pragmatic accomplishments.

Example: Ross Perot's Mars squares his relocated Midheaven in Tehran, Iran, where he pulled off a daring rescue of his employees.

JUPITER CONFLICT MIDHEAVEN/IC
Authorities may challenge your ideals and goals in this region, or your philosophy/religion may feel at odds with the establishment. Moral or ethical issues could arise in your career. Expectations (too much or too little) could clash with reality. You may need to integrate optimism and pessimism; faith and fear; idealism and realism. Necessary duties may compete with your quest for meaning or urge for adventure. You'll work here on the balance between power and truth; expansion and contraction — while learning to ground your visions.

SATURN CONFLICT MIDHEAVEN/IC
In this region, you may clash with authorities over who is in charge. Issues around responsibility, appropriate limits (neither too few nor too many), dedication, and discipline could affect your vocational life. Status and power issues are highlighted; jockeying for position is possible. Traditions and the wisdom of experience may feel restrictive—or your experience contradicts "standard operating procedures." Developing practicality, patience and dedication may be essential to your success. You may feel ambivalent about your responsibilities, or what career to pursue, or balancing work with other needs (e.g., family, relationships, etc.). Time management may be a challenge. Solidifying, contracting, or building structures might become essential in this area.

Example: Clinton's Saturn closely squares his relocated Midheaven in Belgrade, Serbia.

URANUS CONFLICT MIDHEAVEN/IC

Your eccentricity may clash with rules, regulations and established structures in this region, or your independence might rub authorities the wrong way. Your inventiveness may challenge "the real world" (or feel blocked by it). You will be working to integrate theory and practice; the old and new (past and future); tradition and revolution; order and chaos; independence and control. You may feel torn between breaking the rules versus following them. Your humanitarian instincts may clash with the powers that be. You need to find ways to create freedom within a structure and/or to loosen up and change existing structures.

NEPTUNE CONFLICT MIDHEAVEN/IC

Your romantic, dreamy side may compete with your need to achieve in this locale. Rose-colored glasses, romantic imagery, or sensitive compassion could vie with ambition and a need to accomplish. Authorities might challenge your dreams, question your faith. Your imagination may be at odds with practical, worldly demands until integrated. You may feel torn between setting clear limits and structures versus dissolving boundaries and barriers; between being in control and "letting go and letting God." Savior/victim entanglements could affect your professional life. Compassion could clash with pragmatism and the bottom line; both are essential. With integration, you find ways to bring transcendent experiences into the material plane.

PLUTO CONFLICT MIDHEAVEN/IC

Power struggles with authorities or business partners are possible in this region. Issues of sexuality, manipulation, secrecy, possessiveness, addictions, or intense emotions could affect your vocation and status. Money may be used as a club; questions might arise around debts, taxes, or who owes what to whom. Thoroughness (too much or too little) could become an issue. Intimacy urges could clash with status needs until integrated; keep a balance between love and work; between equality and power. You may have to face the dark side of life (and yourself); don't let unconscious needs control your life. Compromises could be challenging; extremism comes easily. Learning to share power will be essential. Rather than obsess, resent, or withhold, know when to release and move on.

CERES CONFLICT MIDHEAVEN/IC

This region accents your susceptibility to the "indispensability trap": overworked and underpaid. You may have to learn when to delegate and when to handle the details yourself. Clashes around the "right" way to do things, duties, common sense, and practicality could arise. Family obligations may compete with vocational demands. A dearth or excess of practicality could be a challenge. You may feel torn between being a taskmaster and a nurturer or between humble service versus executive power. The demands and duties you feel bound by might affect your health if carried to an extreme. Health and healing could become a focus in your job. Realism and getting results are emphasized. You may bring together work and home (family business; working out of home; nurturing work, etc.).

VESTA CONFLICT MIDHEAVEN/IC

This region suggests potential challenges in regard to nit-picking, criticism, tunnel vision, practicality (too much or too little), workaholism, and the desire to have things **just so**. You might fall into the "indispensability trap" or feel overworked and underpaid. If over stressed, health challenges might develop. Colleagues, authorities, and family members may not agree with your definitions of common sense and the "right" way to do things. If you channel your flaw-finding instincts into improving your job performance, you can be highly effective, productive, and helpful in this area.

PALLAS CONFLICT MC

In this region, you may feel more torn (until you achieve integration) between love and work; cooperation (teamwork) and control; partnership and parenting; duty and relaxation; worldly ambitions and social needs. Love needs may conflict with work demands. Issues of justice, fair play, theory versus practice, and compromise may arise at work and at home. You could end up doing a lot of comparing, contrasting, and weighing alternatives. Beauty or aesthetic interests may require balancing with practical necessities. Your skill with people could be helpful on the job and in your home.

JUNO CONFLICT MIDHEAVEN/IC

This region may heighten the tension between love and work in your life. You may put more effort into balancing equality and control needs; partnership and parenting demands; aesthetic interests and practical necessities; the "bottom line" and intense emotions. Power struggles (at work and home) and competition could emerge over issues of shared resources, pleasures, possessions, and finances. You might associate too much security with a committed relationship. Compromises with authorities regarding money and relationship matters may be necessary.

CHIRON CONFLICT MIDHEAVEN/IC

This area highlights your conflict between pursuing variety, travel, intellectual seeking, spiritual truths and your desire for status, authority, control, and power in the material world. Ethical issues could arise vocationally or with authorities. Perfectionism and restlessness may challenge achievements and work satisfaction until you compromise. Traditions may vie with progress until you achieve balance. Your freedom needs could compete with your desire to work within the limits and to establish a home base. With integration, you can make your dreams real, balance independence with emotional connections; and keep a degree of openness and stimulation in your career and at home.

CHAPTER FOUR
ASPECTS TO THE ANGLES FROM HOUSE RULERS

The zodiacal positions of the planets do not change when you relocate, but the angles of the horoscope (Ascendant, Descendant, Midheaven, IC) will be altered. Thus, your aspects to the horoscope angles will also change. You never lose the natal patterns, but must factor in the relocated ones as well. If aspects were present natally and disappear in the relocation, those themes remain for you, but are less relevant in that area. If aspects were not present natally, but are in the relocation, those are issues you will face in that region but are not innate themes for you. If you move from natal harmony to relocated conflict, you have the opportunity to prove your mastery of those issues. If you move from natal conflict to relocated harmony, you have a bit of "ease" in facing the natal challenges, the potential of integrating some of your dilemmas.

This section will examine **relocated aspects (harmony or conflict) from house rulers to angles**. The angles discussed include the Ascendant, Descendant, Midheaven and IC. Since the angles are axes, harmony aspects (sextiles and trines) to one end (MC or IC; Ascendant or Descendant) also make harmony aspects to the opposite. This is usually the case with conflict aspects as well. Squares automatically square both ends of an angle axis. One could, however, have a quincunx (conflict aspect) to one end of an angle axis and a semi-sextile (neutral or mixed harmony and conflict) to the other. Similarly, a conjunction to one end of an axis will oppose (conflict aspect) the other end. Conjunctions are not discussed here **Any conjunction of a house ruler to an angle simply puts the matters of that house in higher focus.** Give them more weight in that location.

Rulers of 1st House

HARMONY TO ASCENDANT:
Inner agreement. Your basic drives and instincts reinforce each other. Your energy moves easily into self-expression. (Consider chart as a whole for what is most natural to you.)

CONFLICT TO ASCENDANT:
Inner ambivalence. You may sabotage yourself. You feel torn in different directions. Approach/ avoidance feelings. You must make peace within, finding avenues for all your various drives.

HARMONY TO DESCENDANT:
You can cooperate easily with others. You have a knack for interpersonal relationships. Self-other connections run relatively smoothly.

CONFLICT TO DESCENDANT:
You may clash with others on occasion. You could feel torn between doing your own thing and sharing life with someone else, or between asserting yourself versus accommodating another individual. A middle ground is essential.

HARMONY TO MIDHEAVEN:
Your immediate urges support your career efforts. You know how to fend for yourself as well as fit into society's structures. You naturally put yourself into vocational achievements.

CONFLICT TO MIDHEAVEN:
You may experience clashes with authority figures, or between what you want and what society demands (by law, convention, structures, etc.). Avoid extremes of giving up too soon or pushing too hard. Find ways to figure out the basic rules and work within them for what you want.

HARMONY TO IC:

Your natural self-expression harmonizes with your desire for a nest. You can nurture and be nurtured by family members or those upon whom you depend. You are able to balance independence and attachments.

CONFLICT TO IC:

Your personal needs may seem at odds with family demands or domestic duties. You could feel torn between independent action versus dependency or nurturance roles. Emotional conflicts are possible until you make room for both freedom and close connections.

Rulers of 2nd House

HARMONY TO ASCENDANT:

What you want as an individual flows easily with your desire for comfort, ease, material pleasures and finances. Your energy flows naturally into gratification. You instinctively seek pleasure.

CONFLICT TO ASCENDANT:

Your natural self-expression may feel blocked by financial or material issues. You may feel limited by the state of your finances and possessions, or feel tied down by them. The challenge is to be able to enjoy spontaneity and independent action as well as sensual and monetary gratification.

HARMONY TO DESCENDANT:

Partners or a cooperative attitude may enhance your material or financial picture. Teamwork could contribute to your pleasure from the physical world. Grace and beauty flow naturally.

CONFLICT TO DESCENDANT:

Partners may challenge your material or financial picture. Clashes are possible around issues of comfort, sensuality, or money. Differing viewpoints may call for compromise in terms of pleasures and possessions.

HARMONY TO MC:

Your career has the potential to support and enhance your financial and material assets. Your contribution to society may bring you greater pleasure, comfort or material gratification.

CONFLICT TO MC:
Your career may challenge your capacity to earn money and enjoy the physical world. Perhaps you work hard for what you get; perhaps you are overworked and underpaid. Perhaps what you most enjoy does not pay well. The challenge is to satisfy your ambition as well as your need for pleasure and material rewards.

HARMONY TO IC:
Family members may contribute to your capacity to enjoy the material or sensual world. Your home, parents or family could enhance your financial situation or bring more gratification and pleasure into your life.

CONFLICT TO IC:
Family clashes could revolve around sensual or financial issues. You may differ with parents or other family members around issues of money, comfort, physical indulgence and pleasure. Find ways to compromise.

Rulers of 3rd House

HARMONY TO ASCENDANT:
Your mental and communicative skills enhance your self-expression and ability to take action on your own behalf. Relatives may contribute to your sense of personal freedom. You enjoy learning and gathering information.

CONFLICT TO ASCENDANT:
Your mental and communicative abilities may be involved in clashes over assertion, anger or self-expression. Conflicts with relatives are possible. Forceful ideas may be involved. Strive for detachment and an objective eye.

HARMONY TO DESCENDANT:
Your social skills and desire to communicate can enhance your relationships. Shared mental connections are possible. You can enjoy learning together. Equality is suggested, with a good capacity to see each other's viewpoint.

CONFLICT TO DESCENDANT:
Communication may be a challenge in relationships. Perhaps one person talks too much, another too little. Perhaps there is a lack of clarity and a reluctance to confront touchy issues. Work toward increased objectivity and empathy.

HARMONY TO MC:
Mental and communication skills could enhance your career efforts. Authorities could assist your learning, and relatives might contribute to your work. You can use your mind to make a contribution to the world, to achieve.

CONFLICT TO MC:
Communication clashes are possible with authority figures. You may feel blocked or inhibited by the criticism of others. Detachment allows you to learn what is useful from the situation and disregard the rest.

HARMONY TO IC:
Family harmony is possible. You can stimulate each other's minds. Lively discussions may occur. Your home could be full of learning. A parent may encourage or support your further training. You can both listen and talk easily with those close to you.

CONFLICT TO IC:
Communication may be unclear, blocked or inhibited with family members. Whether fear, criticism, self-doubts, arrogance, or other qualities are involved, the challenge is to be objective and deal logically as well as sensitively with important emotional issues.

Rulers of 4th House

HARMONY TO ASCENDANT:
Mutual support is possible between you and family members. Nurturing figures may be of assistance to you and you may protect others. You find it easy to pursue your own activities and still have time for the people you care about.

CONFLICT TO ASCENDANT:
A lack of support may be experienced—from your family toward you and/or vice versa. Differing needs could result in push/pull or "come closer; go away" experiences. The challenge is to get more in synch with each other so you can share comfortably sometimes and enjoy independence other times.

HARMONY TO DESCENDANT:
Sharing and caring are accentuated. Relationships are important—on both an equal level and in terms of protecting or being protected. Harmony may flow between parents and partner, or simply between your partnership side and your nurturing side.

CONFLICT TO DESCENDANT:

The degree of closeness desired by you may be in question. You could be torn between commitments to parents (or parenthood) versus commitments to a partner. You need to resolve tension between being an equal versus being cared for or taking care of others. Sensitivity and empathy are your best tools.

HARMONY TO MC:

You have the potential of easily balancing home and career, dominance and dependency. You can commit to both domestic needs and career demands with a reasonable balance. There is a naturally helpful, supportive focus.

CONFLICT TO MC:

You may feel torn between achievement needs and domestic duties. Your time and energy could be stressfully pulled between family and career. You can be both strong and gentle, but need to find a middle ground position.

HARMONY TO IC:

You have inner agreement regarding family and domestic issues. Your attitudes around caretaking and emotional support systems are mutually supportive. (The whole chart will give the character of those attitudes.) Your nurturing and dependency instincts reinforce each other.

CONFLICT TO IC:

You may experience ambivalence regarding family and domestic issues. One side of your nature wants one thing; another side wants something different. Rather than fighting yourself or fighting family members, find a way to have a little bit of each. In that case, closeness strengthens and deepens.

Rulers of 5th House

HARMONY TO ASCENDANT:

You may find it easier to be noticed or to receive positive feedback. Your energy flows naturally into exciting, dynamic, creative activities. Your relationships with children (and/or loved ones) tend to be harmonious. Your actions build self-esteem.

CONFLICT TO ASCENDANT:
Ego conflicts are possible. There could be competition over the limelight, or you might block your need to shine with criticism or anxiety. Clashes could occur with lovers or children over the issue of positive regard. Healthy self-love allows you to also love others in an affirming way.

HARMONY TO DESCENDANT:
Love relationships are highlighted. The desire to be passionately involved with someone else is suggested. There is potential harmony between your children and partners or between your child-like, creative side and your cooperative, other-directed side.

CONFLICT TO DESCENDANT:
Ego clashes could affect relationships. You may experience partners and kids battling for attention or different people demanding your love. The challenge is to integrate your thrill-seeking, risk-taking side with your desire for committed relationships and caring connections. Find healthy avenues for mutual applause and admiration.

HARMONY TO MC:
Your creative, confident, zestful enthusiasm can enhance your career direction and/or your relationships with authorities. Believing in yourself and your ability to shine furthers your vocational ambitions. Children and/or lovers might contribute to your work (and vice versa).

CONFLICT TO MC:
Love and work might seem at odds with one another. You could feel torn between those you love (especially children) versus the demands of your job. Your responsible, hardworking side might vie with your risk-taking, creative side. Keep room for both joy and accomplishment, work and play.

HARMONY TO IC:
Warmth and caring connections are highlighted. The focus is on loving and being loved, and the desire for a family and loved ones to share your world. You find it easy to create and to nurture your creations.

CONFLICT TO IC:

The public and private parts of your life may be at odds. You could be torn between roles as a creator versus as a protector and nurturer. Stress might exist between your children (or a lover) and a parent. You need to integrate caretaking roles and your drive for excitement and drama.

Rulers of 6th House

HARMONY TO ASCENDANT:

You may easily pour yourself into your work. Your energy flows into tangible accomplishments—either on the job or focusing on health. Practical achievements appeal greatly to you. You can cooperate with co-workers.

CONFLICT TO ASCENDANT:

You may feel your work does not really fit who you are, or feel frustrated in some sense by what you do. The challenge is to make your job more a reflection of your basic drives. Clashes with co-workers are symptomatic of the need to work on matters that are more reflective of your identity. Aim toward more tasks which you can perform in your own way.

HARMONY TO DESCENDANT:

You have the capacity to keep partnerships and work complementary and supportive of one another. Your partner might contribute to your work or vice versa (relationships enhanced through your work). You may work more effectively with others.

CONFLICT TO DESCENDANT:

You may feel torn between your work and your relationships, or between colleagues and partners, or between a critical, flaw-finding attitude versus an accepting, empathic approach. The challenge is to make love and work support each other—and not compete with one another. Practicality can enhance your associations and empathy can further your work.

HARMONY TO MC:

Inner harmony is suggested in terms of your approach to the material world and earning a living. Your handling of details and duties can further your broader career and contribution to society. Skill at gaining tangible results and getting things done is likely.

CONFLICT TO MC:
Some inner conflict is suggested in terms of your approach to the physical world and making a living. Perhaps you clash with authorities over details and duties. Perhaps criticism and nit-picking is a problem. The challenge is to be efficient without (a) trying to be indispensable or (b) refusing to handle the boring but essential parts of a job. With integration, focus, concentration, and accomplishment are highlighted.

HARMONY TO IC:
You have the ability to nurture your family in practical ways and gain support from those you love for your vocational efforts. You are able to be sensible as well as warm, to harmonize family needs and vocational duties.

CONFLICT TO IC:
You may experience some stress between family needs and work duties. The challenge is to make your job supportive of those you love and vice versa. You could vacillate between warm compassion and hard-nosed practicality. Both can be helpful, if you choose your times and places wisely.

Rulers of 7th House

HARMONY TO ASCENDANT:
You have the capacity to blend personal and interpersonal needs. You can be your own person and still share a warm relationship with a partner. Harmony between you and others is implied; cooperation comes naturally.

CONFLICT TO ASCENDANT:
Clashes between you and others are possible. You may feel torn between meeting your own needs versus those of a partner. You could swing between too much focus on yourself, to too much on other people. Find a balance.

HARMONY TO DESCENDANT:
Inner agreement is suggested in your approach to partnerships. This could be cooperative, competitive, protective, etc. (See whole chart for the focus.) Grace, beauty and harmony are potential strengths.

CONFLICT TO DESCENDANT:

Some inner conflict is implied in the area of relationships. You may have clashing desires. Your partner(s) may be ambivalent. The challenge is to find ways to compromise and take turns between differing drives. Practice helps balancing and harmonizing come more easily.

HARMONY TO MC:

You keep relationships and work supportive of one another. You have a positive potential for partners enhancing your career and/or your work enhancing your relationships. You can create a constructive blend of empathy and practicality, sharing and responsibility.

CONFLICT TO MC:

You may feel your relationships compete with your career—each taking time and energy from the other. Or, your partner may clash with you about work, responsibility, or power. An authority figure might be at odds with a partner. You need to make peace between your sharing side and your side that wants control.

HARMONY TO IC:

Relationships with those you care about may flow rather well. You have the potential of harmony between family and partners, between a nurturing figure and a spouse. This indicates you can operate well as an equal and also as a protector, and find it easy to switch from one role to the other.

CONFLICT TO IC:

Close relationships may be an arena of some ambivalence. Clashes might occur between a partner and your family, especially a nurturing figure. You may feel torn between your position as an equal versus your position as a dependent or a nurturer. Establish appropriate times and places for each.

Rulers of 8th House

HARMONY TO ASCENDANT:

You may find it easy to direct your energies into intimacy, sexuality or shared pleasures. A passionate focus is possible. Agreements around shared finances and resources may flow easily. You can share power wisely.

CONFLICT TO ASCENDANT:

You may feel torn between solitary activities and intimate exchanges. Clashes over finances, sexuality, or shared possessions are possible with a mate. The challenge is to be able to share power over monetary and sensual matters for mutual satisfaction. Rising to the challenge will increase your personal power and mastery as well.

HARMONY TO DESCENDANT:

Inner agreement is suggested in your approach to partnerships and intimacy. (Consider whole chart for major themes.) You may find associations flow rather smoothly, or at least you are comfortable with your general approach and style of interaction where others are concerned.

CONFLICT TO DESCENDANT:

Some ambivalence is suggested in terms of interpersonal relationships. This could indicate clashes with partners, especially when monetary or sexual issues are concerned. The challenge is to share power, to truly be equal with one another—without domination, intimidation or manipulation. Attention to issues of mutuality will strengthen your intimate connections.

HARMONY TO MC:

Your intense, intimacy-oriented side can support your career ambitions. A mate may contribute to your career (or vice versa). Your follow-through and endurance enhance your status and contribution to society.

CONFLICT TO MC:

Intimacy may seem at odds with achievement needs. Your mate may conflict with your boss, or your sexual, financial, and sensual needs in a relationship may take you away from career attainments (and vice versa). The challenge is to intensely relate to another while still accomplishing enough to feel personal satisfaction.

HARMONY TO IC:

Emotional closeness is indicated as a significant theme. You may find natural harmony between your mate and your family. You may find your sensual and sexual connections enhance your capacity to nurture. Empathy and compassion make financial matters and division of resources easier.

CONFLICT TO IC:
Mate themes may clash with nurturing needs. Beware of parenting or being parented by a mate—take turns. Parents or children could compete with your mate for your time and energy. Sexual or financial needs might seem at odds with emotional yearnings. Focusing on deeper feelings and hidden motives will help resolve challenges.

Rulers of 9th House

HARMONY TO ASCENDANT:
Confidence and faith feed your urge to act and express yourself. Your behavior is strongly influenced by beliefs, ethics and values. You may receive assistance from in-laws, religious or spiritual involvements, or further education and training. Optimism is likely.

CONFLICT TO ASCENDANT:
You may sometimes act against your better judgment. Tension may arise around issues of morality, values, beliefs, or ethics. Disagreements with in-laws are possible. Focusing on constructive faith — enough but not too much — and trusting in appropriate areas is advisable.

HARMONY TO DESCENDANT:
Harmony in relationships is suggested around the themes of beliefs and values. You can agree with partners in terms of ethics, morality and faith. Your ideals may be in harmony. You have the capacity to see the best in each other.

CONFLICT TO DESCENDANT:
Idealism is an issue in interpersonal relationships. You may want more than is humanly possibly—or attract partners whose expectations are very grand. Ethics, moral principles and religious or spiritual beliefs may require discussion and compromise. Encourage the positive without falling into perfectionism.

HARMONY TO MC:
A confident approach can enhance your career prospects. Your faith and willingness to do more and better will support your vocational endeavors. Your work efforts may be enhanced through further education or training, support from in-laws, or your willingness to try something bigger and more exciting.

CONFLICT TO MC:

Expectations are an issue in your career. You may set your sights too high, wanting more than is reasonable—or be afraid to try if you cannot do some great, wonderful project. The key is **reasonable expectations**—combining your desire for more with practicality. Be clear about ethics and values with authority figures.

HARMONY TO IC:

You have the capacity to combine domesticity and adventure. You can reach out into the world for more travel, education, understanding or excitement, while still maintaining important emotional ties. You may broaden your home base and enlarge your comfort with new experiences.

CONFLICT TO IC:

You may feel torn between the attractions of your home and emotional security versus the lure of the open road, adventuring, and the quest for meaning in the wider world. Both are necessary. Family conflicts might arise over safety versus risk-taking unless compromises are made. Seek a sense of security within an open, exploratory framework.

Rulers of 10th House

HARMONY TO ASCENDANT:

You can easily direct your energies toward vocational accomplishment. Your natural instincts support practicality, responsibility and achievement. You can get along with authority figures.

CONFLICT TO ASCENDANT:

You may feel torn between doing what you want and fitting into societal structures or limits. Don't succumb to the extreme of fighting all the rules (or authorities), nor to the extreme of feeling blocked and inhibited by what is necessary. You need to determine what is possible and do what you can within that framework.

HARMONY TO DESCENDANT:

You have the capacity to blend love and work needs. You can maintain close ties while still meeting your achievement needs. You can make relationships and career supportive of one another, and create a reasonable balance between shared emotional ties and outer world accomplishments.

CONFLICT TO DESCENDANT:

You are working on the integration of love and work needs. You may feel torn between time and energy demands of a career versus close relationships. Your job may take you away from a partner or vice versa. Compromise allow you to make room for caring and competence, sharing and success.

HARMONY TO MC:

Ability and talent is suggested for handling responsibilities and career demands. You can be practical, assess reality, and do what is necessary. You have the capacity to work toward more and more authority. Taking control, particularly vocationally, is a natural for you.

CONFLICT TO MC:

Some conflict is possible around issues of structure, authority and power. This might include stress with authority figures, or simply your own ambivalence about responsibility and the degree to which you want or are willing to take control in life. Be sensible and work within practical limits.

HARMONY TO IC:

You can make your family and career supportive of one another. Those closest to you can support your working endeavors, and your vocational responsibilities contribute to domestic well-being. You are able to make a comfortable combination of caring and competence. You can be warm and effective.

CONFLICT TO IC:

You may experience some tension between family and work demands, or a push/pull between dominance and dependency, or warm caring and pragmatic performance. Compromise allows both sides expression. Find ways to make your career and domestic areas mutually supportive—or, at least, enjoy each — in turn — without guilt.

Rulers of 11th House

HARMONY TO ASCENDANT:

Your independent, unique, innovative side is easier to express. Harmony is likely with friends and you may receive support from organizations, new technology, or anything on the cutting edge of change. You can enjoy the unusual and the different.

CONFLICT TO ASCENDANT:
Independence issues are possible; you may overdo freedom urges, or unnecessarily restrict your unique individualism. Stress with friends or around groups, organizations, and causes is possible if you lack a constructive focus for the draw of the new, unusual or different. March to a different drummer where it truly matters to you.

HARMONY TO DESCENDANT:
Harmony is suggested in terms of relationships. Friends cooperate with partners and vice versa. Some people may go from friend to partner (and vice versa). Sharing flows rather easily. You appreciate people's unique gifts and individuality.

CONFLICT TO DESCENDANT:
Issues of individuality and freedom may surface in relationships. Friends could clash with partners, or you may be torn between sharing with someone versus treading your own path. Independence needs to be acknowledged without disrupting relationships. Objectivity can be an asset for you.

HARMONY TO MC:
Innovative approaches and new ideas can enhance your career. You may receive assistance or vocational support through friends, organizations, or new technological advances. A fresh perspective and willingness to break the rules constructively can contribute to your status and accomplishments.

CONFLICT TO MC:
Innovative impulses and the desire for independence may create some stress with authority figures or your achievement drives. Conventionality and unconventionality could be at war. You must creatively combine the old and the new, structure and flexibility, for constructive outcomes.

HARMONY TO IC:
Openness, tolerance and a focus on individuality can enhance your domestic experiences. Your friendships enrich your home life and vice versa. You have the capacity to be warm as well as objective, committed as well as independent. The focus is on caring without strings.

CONFLICT TO IC:

Conflict is possible between your desire for warmth and commitment versus your urge for independence and going your own way. Friends may compete with family and vice versa. The challenge is to keep a balance between attachment and detachment, between individuality and caring connections. Try treating friends as family (loving, warm) and family as friends (open-minded, tolerant, accepting).

Rulers of 12th House

HARMONY TO THE ASCENDANT:

You can naturally direct your energies toward helping, healing, or artistic endeavors. Idealism complements your self-expression. Your compassion feeds your willingness to act and to make a difference.

CONFLICT TO THE ASCENDANT:

Your idealistic, compassionate side may be at odds with your need to be independent. You could feel torn between self-assertion and self-sacrifice. Your visionary side or utopian images might lead to unwise actions. You can put your grace and beauty into physical action. Pay attention to your Higher Self.

HARMONY TO THE DESCENDANT:

Your capacity to visualize the best can enhance your relationships. You can see the highest potential in a partner and encourage its development. Your willingness to work toward enlightenment and the positive possibilities in life will enrich your people interactions.

CONFLICT TO THE DESCENDANT:

Your quest for infinite love and beauty may challenge human relationships. If overdone, you may want more than is possible or fall into savior-victim (co-dependent) associations. You have a talent for imagining utopian prospects; be sure you are sufficiently grounded to help make them real.

HARMONY TO THE MC:

Your visualization skills may enhance your career. Your intuition could be an asset in your work, or you could use talent for beauty, healing, or assisting people. Compassion and an understanding of the underlying processes and patterns of life will contribute to your work in the world.

CONFLICT TO THE MC:
Your yearning for the ultimate may challenge your professional aspirations. If carried too far, you could seek the "perfect" job that doesn't exist, or want more than is reasonable of yourself as a worker. Your visions **can** be made real; just keep a balance between doing and dreaming.

HARMONY TO THE IC:
Your sensitive, compassionate side may enhance your domestic environment (literally with beauty or emotionally with idealism). You are likely to recognize and feed the highest potential of those you care about. Family members will be encouraged to dialogue with their Higher Selves.

CONFLICT TO THE IC:
Your idealistic caring may affect your home and family. If overdone, sensitivity could be a problem. You or those you care about might be susceptible to escapism or martyrdom. If integrated, you can make your home a sanctuary, a place that feeds the soul.

CHAPTER FIVE

RULERS CHANGING HOUSES

A relocation often gives us different planetary rulers for our houses. Even if the rulership stays the same, that **planetary ruler may move to occupy a new house**. This section considers the rulers of the Ascendant (1st house) and Midheaven (10th house) only. They are, after all, considered the two most important angles by most astrologers.

The ruler of the Ascendant (and then of the Midheaven) is interpreted through every possible combination of original natal placement coupled with relocated placement. (Readers can create their own delineations for the other houses, following similar principles.)

Stellia changing houses are also considered.

Ascendant (1st House) Rulers: from 1st to...

2nd: You will retain a strong need to be yourself and be independent (with ruler of 1st in the 1st natally), but your self-expression is tied more to money, possessions, and pleasures now. Being self-sufficient financially may feel more important. You probably pursue beauty, comfort, and gratification here.

3rd: You will retain a strong need to be yourself (with ruler of 1st in the 1st natally), but your self-expression is more connected to the mind and communication in this area. You may find your mind and tongue work a bit more quickly (perhaps even impulsively). You could become more active in terms of classes, teaching, learning, neighborhood events, relatives, transportation or media.

4th: You will retain a strong need to assert your basic nature (with ruler of 1st in the 1st natally), but have a gentler overlay in this location. Home and family may become more important to your identity. You could feel some tension between independence and closeness needs. You might express more at home, with the public, or could become active in terms of land, commodities, food, roots, etc.

5th: You still have a strong need to be uniquely yourself (with ruler of 1st in the 1st natally), but need a wider scope of ego-expansion in this region. You will probably want to shine and be noticed. Love, admiration, attention and approval for who you are and what you do become more central. Children or creativity could be vital to your self-expression and personal action.

6th: You retain a strong need to express yourself (with ruler of the 1st in the 1st natally), but a sense of efficiency and productivity becomes more central to your self-expression in this locale. You need to do things well—in terms of your job and also in terms of physical health. Frustrations could affect either area. You probably have plenty of energy for activities that seem useful to you or provide a sense of accomplishment.

7th: You still have a decided need to express yourself and be your own person (with ruler of the 1st in the 1st natally), but relationships become more of a focus in this area. You are likely to meet partners or other people who reflect back sides of yourself. Through interacting with them, you learn more about who you are. The challenge is to balance your personal and interpersonal needs without going overboard on assertion or accommodation.

8th: You retain a need to be your own person (with ruler of 1st in the 1st natally), but deal more directly with power issues in this location. You will face issues of personal power versus shared power and may butt heads with other people or deal with manipulation and intimidation until you can share power wisely—particularly where money, sex and possessions are concerned.

9th: You have a strong need to be your own person (with ruler of 1st in the 1st natally), and this region reinforces your courage and your adventurous spirit. You may be drawn to seek the truth (through education, religion, spiritual quests, travel, etc.) or simply to wander the world or expand your horizons intellectually. Self-confidence and optimism may increase.

10th: You retain a strong need to be your own person, but will face the need to integrate self-expression with the "rules of the game" in this area. You may learn to control yourself for career ambitions, or clash with authority figures. You could overdo self-criticism or push too hard against the limits of the world. The challenge is to do as much as possible, in a realistic fashion.

11th: You still have a strong drive to be uniquely you (with ruler of 1st in the 1st natally), and this region accentuates your drive for individuality. Independence (particularly of mind) remains vital to your self-expression. You may be active in groups, causes, politics, social causes, new age ideas, computers, astrology, or anything on the cutting edge of change. You seek stimulation!

12th: You retain the urge to be fully yourself (with ruler of 1st in the 1st natally), but your personal expression may be more subdued in this location. You could have a mysterious, gentle or compassionate overlay to your approach to life. Helping, healing or artistic activities may draw you. Your intuition may develop further. You could experience mysticism personally, or tune in to your Higher Self.

Ascendant (1st House) Rulers: from 2nd to...

1st: Your identity remains connected to pleasures, possessions and finances (ruler of 1st in 2nd natally), but the focus on self-expression, assertion and doing your own thing is stronger here. Your experiences may challenge you to be true to yourself and to enjoy life on your own terms. You're best off being financially self-sufficient.

3rd: Pleasure, possessions and finances remain central to your sense of identity (ruler of 1st in 2nd natally), but a mental overlay is relevant in this area. You probably seek to express yourself through the world of the mind and may enjoy word play, mental games, arguments, quick wits or other forms of intellectual versatility.

4th: Your basic identity and sense of self remain caught up with pleasure and comfort issues (ruler of 1st in 2nd natally), but this area focuses more on emotional security. You may look to family, land, commodities or other resources for financial security, or depend upon them emotionally. Your home may become more important to you, and nurturing issues crop up.

5th: Your identity remains connected to pleasures, possessions and finances (ruler of 1st in 2nd natally), but you are probably more willing to take chances in this area. Investments, speculation, gambling or other risk-taking activities may appeal. You may gain increased pleasure in creativity or children. You'll probably seek ways and means to increase your pay-offs in life, to gain more of life's goodies.

6th: Pleasure, possessions and finances remain central to your sense of identity (ruler of 1st in 2nd natally), while your focus turns to discipline and productivity. Work is pursued not just for remunerative rewards, but also for the sake of doing something **well**. Health interests may arise. You can learn to enjoy functioning efficiently on all levels.

7th: Your basic identity and sense of self remain caught up with pleasure and comfort issues (ruler of 1st in 2nd natally), but the focus can enlarge from material, financial realms to incorporate social realms as well. You may get more involved in relationships, and deal more with issues of balancing personal and interpersonal needs. You can enjoy people as well as sensuality and beauty pursuits could continue to be highly gratifying.

8th: Your identity remains connected to pleasures, possessions and finances (ruler of 1st in 2nd natally), but a polarity issue emerges here. You may face tensions between self-indulgence versus self-control (over food, alcohol, smoking, sex, sensuality, etc.), or you may feel torn between earning your own way versus depending on/receiving from others (or providing for them). Questions of "mine" versus "ours" could arise in terms of money, sexuality, and possessions until you achieve balance. Integration deepens your mastery of self and increases your inner understanding.

9th: Your basic identity and sense of self remain caught up with pleasure, comfort issues (ruler of 1st in 2nd natally), but you are expanding horizons now. You may be drawn toward expressing yourself in travel, studies, religion, philosophy and any meaning-oriented activities. Optimism and humor could increase. Your dreams and goals are likely to be bigger; don't reach too high, or demand too much from yourself and/or life.

10th: Your basic identity remains connected to money, possessions and pleasures (ruler of 1st in 2nd natally), with an increased sense of responsibility probable in this location. You are likely to feel the need to make a contribution to society and could succumb to guilt if not doing what you "should." Your personal will may be tested against that of authorities or the laws of life. You can accomplish much if you avoid the extreme of pushing too hard or giving up too soon.

11th: Your sense of self is still connected to money, pleasures and possessions (ruler of 1st in 2nd natally), but a more mental flavor permeates here. Individualism becomes more central to your self-expression and you might become actively involved with groups, social causes or new age activities. Your former security focus could open to more change and variety.

12th: Your basic identity and self-expression remain tied to pleasure, comfort, possessions and money (ruler of 1st in 2nd natally), but you may develop a more inclusive perspective here. Philanthropic, healing, or helping concerns may move you. Beauty and aesthetics could be an ongoing focus, or activity which is inspirational and uplifting.

Ascendant (1st House) Rulers: from 3rd to...

1st: Your identification with the mind is likely to continue (ruler of 1st in 3rd natally), but you move toward more assertion and personal expression in this area. You face more issues around being yourself and number one. You are learning to handle personal will constructively.

2nd: Your identification with the mind is likely to persist (ruler of 1st in 3rd natally), but you could be a bit more laid-back in this region. You may be more pleasure-oriented or focused on money or ownership. The material, sensual, and financial realms gain increased importance to your personal actions.

4th: Your identification with the mind is likely to continue (ruler of 1st in 3rd natally), but you may be a bit more home-oriented here. You might want to center your actions in the domestic arena, or around issues of warmth, nurturance, protection, and the land. Family could become more important.

5th: You retain an identification with mental issues and communication (ruler of 1st in 3rd natally), but you may be more willing to take center stage in this area. Your need to shine, to be noticed, recognized, admired, or loved could increase. Your charisma quotient is higher in this locale, and promotion, sales, or teaching come more naturally to you. You can be quite dynamic here.

6th: Your personal focus on the mind and communication persists (ruler of 1st in 3rd natally), but you will probably want to ground it now. You could become interested in obtaining tangible results from your thinking or communicating. Simple curiosity no longer seems enough. You seek intellectual productivity and efficient analysis. You may focus more on your work and/or health.

7th: Your identification with the mind is likely to persist (ruler of 1st in 3rd natally), but you will increasingly share ideas with others. In this area, relationships are a strong personal focus, and you are learning about yourself through the mirror of other people. Avoid the extremes of giving away all your power, or trying to have everything your way and find the constructive middle ground of compromise, negotiation and balance.

8th: You tend to retain an identification with the mind and tongue (ruler of 1st in 3rd natally), but your focus is deeper and more intense now. You may analyze yourself (and others) on many levels, seeking root causes. Power issues could emerge, especially the question of personal power versus shared power. Communication around issues of intimacy, joint finances, and sensuality will be particularly important.

9th: You probably will continue your personal identification with your mind (ruler of 1st in 3rd natally), but expand the horizons of your questioning. You may experience an increase in your desire to adventure, explore, and go further than you have gone in the past. You may be drawn toward education, travel, philosophy, spiritual quests or any form of searching for your ultimate values.

10th: You are likely to continue your identification with the intellect (ruler of 1st in 3rd natally), but wish to manifest that in the world somehow. You may use your communication skills professionally, or put networking and information gathering to work in the world. An increasing sense of responsibility or susceptibility to judgment could affect your mental capacities. You'll want to apply your concepts to the "real world" — make them useful.

11th: You have an ongoing identification with the mind and communication (ruler of 1st in 3rd natally), but this area further emphasizes objectivity, tolerance, openness and a variety of options.

You could be even more restless, variety-oriented, and eager for the new and different. You may explore mental arenas with astrology, friends, groups, causes, or social organizations.

12th: You retain a personal identification with the mind (ruler of the 1st in the 3rd natally), but can add an element of intuition to your logic and rationality. You may be able to blend facts and fancy, or your feeling, compassionate, sensitive side could seem at odds with your cool, objective side. You are likely to continue to have broad interests and need to guard against scattering your focus by establishing clear priorities.

Ascendant (1st House) Rulers: from 4th to...

1st: You will retain an identification with closeness, nurturing, family or emotional security issues (ruler of 1st in 4th natally), but this area further emphasizes the development of personal will and assertion. Despite empathy and an emotional focus, you can move toward more self-expression, freedom, and energetic action.

2nd: Your identity remains tied to emotional issues (ruler of 1st in 4th natally), but this area highlights the desire for physical security, comfort and pleasure. Having power over your material and financial base is probably more important here to your sense of self and inner security.

3rd: You keep your personal identification with domestic and closeness issues (ruler of 1st in 4th natally), but may have a more objective overlay in this area. You can use logic as well as feelings. Family might be a significant focus. Your emotions will affect communication and the information you process.

5th: You are likely to retain an identification with closeness, nurturance, family or emotional security issues (ruler of 1st in 4th natally) while loving and being loved becomes more central. Children, creativity or any forms of ego expansion become more essential to your self-expression in this locale.

6th: Your identity remains tied to emotional and closeness issues (ruler of 1st in 4th natally), but this region emphasizes the desire for productivity and tangible results. You need a sense of personal accomplishment. You can find security in doing a **good job** and maintaining a healthy body.

7th: Dependency/nurturance issues remain significant in your personal action and identity (ruler of 1st in 4th natally), but this location highlights meeting yourself through partners and partnership. You need to find a reasonable balance of dependency and nurturance with a partner — neither one doing too much for the other. Relationships are important to your self-expression here.

8th: Emotional security needs remain strong in your basic identity (ruler of 1st in 4th natally), but the learning ground tends toward sensuality, sexuality, shared resources, and pleasures. You may develop more strength and self-mastery through interaction with a mate—learning to give, receive and share equally in financial and sensual areas. You are likely to feel deeply.

9th: Although emotional closeness remains an important part of your identity (ruler of 1st in 4th natally), you are more inclined to wander, explore and take risks now. This location highlights your quest for meaning—whether through education, travel, philosophy, religion, ideals, etc. Wanderlust may compete with domestic issues. Your security may be sought through beliefs.

10th: Domestic issues and the need for emotional security and closeness remain central to your personal identity (ruler of 1st in 4th natally), but this area puts additional focus on the drive to achieve, to be responsible, to have a career, and attain a sense of status and competence. You will need to balance dominance and dependency, feelings and pragmatism.

11th: Dependency/nurturance issues remain significant for your personal identity (ruler of 1st in 4th natally), but this area highlights the contrasting desire for independence and uniqueness. You will have to balance freedom and closeness needs in your self-expression and actions. You may seek emotional security through friends, causes, organizations or new-age knowledge and technology.

12th: Emotional security needs are a significant theme in your basic identity (ruler of 1st in 4th natally), and this area suggests even more sensitivity, empathy, compassion and drive for infinite love and beauty. Aesthetic or healing roles may appeal. If you get carried away with helping, you could fall into martyr or victim positions. Use your caring wisely.

Ascendant (1st House) Rulers: from 5th to...

1st: The need to shine, to be recognized and gain positive esteem is still central to your self-expression (ruler of 1st in 5th natally), but the impetus is now more toward doing your own thing, being true to yourself, and allowing your spontaneous instincts out.

2nd: The desire for love, attention, limelight and public recognition remains central to your identity (ruler of 1st in 5th natally), but some of the positive regard may be sought through financial, material, or sensual channels. Feeling good and indulging sensually may become more important to you here.

3rd: Your creative drive for recognition, love, attention, and applause remains a significant facet of your identity (ruler of 1st in 5th natally). You may, however, seek some self-esteem through intellectual functions. Shining with the mind is possible, gaining positive feedback through learning, dexterity, teaching, speaking, or information exchange.

4th: Your drive to do more than has been done before and to achieve positive acknowledgment for it (ruler of 1st in 5th natally) remains, but some of that need for recognition could be channeled into emotional arenas. Home and family may satisfy your desire for love and positive feedback, or you could be extremely creative in terms of land, the public, commodities, structures.

6th: Your identity is still connected to a need for recognition and applause (ruler of 1st in 5th natally), but that may be channeled through productive efforts in this region. You may center your seeking of self-esteem around your work or health, expressing your creativity and looking for positive attention through those areas.

7th: Creativity, self-expansion, pride, and the drive to receive favorable notice remain central to your identity and action (ruler of 1st in 5th natally). Some of your sense of self, however, is now tied to partners and partnership. You may be ego-vulnerable to the opinions of others. Aesthetic abilities could be enhanced. Charm and charisma might increase.

8th: Your need to do more, to risk, to be creative, and to gain positive feedback remains strong (ruler of 1st in 5th natally), while power issues become more central. Sensual/sexual needs are highlighted, and learning to share power, resources, and pleasures is a key challenge in this area. Your strength of will may increase.

9th: Your identity is still tied to shining, being significant, loved, noted, and appreciated (ruler of 1st in 5th natally). This location highlights your courage, willingness to dare, to explore, adventure, and seek the best in life. Your optimism and self-confidence may be excellent. You seek expansive paths to self-expression.

10th: Creativity, self-expansion, pride and the drive to receive favorable responses from others remain central to your identity (ruler of 1st in 5th natally), but you may center your efforts around a career or contribution to society. You are likely to seek the limelight through professional routes.

11th: Your desire for attention, love, esteem, and recognition remains central to your sense of self (ruler of 1st in 5th natally), but your world may expand. A larger circle of acquaintances is possible; you may relate to all of humanity. Social organizations or political causes could be a setting for your desire to act decisively and to make a difference.

12th: Creativity, charisma, self-esteem, and the desire for positive feedback are still major forces in your identity and personal action (ruler of 1st in 5th natally). This region highlights your persuasiveness, emotional impact and ability to "sell" others. Romance is more important and likely to be idealized. You can rouse intense emotions in yourself and others, perhaps to the point of excess. Balance faith in yourself with faith in a Higher Power.

Ascendant (1st House) Rulers: from 6th to...

1st: Your sense of self remains tied to your productive efforts (ruler of 1st in 6th natally), but this region highlights the need for personal action. Doing your own thing could feel more imperative: to achieve results on your own, and to be active and independent on the job and in your self-expression.

2nd: Efficient functioning remains a core theme for your personal identity (ruler of 1st in 6th natally). In this area, you may channel that desire to be productive more into financial or sensual realms. Material accomplishments and control of your own resources are essential for personal satisfaction.

3rd: Doing things right and working well on the job and in your health remain central themes for your self-expression (ruler of 1st in 6th natally). This area ties some of that personal action into thinking, communicating and sharing information. You may be mentally productive or enjoy achieving with people and ideas.

4th: Your sense of self remains tied to your productive efforts (ruler of 1st in 6th natally), but some of your desire to work and serve could be directed toward domestic or family matters. You may desire to improve or enhance your home environment, or focus on success within the family or work in the home or for the public.

5th: Efficient functioning remains a core theme for your personal identity (ruler of 1st in 6th natally), but you will probably want more attention in this location. The need for positive feedback is highlighted, with a desire to shine through your work or health. Praise and recognition are sought in addition to a sense of accomplishment.

7th: Doing things right and working well on the job and in your health continue to be significant themes in your self-expression (ruler of 1st in 6th natally), while partnership also moves into high focus. You may work on relationships (be wary of criticizing or being criticized too much), work with people, or partnerships may affect your work prospects.

8th: Your sense of self remains tied to your productive efforts (ruler of 1st in 6th natally), with an increased desire to be thorough, exacting, disciplined, and enduring. Your organizational skills are encouraged here, along with a desire to get to the end and to the bottom of things.

9th: Doing things right and working well on the job and in your health continue to be significant themes in your personal action (ruler of 1st in 6th natally), while ideals, beliefs and values become more central. You may develop greater faith or confidence, question your world view, or alter some of your basic assumptions about life, reality, and ultimate meaning and change some long-range goals.

10th: Your sense of self remains tied to your productive efforts (ruler of 1st in 6th natally), with an increased drive toward personal responsibility, power, authority and control. Beware of overdoing (taking on too much) or giving up too soon. You are capable of achieving much!

11th: Efficient functioning remains a core theme for your personal identity (ruler of 1st in 6th natally), as you move toward increased openness, individuality, liberty, and unconventionality. You may become more willing to break the rules, particularly if it seems to "make sense."

12th: Doing things right and working well on the job and in your health continue to be significant motifs in your self-expression (ruler of 1st in 6th natally), with an increased sense of inspiration or connection to mystical or inspired experiences. You yearn to be uplifted, and healing or aesthetic efforts can be an important part of your competence drives. Look for and carry out the small steps that will make your dreams come true.

Ascendant (1st House) Rulers: from 7th to...

1st: Interpersonal issues remain and you may meet yourself through other people (ruler of 1st in 7th natally), but this area puts a stronger focus on expressing your own desires and doing your own thing. You are learning balance between self and others, but constructive self-assertion is more the focus here.

2nd: Relationships remain an important source of your sense of self (ruler of 1st in 7th natally), but this region emphasizes a desire for personal control of resources and the need for aesthetics and pleasure. Beware of passivity if the drive to keep things pleasant and easy is carried too far. You could become more involved with art, beauty, sensual gratifications, or financial matters.

3rd: You are learning about yourself through interactions with other people (ruler of 1st in 7th natally) and this region particularly highlights issues of communication and the light touch. Peer relationships are important to your sense of self. You express best with other people.

4th: Your sociable side which seeks identity through interacting with others persists (ruler of 1st in 7th natally), but this region suggests a stronger home focus. You may become more involved with family members, the public, land, commodities, but your ability to share, balance and negotiate remains central to the picture.

5th: Interpersonal issues remain central to your self-expression, meeting yourself through other people (ruler of 1st in 7th natally), with an increased need for positive feedback. Love relationships are apt to be quite important here. Creative or aesthetic outlets may be satisfying. You need love, admiration, attention, and applause from others, but try not to let your sense of self-worth become too dependent on the attitudes of others. Your charisma may increase.

6th: Other people remain involved with your sense of self and ability to express (ruler of 1st in 7th natally). In this region, however, some of your social and relationship needs may be met through your job. Your feelings about partners might affect your health or your job may impact your emotional ties. You are learning to balance enjoying yourself and working hard; critical judgment and acceptance.

8th: You remain vulnerable to the actions and opinions of others (ruler of 1st in 7th natally), and this region accentuates the issue of personal power versus shared power. The goal is avoid intimidating or being intimidated by others. Your challenge is to achieve comfortable sharing and exchanges in terms of monetary, sensual, and material gratifications.

9th: Other people, especially partners, remain a significant factor in your identity and ability to express yourself (ruler of 1st in 7th natally). This region puts expectations in high focus. You may demand more than is reasonable, from yourself and from others, in terms of sharing. The challenge is to have goals, ethics and values, while still being able to compromise.

10th: Interpersonal issues remains central to your self-expression and sense of who you are (ruler of 1st in 7th natally), but this region channels some of your focus into a career or contribution to the world. You may need to balance love needs and achievement drives, equality urges with the need for control. Life is big enough for peers and productivity.

11th: Other people remain involved with your sense of self and ability to express (ruler of 1st in 7th natally), with a wider focus in this region. You may expand your social circles, become more active in terms of groups, causes, politics, organizations, or anything on the cutting edge.

12th: Other people, including partners, remain a significant factor in your identity and ability to express yourself (ruler of 1st in 7th natally). You may seek inspiration through relationships, or strive to share with others on the highest levels. Be wary of rose-colored glasses or too much sacrifice, but do appreciate the ability to see and support the best in yourself and in others (and hopefully others will share your gifts).

Ascendant (1st House) Rulers: from 8th to...

1st: Issues of self-mastery, self-control and power remain central to your basic identity (ruler of 1st in 8th natally). This region highlights assertion, self-expression, spontaneity, anger when you do not get your way, and the desire to be #1. Try to maintain positive manifestations of your personal will power, avoiding overdoing it or too much self-blocking and over control.

2nd: You continue to face issues of self-mastery, self-control and power (ruler of 1st in 8th natally), but this region highlights the polarity between appetite indulgence and appetite mastery.

Swings (feast versus famine) are possible in terms of food, sex, money, pleasures or possessions. You may be at odds with a partner regarding this issue, until inner balance is achieved and moderation is attained. Giving, receiving, and sharing with a partner may also be an important issue here.

3rd: Issues of self-mastery, self-control and power remain central to your basic identity (ruler of 1st in 8th natally). This area emphasizes communication, relatives and learning. You may seek control over your sources of information; face power issues with relatives; study subjects in depth; or seek a thorough understanding of the people around you.

4th: Motifs revolving around self-mastery, addiction, self-control, and shared resources or pleasures continue to be significant for you (ruler of 1st in 8th natally), with an increased focus on the desire for emotional security. Feelings are central and unconscious motivations may sway you. In this region you are learning to control the depths of your psyche and to balance dependency with nurturance.

5th: Personal issues around self-mastery, self-control and the sharing of pleasures and possessions will persist (ruler of 1st in 8th natally). This area emphasizes the need to be loved, admired, and noticed. Power struggles with lovers and/or children are a danger until all parties have a positive place to shine, to be recognized, and to enhance their self-esteem.

6th: Self-mastery, self-control and power over financial, sexual matters are likely to be continuing personal issues (ruler of 1st in 8th natally). This area highlights the need for efficient functioning, so self-discipline might be enhanced and you may adopt health regimes that further your sense of self-control. You could also deal with financial or sensual matters in your work.

7th: Motifs revolving around self-mastery, addiction, self-control, and the capacity to share the sensual, sexual, and financial world persist for you personally (ruler of 1st in 8th natally). This area particularly brings up relationship themes in terms of learning to be comfortable giving, receiving, and sharing possessions, pleasures and power.

9th: You are likely to remain involved with issues of power, sensuality, sexuality, shared finances, and self-mastery (ruler of 1st in 8th natally). This area emphasizes high expectations. Beware of demanding more than is reasonable of yourself or others, particularly in touchy emotional areas. You can direct much intensity toward reaching your highest potentials.

10th: Issues revolving around self-mastery, addictions, shared resources and pleasures remain central to your identity (ruler of 1st in 8th natally), with a stronger sense of responsibility. Self-control and self-discipline are in higher focus. Beware of overdoing self-denial. You can be more thorough, exacting, organized, skilled at concentrating, and focused on career.

11th: Self-mastery, self-control and power over financial/sexual matters are likely to be ongoing personal issues (ruler of 1st in 8th natally). This region suggests an overlay of detachment to these touchy emotional areas. You may feel torn between your head and gut, or between security and taking risks, but are capable of getting the best from both.

12th: Issues centering around self-mastery, addiction, self-control, and the handling of sensual, sexual, and financial matters persist for you personally (ruler of 1st in 8th natally). This region highlights compassion, mysticism, and the quest for the beautiful dream. Gratification could be idealized and overdone, or self-mastery could be seen as an ultimate value. The goal is to manifest your Higher Self in handling matters which arouse deep emotions.

Ascendant (1st House) Rulers: from 9th to...

1st: Your beliefs, values, and ideals remain central to your identity (ruler of 1st in 9th natally), but this region puts a strong focus on finding your own truth. You are more likely to assert yourself in matters of faith and ethics. You will tend to trust your own personal experience.

2nd: Your world view, faith, metaphysics, and visions retain importance in your personal identity and action (ruler of 1st in 9th natally), but this area highlights issues of sensuality, comfort and finances. You may want to ground your beliefs, balance the material and spiritual, enjoy the process of seeking, or search for the ultimate pleasures.

3rd: What you trust, value, idealize and believe in continues to influence your self-definition and personal actions (ruler of 1st in 9th natally), while you seek more information, learning, communication or interaction. A mental focus is strong with an accent on teaching, sharing information and communicating knowledge. Travel could also continue or increase.

4th: Your beliefs, values and ideals retain their core connection to your identity and instinctive actions (ruler of 1st in 9th natally). In this area, however, some of your quest for meaning will be directed toward the home front. Emotional security may become an ultimate value and you may need to balance adventures versus safety, high expectations versus empathic caring.

5th: Faith, values, goals, ethics and aspirations are central to your sense of personal identity and action (ruler of 1st in 9th natally). In this area, your desire to do, to shine, to be noticed and appreciated is accentuated. Charisma comes more naturally. You may gain attention through your metaphysics, morality or long-range goals and values. You may be increasingly willing to try, to risk, to aim for more because you trust the future.

6th: Your world view, faith, metaphysics and visions still have importance in your personal actions and sense of self (ruler of 1st in 9th natally). In this area, you will be seeking ways to ground your dreams, to work toward your aspirations. Excessive perfectionism could lead to frustration. Take small, sensible steps toward what you value most.

7th: Your beliefs, values and ideas remain central in their connection to your basic identity and actions (ruler of 1st in 9th natally). In this region, relationships become more central, as you meet parts of yourself through interactions with others. High ideals and expectations may affect your view of yourself and others. Look for the best, but don't demand impossible perfection.

8th: Faith, values, goals, ethics and aspirations contribute to your sense of identity and personal action (ruler of 1st in 9th natally). In this region, your seeking of the best is tied to issues of sharing sensually, sexually and financially. High expectations could affect relationships with a mate or your capacity for self-mastery and self-control. You may intensely commit to seeking the best, including knowledge of your own inner depths.

10th: Your world view, faith, beliefs, morality and goals are central aspects of who you are (ruler of 1st in 9th natally). In this region, you are striving to bring your dreams down to earth, and ground your aspirations in a career or some kind of work in the world. High ideals for your job, how you work, or what your work does for the world are likely.

11th: Beliefs, values, goals, ethics and faith are central to your personal actions and sense of identity (ruler of 1st in 9th natally). Your search for meaning is likely to expand in this areas as you consider more options and alternatives. You will probably be encouraged to go beyond traditional boundaries and to appreciate freedom and uniqueness in your quest to understand life's purpose.

12th: Your identity is tied to a search for meaning and understanding in life; beliefs, values, ethics and ideals may be central in your personal actions (ruler of 1st in 9th natally). In this area, you are likely to persist in having high standards for your own behavior, and are learning to integrate intellectual insights with emotional understanding. Faith in something beyond the physical world is apt to be a significant issue.

Ascendant (1st House) Rulers: from 10th to...

1st: Responsibility, power, achievement and facing realistic limits are central themes for your identity and personal actions (ruler of 1st in 10th natally). In this area, you are likely to want things more on your own terms, to seek control over your accomplishments, to strive for independence and doing things **your way** in your career.

2nd: Your actions and self-expression could incline toward overdrive (trying to carry the whole world), self-blocking (feeling inhibited, inadequate, unable to cope) or realistic accomplishment [ruler of 1st in the 10th natally]. In this area you are apt to seek pleasure in your work, and put emphasis on the material rewards of your attainments. Results will matter to you.

3rd: You may identify with your work or center your actions around issues of duties, limits, obligations and necessities (ruler of 1st in 10th natally). This region highlights your need to be involved with the mind, communication or information-processing. You could work with words, ideas or dexterity. You may feel responsible for relatives or labor mentally.

4th: Your personal actions are connected to a sense of responsibility, realism, authority or limitation (ruler of 1st in 10th natally). This region highlights your need to integrate practical and emotional matters. Your achievement urges may affect the domestic arena, or you could feel torn between home and career; dominance and dependency. You can be highly effective in dealing with matters of emotional safety and security.

5th: Responsibility, power, achievement and facing realistic limits are significant motifs within your personal identity and actions (ruler of 1st in 10th natally). In this region, ambition is highlighted, and your career drives are likely to be focused toward gaining more power as well as recognition, rewards, attention and renown. You need to shine and to be noticed.

6th: Pragmatism, realism, duties, achievement and doing what is necessary are basic themes in your identity and actions (ruler of 1st in 10th natally). This area highlights the need to express yourself through work and tangible results. You may also wish to improve your health habits. The general focus is on good craftsmanship and doing something well. If flaw-finding is carried to an extreme, self-criticism could become a problem to be mastered. You can get a lot done — one step at a time.

7th: Your sense of identity and personal actions are tied to work, discipline, realism, limits and authority issues (ruler of 1st in 10th natally). This area emphasizes relationships issues, with you facing the balancing act between your power and that of other people. Issues of criticism (from you or toward you) may affect relationships. Be practical about people. Make room for equalitarian sharing and control in your work.

8th: Power, responsibility, authority, control and limits are still central motifs in your personal identity and action (ruler of 1st in 10th natally). This region highlights the issues of dominance, force and discipline. You can increase your self-control and self-mastery in many areas. Avoid excessive restrictiveness toward yourself or others. Channel your need to win or to be on top into competitive businesses, games, sports or political action.

9th: Pragmatism, realism, duties, achievement and doing what is necessary remain major themes for your personal action and sense of self (ruler of 1st in 10th natally). You can balance pessimism with optimism, visions with dreams. Your career aspirations may increase. Your beliefs, values, faith, education, urge to travel, or adventurous spirit could contribute to your profession.

11th: Your sense of identity and personal actions remain tied to work, discipline, realism, limits and authority issues (ruler of 1st in 10th natally). This area puts a stronger focus on individuality and inventiveness. You may explore alternatives in terms of your career, or make changes in your dealings with structures and rules. You may increase your capacity to blend the old and the new, the conventional and the unconventional.

12th: Power, responsibility, authority, control and limits are still significant motifs in your personal identity and action (ruler of 1st in 10th natally). This area emphasizes compassion, sensitivity, and idealism. You can bring inspiration, art, or healing into your career. You also could want more than is reasonable from life and your own behavior. You can expand the capacity to work hard for your vision of infinite love and beauty.

Ascendant (1st House) Rulers: from 11th to...

1st: Individuality and uniqueness are central to your identity and basic instincts [ruler of 1st in 11th natally]. This area emphasizes your need for personal freedom. Spontaneity, self-expression and doing your own thing will probably matter even more.

2nd: Your personal action and natural instincts incline toward being an individual and expressing your independence [ruler of 1st in 11th natally]. This region accentuates a focus on comfort and security needs. Don't fall into a struggle between stability and change; do keep room in your life for both the new and the tried-and-true, the material and the intellectual, the unusual and the familiar. You may alter your handling of finances and possessions.

3rd: Being true to your own inner nature and coming from your own center is central to your being [ruler of 1st in 11th natally]. This part of the world highlights a mental focus and expression in your life. Intellectual stimulation becomes more important to you. Teaching, learning, gathering and disseminating knowledge and information may be more central to your identity and self-expression.

4th: You are not quite like anyone else and instinctively follow your own way rather than conventions [ruler of 1st in 11th natally]. This area brings emotional needs into a stronger focus. You could sometimes feel torn between feelings and logic, family and friends, or security needs versus the desire for something new, different and exciting. It is possible to have them all with a little compromise!

5th: Individuality and uniqueness are central to your identity and basic instincts [ruler of 1st in 11th natally]. This region emphasizes your creativity and ability to take risks, to do, to try, to aim for something more exciting and dynamic in life. Your confidence and thrust toward the future may increase.

6th: Your personal action and natural instincts incline toward being an individual and expressing your independence [ruler of 1st in 11th natally]. This area accentuates a need for tangible results and to do things **well**. You may become more identified with your work and look for individualistic forms of competence and achievement. Your variety needs could compete with your precision side, but they can also support each other. You might focus more on a healthily functioning body and explore alternative forms of healing.

7th: A sense of independence and uniqueness is very important to who you are. You are naturally inclined to make your own rules [ruler of the 1st in the 11th natally]. This region accentuates the focus on objectivity, logic and the ability to keep perspective, but lends a more relationship-oriented focus. You could discover more about yourself through relationships with others (cooperative and competitive).

8th: Personal independence, individuality and progress are central keys in your basic identity [ruler of the 1st in the 11th natally]. This placement implies the need to blend intimacy instincts and freedom drives. You could feel torn between attachment and detachment or emotions and the intellect. You are learning to balance security and risk, to be able to dive deeply into life as well as seeing the broad overview.

9th: Uniqueness remains a core thread in your identity and intellectual, progressive, networking or scientific interests may be important in your personal actions [ruler of 1st in 11th natally]. This area highlights your need for adventure, freedom, risk-taking, the new, and to move forward in life. Confidence is accentuated along with an orientation toward larger issues—ideals and ideas. You may express increasingly in the transpersonal realm.

10th: Your identity and personal action are tied to independence, uniqueness and the urge to go beyond traditional limits [ruler of 1st in 11th natally]. This region suggests that limits, rules, regulations and expectations (vocational, societal, cultural, etc.) will need to be integrated with your freedom-loving, unconventional side. You can bring together the old and new, the revolutionary and reactionary, if you choose to work creatively with essential structures.

12th: You have a strong instinctive urge toward freedom, individuality, progress, and anything on the cutting edge of change [ruler of 1st in 11th natally]. This region suggests a strong focus on transpersonal issues such as ideals, goals, humanitarian principles, philanthropic hopes and anything dealing with large groups of people. You may want more than is reasonable of yourself; keep expectations reachable. You may be drawn toward mystical or healing paths. If you avoid the pitfalls of rose-colored glasses and savior/victim interchanges, you could increase your intuition and contact with your Inner Wisdom.

Ascendant (1st House) Rulers: from 12th to...

1st: You have a strong drive for aesthetics and inspiration [ruler of 1st in 12th natally]. This region puts more focus on doing your own thing. You may put beauty into motion or fight for causes. You need to act on your ideals.

2nd: Your basic identity and personal action are tied to compassion, intuition and mystical themes [ruler of 1st in 12th natally]. This area highlights your feeling for beauty and grace. Comfort, pleasure and indulgence are likely to be important (and might be overdone). Don't let rose-colored glasses rule your financial picture. Ease appeals. You can enjoy yourself.

3rd: You have the capacity to express yourself through helping, healing or aesthetic channels—or through escapism [ruler of 1st in 12th natally]. This placement emphasizes restlessness and the desire to absorb anything and everything. Beware of scattering your forces in trying to know and do it all. You can develop the ability to blend logic and intuition, facts and fancy.

4th: You are naturally concerned with inspiration, compassion, beauty and grace [ruler of 1st in 12th natally]. This region further emphasizes your sensitivity, concern with feelings, and need for emotional attachments. You may express some of your aesthetic or healing talents in the home or for the public.

5th: You have a strong drive for aesthetics and inspiration [ruler of 1st in 12th natally]. This region puts increased focus on your need to express creatively and do more than you have done before. You may seek the limelight or gain attention through grace, healing, beauty, drama or magical motifs.

6th: Your basic identity and personal action are tied to compassion, intuition and mystical themes [ruler of 1st in 12th natally]. This area highlights your desire for results. You will want to ground your ideals and achieve something tangible. Your work or health could become a focus for your need to transcend.

7th: You have the capacity to express yourself through helping, healing or aesthetic channels—or through escapism [ruler of 1st in 12th natally]. This placement emphasizes a feeling for beauty and balance. You may further develop artistic talents or focus more on relationships. Beware of wanting more than is possible where people are concerned. Your capacity for empathy may increase.

8th: You are naturally concerned with inspiration, compassion, beauty and grace [ruler of 1st in 12th natally]. This region further emphasizes your need to understand root causes, to grasp the underlying patterns and issues in life. Your personality could become even more complex and many-layered, letting few people see the depths of your psyche. Yet your own intuitive understanding may deepen through emotionally intense personal relationships. Guard against expecting too much of relationships. You may become able to merge with a partner, tuning into one another and feeling a "soul mate" connection.

9th: You have a strong drive for aesthetics and inspiration [ruler of 1st in 12th natally]. This area puts your idealism in high focus. You may expect a lot of yourself, act for a Higher purpose, fight for causes, or be otherwise involved in seeking the best (or demanding the impossible). More and more, you may sway others with your beliefs.

10th: Your basic identity and personal action are tied to compassion, intuition and mystical themes [ruler of 1st in 12th natally]. This area highlights your need to accomplish something with your dreams. You will want to establish your vision (artistic, healing, escapist, rescuing) through your career and somehow make your fantasies into reality in the physical world.

11th: You have the capacity to express yourself through helping, healing or aesthetic channels—or through escapism [ruler of 1st in 12th natally]. This placement highlights a transpersonal focus—your personal concern with large-scale issues, humanitarian or philanthropic causes, groups, networking and making a difference in the world. Your perspective may broaden.

Midheaven (10th House) Rulers: from 1st to...

2nd: You need to have your world under your own personal control here. Accomplishment, for you, should be when, where and how you choose. You may resist outside authority. Strength and determination are likely on the job. Your laid-back side may vie with your desire for energetic accomplishment. You might seek more comfort and adequate recompense for your work.

3rd: You probably prefer a flexible approach to the job in this locale, and have a strong need for variety in the working environment and in your tasks. Your energy level is high for matters involving communication and information exchange. Coordination and dexterity could contribute to your professional skills.

4th: You may feel ambivalent about your worldly ambitions—torn between work which allows you freedom and independence versus work which satisfies emotional needs and provides safety and security. Competitive instincts could vie with compassionate inclinations. Your reality requires a bit of both.

5th: You are increasingly drawn toward exciting work here. You are likely to need to move on the job and may abhor the ordinary. You can put tremendous vitality, enthusiasm and charisma into your world and handling the power structure.

6th: Productivity, accomplishment and general competence are even more important to you in this region. You could measure yourself by what you do. You might be overly harsh in judging your achievements, or demand that you work only on your own terms. Your challenge is to blend self-will and limits or laws, personal desires and the duties of the everyday reality.

7th: Your contribution to society might involve give-and-take with other people as you learn how to balance the power between you and others. You may feel torn between assertion and accommodation. You need some independence as well as some teamwork and cooperation in the world.

8th: You may be more drawn toward power and control in your world. Talent could surface in fields involving medicine, assertion, business, probing beneath the surface, or power relationships. You could make a contribution to society which involves physical danger or fascination, hidden matters, or strong emotions.

9th: You could deal well here in a career involving fun, humor, verve and action. Restless, you may continually expand your vocational horizons. Without new challenges, you might job-hop (or unconsciously set yourself up to be fired when you're feeling bored). Find a stimulating focus!

10th: You may need to balance your way of doing things with the rules (especially the "establishment" or boss's rules). You might push too hard for what you want or give up too soon on what you **could** do. Integrate your desires and needs with the basic regulations and structure of the "real world."

11th: Freedom of action is likely to become even more important in your work. If you start to feel confined, you may be tempted to leave. You can be quite innovative and creative in your world. You function best on your own.

12th: You may prefer work which advances your personal ideals or vision. Your contribution to society might come to involve healing, helping, fighting for causes. You may feel torn between competition and compassion. You can be energetic on behalf of your dreams.

Midheaven (10th House) Rulers: from 2nd to...

1st: You probably want close personal control over your resources and the way you work in this locale. You prefer to labor when, where and how you choose. Material and financial rewards matter to you, but on your own terms. You have much strength, determination and forcefulness to apply to the "real world."

3rd: You may find pleasure through communication in your work here. You could be drawn toward fields involving beauty through language (singing, poetry, song writing, lecturing). You may have a casual, comfortable attitude toward your world and place in society. Relatives could affect your finances. You could achieve more objectivity about resources and possessions.

4th: Your career might come to involve basic security and resources (banking, land, commodities, food...). Safety and stability are increasingly important to you in terms of vocation. Family may affect your professional prospects. Material gratifications are important to your work satisfaction.

5th: You may experience ambivalence between a career which involves a steady, dependable situation and income versus a career involving risks, excitement, and the possibility of making a big splash in the world. Financial matters could become a professional focus, as could artistic creativity.

6th: You are likely to focus on work satisfaction and seek pleasure through doing a good job. You may value established routines more, constantly striving to hone your skills to a higher level of efficiency.

7th: Your contribution to society in this area could involve pleasure and/or beauty. You are apt to prefer a comfortable, easygoing attitude about achievement (and might even be **too** laid-back). Harmony at work matters to you.

8th: Business skills are highlighted here, especially in fields involving finance. You may also exhibit more talent in physical manipulation (massage, acupressure, chiropractic, physiotherapy, etc.). You can be very practical and sensible about your world and appreciate security and material gratifications.

9th: You may feel torn between a tangible, earth-centered, practical work (pay the bills) versus a more philosophical, abstract or idealistic career. Integrating physical and intellectual or material and spiritual needs could become a focus in your approach to the world.

10th: You can manifest a grounded, practical, reasonable attitude toward the world while residing here. Sensible and stable, you are likely to be a good, steady worker who values the rewards of success. You may sometimes be torn between effort versus ease, but are generally focused on getting results and material rewards.

11th: You may experience an inner conflict between work which is routine and predictable with a stable base versus work which is full of challenges, changes, and allows you to be original. You may uncover unique ways to increase your income.

12th: You are likely to desire a smooth, easy working environment. You could develop talent in the beauty fields. You may prefer to avoid unpleasantness in the work arena. Don't compromise too much. You might operate as a peacemaker, a source of grace and harmony in the world.

Midheaven (10th House) Rulers: from 3rd to...

1st: Variety and flexibility probably appeal to you in your world. Communication, especially if direct, could be one of your talents. Your coordination and dexterity might prove useful on the job here. You need a lively, active working situation which allows much information processing and mental stimulation. You could make multiple contributions to society.

2nd: You may enjoy communicating in your work, or make a living through your mind, hands, tongue. You probably have talent for beautiful language (poetry, song writing, lecturing, writing). You can become quite casual and comfortable on the job, able to relax and be open.

4th: You may start working with the mind and/or emotions. This could include conveying ideas to the public, communicating feelings through your work, articulating or processing information in terms of security, land, commodities, etc. Your job might become more family-oriented or involve family members.

5th: You could further develop a talent for communication and persuasion. This combination is a natural for sales, promotion, advertising, teaching, and entertaining. (It can also denote the person who plays rather than working.) Charismatic communication is a keynote.

6th: Your mind should be central with your work here. You probably have a talent for details, yet a breadth of interests can lead you to scatter and become overextended. You're apt to be eager to gather and process information. Decide what is worth doing well, and what you can just investigate, look over, and drop.

7th: With a sociable orientation, your contribution to society might easily involve people. You probably have a flair for communication and interpersonal relations. You can meet people on their own level, be comfortable, open, and equalitarian.

8th: You may feel torn between a depth approach (persevering, enduring, tenacious) to your world versus a "once-over-lightly" style. Decide what you can play at and be casual about, and what requires true concentration. Your analytical skills may increase in this area. You can communicate well even when intense emotions are involved.

9th: Mental agility and verbal skills are highlighted for your societal contribution here. You have excellent potential for any work involving communication, information exchange, travel, writing, teaching, etc. You may feel a bit restless and do need variety and stimulation on the job.

10th: In some way, you need to blend a casual, lighthearted, flippant approach with a more serious, grounded, disciplined attitude. You can be mentally quick, yet also thorough. You need scope for your restless mind as well as your desire to be dedicated.

11th: Your world needs to involve variety—changes of routine, environment, people, etc. A mental focus is likely in your career. You can further develop communication skills and an instinctively equalitarian approach. Teamwork is likely to come naturally to you here. You can be a good networker.

12th: You may be tempted to scatter your forces vocationally, as it is easy for you to be drawn in many different directions. You will need clear priorities so you can work on what is most important. Versatility, adaptability, flexibility and the capacity to use both logic and intuition are highlighted for you in this region.

Midheaven (10th House) Rulers: from 4th to...

1st: Your work is a source of security (emotional, physical), but becomes more of a basis of your identity and sense of self. You need to make a contribution. You may feel torn between compassion versus competition on the job. You could strengthen your talent for fields involving the public, the land, family members, family issues, emotional needs or commodities—if you can operate on your own terms.

2nd: Pleasure and comfort are important needs to be served by your career. You may develop increased talent for working in fields involving basic security or resources (possessions, money, commodities, land, hotels, restaurants, etc.). Family may influence or become involved in your work. You are likely to seek more vocational stability.

3rd: Your career may involve family members, but might also involve basic needs (food, shelter, clothing) and/or ideas. You could become active in communicating feelings through your work, conveying ideas to the public, or articulating security needs.

5th: You have a great deal of warmth and caring to share through your work. This can include working with family members, or in a nurturing career (nanny, coach, homemaker, etc.). A career in the public realm, especially involving publicity, advertising, promotion or sales might develop. Recognition and emotional support are vital to your vocational satisfaction here.

6th: You are apt to take your role in society rather seriously, and might incline toward carrying more than your share of the load. Eager to assist, you can end up taking on other people's duties (and troubles) if not careful. Caretaking fields will probably appeal, or any job which allows you to be helpful. Your job performance here is more sensitive than most people's to emotional stress.

7th: You probably have a natural affinity for working with people in this region. A partner or family members could share a business or a job with you, or you may become closer than usual to co-workers. You have a good spirit of teamwork, but may need to balance cooperation with the tendency to mother or be mothered on the job.

8th: Your intuitive or feeling nature may help you contribute to society. You can be more sensitive than the average person to nonverbal and subtle nuances in your world. You can tune into underlying patterns and may have talent for working with resources, commodities, land, investments or in any field requiring depth.

9th: You may feel somewhat ambivalent about your work direction, with part of you oriented toward a home-centered or security-oriented field, and another part of you eager to explore, expand, take chances and risk for a big pay-off. You need to take your support system out into the world and go for it!

10th: You are facing polarity issues in your work: the balance between home and family versus professional ambitions and a desire to contribute to society. One integration is to work from your home, with family members or in fields involving domestic issues, the land, etc. You can balance compassion and common sense.

11th: Your natal focus is more on security through a career, while your relocated placement emphasizes the need for variety, change and the new. Some of both is healthy. Friends and/or family may affect your vocation here. You can revolutionize and revitalize ways of working with the public.

12th: You can work well in a protected environment. Your intuition may contribute to your career in this region. Sensitive to the "vibes" in your world, you need some alone time to process your impressions and make sense of the patterns you are grasping. Your compassion may make a significant contribution to society, but don't go overboard in rescuing others!

Midheaven (10th House) Rulers: from 5th to...

1st: You need excitement in your world! Action and activity are probably important. You can put out much vitality, enthusiasm, charisma and sparkle professionally. You probably work best on your own here and tend thrive on recognition and applause. Humdrum details may not appeal, but you are happy to keep things hopping!

2nd: You may feel somewhat torn between your risk-taking (natal placement) and your security-oriented (relocated placement). Part of you is willing to speculate for greater return, but another part just wants safety and dependability. You may strengthen your talents for investment or artistic creativity here.

3rd: Silver-tongued oratory is within your talents! You may exhibit increased sales ability or skill at advertising, promotion, persuasion of all kinds. A natural teacher and entertainer, you have a good sense of humor. (Con artistry is also possible.) Your charisma expresses well through your mind and tongue.

4th: Your need for recognition through your work can lead to public or on-stage roles (such as the entertainer, the promoter, the advertiser, the teacher), or it could lead to professional involvement with people you love (family businesses, working with children, etc.). Your work must include an element of warmth and caring here for fullest satisfaction.

6th: You can put together initiation and follow-through for the best of both worlds here. Blessed with confidence as well as perseverance, you are potentially highly capable. You **need** to be recognized for your competence, however, so beware of being too ego-vulnerable to people's assessments of your work. You can be enthusiastic as well as practical in this locale.

7th: Sociability could be the name of the game for your career. You have a talent for persuading people and can be extremely charming. Your charisma flows naturally into your work here. Any field using your outgoing and expressive skills is appropriate.

8th: You probably need to be in charge of your work here. Taking orders is **not** an easy task for you! Control, mastery and authority appeal to you—whether in the corporate world, your own business, or a leadership role. You are apt to feel very strongly about your work and could succumb to power struggles if you get too stubbornly set on what you feel is worthwhile. Compromise!

9th: You are looking to do things in a **big** way here. Mundane, ordinary work has little appeal. You need lots of excitement, thrills and the chance of a large pay-off. Your level of enthusiasm and zest is very high; make sure there is practicality to back it up. You can aim for success on a grand scale.

10th: Ambition is a keynote for you here. Control of your world is probably vital to you; you are a natural leader and executive in terms of career. You have the potential of good self-confidence along with a willingness to work. You may need to balance love and work demands. Pushing to the top is instinctive for you in this region.

11th: You are dealing with a polarity in your work—between your (natal) side which wants excitement, stimulation, recognition, approval and high visibility versus your (relocated) side which wants to be rational, detached and cool on the job. You can be highly creative and innovative here.

12th: Magic is in your aura! You can become a spellbinder, with natural dramatic, persuasive talent. Ability is likely to increase for sales, teaching, politics, comedy advertising, promotion and similar fields. You'll learn how to cast a spell on your audience.

Midheaven (10th House) Rulers: from 6th to...

1st: Productivity and accomplishment matter to you. Disciplined, you are willing to work and do what is necessary. You have a tendency to measure yourself in terms of performance and may sometimes be too self-critical. You can achieve a great deal here, blending initiative and follow-through.

2nd: Tangible results are highlighted. You may take great satisfaction in achievements which can be seen, heard, felt or measured. You want something real for your efforts in this region. You are generally willing to work hard, but also can enjoy what you do!

3rd: Potential talent for ideas, speaking, writing, paperwork, numbers, media or analysis is highlighted in this region. You may feel torn between focused attention and the desire to spread yourself thin—a finger in many pies. You need mental stimulation on the job.

4th: You are usually eager to fix things up and have a natural skill for repairs (physical, mental, emotional). You may sometimes overdo compassion and the "need to be needed" to the point of offering solutions others may not want. You can be a natural caretaker and do well in assisting fields in this region.

5th: Getting the job done could be a primary focus with you. You can be quite disciplined, yet have high energy for achievement. Your work might provide an arena to shine, and you are primarily oriented toward competence and efficiency.

7th: You can be a good problem-solver on the job. Logic and practicality are at your fingertips here. Sometimes, you may delay decisions, trying to collect all the information. You can be practical about people and may consider work in areas such as personnel or related fields.

8th: You have potential talent in handling details, in being focused and able to concentrate. You could have great endurance and stamina for your work in this locale. Your discipline might sometimes be obsessive, but you are highly skilled for just about any business, research or other field involving careful analysis.

9th: You can potentially put a lot of sweat and effort into making your dreams come true here. Dangers include wanting more than is possible from your job or yourself as a worker — or demanding "perfect or not at all" in terms of a career. Mental stimulation is important in your profession.

10th: You tend to believe that work means work, and are willing to be dedicated, disciplined, hardworking, etc. Beware of slipping into a workaholic mode in this area. If frustrated by your work, illness can offer an escape (or a vacation for the workaholic). You **need** to achieve, but don't overdo your responsibilities.

11th: You could feel torn between a practical, sensible (natal) focus in your work versus a willingness to take chances, to change, to break new ground (relocated focus). You have potential talent for any fields involving logic, rationality and a sensible assessment. You can handle details **and** a broad perspective.

12th: You may manifest your visions in your profession in this locale. You could become a realistic mystic, a practical idealist. If these two sides of your nature fight each other, you could be chronically dissatisfied with your work (no "perfect" job) or how you work. Job-hopping is possible. Integrate self-discipline and inspiration.

Midheaven (10th House) Rulers: from 7th to...

1st: Self-other interactions are likely to be significant in your work here. You may be learning to balance assertion and accommodation. Counseling, personnel work, the law, or any one-on-one encounters are appropriate. Partners or partnership could affect your work.

2nd: Talent in beauty fields is likely to increase in this region. You'll want to enjoy your work and find it pleasurable. (If overdone, this can indicate passivity.) Harmonious interactions with co-workers are probably important to you.

3rd: Communication and/or people involvement is natural for your job in this area. You may have good social instincts in terms of your career and a flair for meeting people on their own level. You can be a good team player.

4th: People fields would be natural for you here. You'll tend to become more emotionally involved with people you work with, and might even work with family members. You are learning to balance dependency, nurturing and equality needs through your interactions on the job.

5th: Grace and charm may become vocational assets for you here. Your charisma flows easily into social interactions and communications with others. You may further a flair for sales, entertainment or any persuasive fields. You are likely to be outgoing, expressive and sociable in the world.

6th: You probably want your working relationships to be sensible and practical in this region. Colleagues or teamwork may be important, but efficiency is also apt to be a priority for you. You'll tend to be logical and rational on the job and want people to make sense. (Sometimes they don't.) You may develop more skills with handicrafts, artistic endeavors, or repairs.

8th: Your professional instincts for people are probably excellent here. You may direct your talents into personnel work, the law, politics, counseling, marriage, or other people-oriented vocations.

9th: You can apply social skills to your career in this locale. A strong sense of justice is likely, so you may be drawn to work with law, courts, politics, social causes, etc. Your work could bring together people and ideas or ideals.

10th: You are moving from a teamwork, cooperative focus with your natal placement to a need for more authority and power in your relocation. Encourage your executive side without losing your natural empathy. Keep a good balance between relationship needs and job demands.

11th: Your intellectual and social skills are in high focus here. Talent for networking is likely. Objectivity could become one of your vocational assets. You may work well with groups, or as a team player. You could have a good sense of fair play and justice on the job.

12th: You may strengthen your talent for aesthetic or beauty fields here. You are likely to prefer work that is pleasant, attractive and easy. (You might sometimes be a bit passive or let others help out.) You can be graceful and charming on the job. You may help people pursue their dreams.

Midheaven (10th House) Rulers: from 8th to...

1st: You'll probably want to control your work here and function best independently. You may enhance your talent for medicine, business, anything involving assertion, power or hidden matters. You are learning to balance direct confrontation and subtle forms of power plays and power seeking.

2nd: Material gratification, satisfaction and security are important in your work in this area. You may develop more talent for business, especially financial fields, or anything involving physical manipulation (massage, physiotherapy, acupressure, chiropractic, etc.) or which digs beneath the surface of life.

3rd: You need a career that you find deeply fascinating and compelling. You may be drawn toward areas that are hidden, taboo, or deal with power issues. You could have excellent analytical abilities and might be a natural investigator.

4th: You may use intuition or psychic insights in your work in this region. Subtle emotional cues can affect your performance on the job. You'll need to deal with nonverbal (and other) manipulations or ploys for fullest effectiveness. You could work with family, or colleagues could strongly affect your feelings.

5th: Ambition comes naturally to you here, as you are apt to be drawn to a position of authority or leadership. Your will power is likely to be very strong where vocational issues are concerned. You tend to get involved in projects which arouse intense emotional reactions.

6th: You may strengthen your talents for organization, handling details, concentration and follow-through. Business skills are likely to increase, especially in the financial realm. You can be a very disciplined worker, but may sometimes be a bit obsessive or overdo critical judgment. You may be very thorough here.

7th: People vocations are natural for you here. You career may increasingly involve relating to others: marriage, counseling, astrology, the law, personnel work, etc. You might work with a partner, or meet a partner through your job. Teamwork and sharing the load are appropriate.

9th: For greatest satisfaction in this area, you need a career which rouses intense feelings in you. You are capable of aiming very high, yet also have perseverance. You may develop talent for fields involving physical, mental, emotional or spiritual power; hidden knowledge or ideals and beliefs.

10th: You probably have good management skills, with a penchant for organization, thoroughness, and discipline. You can focus more easily in this region, and finish what you start. A pragmatist, you are likely to seek control and security in your world.

11th: You are learning to balance your desire for control, power, intensity and hidden knowledge (natal placements) in your career versus your quest for equality, change, the new and the cutting edge (relocated placements). You may transform yourself, others, or the world in your work.

12th: Your inner wisdom or intuition can contribute to your work here. You're apt to increase your natural empathy and tune into those around you. You can spot underlying patterns and deal with subtle issues in the outer world.

Midheaven (10th House) Rulers: from 9th to...

1st: You are probably attracted to active, lively careers. Your sense of humor, faith, confidence or self-expression may be important in your work in this locale. Restless, you could seek constant expansion, pioneering, newness in your work. You may quit or get fired if things seem humdrum. You're apt to go after excitement in your world.

2nd: You are generally drawn toward work that is larger than life, promotes ideas and ideals, expands your horizons, stimulates your mind or deals with ethics, principles or meaning in life. Yet the relocation focuses on grounding these aspirations, bringing them into practical, tangible manifestation.

3rd: Teaching, preaching, traveling, collecting and disseminating knowledge and information are natural careers for you. Mental agility and verbal skills are highlighted in this region. You probably need a lots of variety and intellectual stimulation on the job.

4th: Your (natal) aspirations, dreams, seeking of expansion, enlightenment and something **more** in your work need to be balanced with security drives and a home-centeredness (suggested in the relocation). Adventure vies with domesticity; public with private. Your work could bring the world closer to others.

5th: You can put a lot of zest and enthusiasm into your job! A high-energy worker, you need action, excitement and stimulation in your career. Ambitious, you are likely to seek expansion and a sense of doing more than you have done before. You may sometimes overreach or come across as a bit arrogant, but you can be quite charismatic and fun to work with.

6th: You are learning to balance inspiration and application in your work— to somehow ground your dreams, visions, quest for **more**. Skill is likely in working with the mind. You may sometimes want too much, too fast, but have the capacity to work toward your heart's desire.

7th: Your work in this locale may well involve people and/or ideas. Communication skills are in focus, and persuasion may come naturally to you. Probably blessed with a sense of justice, you may be drawn to the law, politics, social causes, etc. Your personal magnetism may be an asset in your career here.

8th: You may have high aspirations for your work—perhaps sometimes wanting more than is possible. You need to be intensely moved by your career; halfway measures are unsatisfying. You want to go all-out in what you do. A compelling urge to contribute to the world is highlighted here.

10th: You are likely to seek the best in your world. This can lead to tremendous accomplishments, but another option is disillusionment (nothing is ever as ideal as you imagined it would be). Your skill lies in visualizing the best potentials and working to make them real.

11th: Your world could involve the future in some sense: new ideas, ideals, technology, networking or something on the cutting edge. Optimism about career options probably comes naturally to you. If your work is not sufficiently stimulating, progressive or varied, you may quit, be fired or job-hop. Your career may become more transpersonal: affecting the wider world.

12th: Idealism is central to your efforts in this area. This could manifest as searching for the perfect job (and perhaps never being satisfied, sometimes with multiple jobs), trying to do your work perfectly, placing a high value on the work ethic or trying to make a more perfect or a more beautiful world.

Midheaven (10th House) Rulers: from 10th to...

1st: You are likely to have a strong sense of responsibility in terms of work, and deal best under self-direction or being the executive. You can be a high achiever here, but may need to deal with issues of limits. You might unnecessarily restrict (inhibit) yourself—or ignore needed rules/regulations. Discipline linked to initiative can reap noteworthy results.

2nd: Slow and steady probably wins the race in this region. You can be quite disciplined, but also know how to relax. Sensible and stable, you are likely to be a dedicated and dependable worker. Tangible results are important to you, and you probably prefer a practical, grounded, reasonable approach on the job.

3rd: You are apt to seek authority and responsibility in your work, but also value variety and mental stimulation in this locale. It may not be easy to blend your serious and flippant sides, but both can make a contribution to your job. You can use your organizational skills to deal with information and ideas.

4th: Competence and achievements matter to you, but your relocation brings the focus back to the home. Career must be balanced with family, emotions with pragmatism. You may work more from your home or with family members. Security and safety are more important to you here.

5th: A position of authority and power probably seems instinctive to you; you would prefer to run the show. Potentially highly effective and capable, this region highlights both energy and endurance on the job. You're a natural for making things happen, getting things done.

6th: Hard work is something you are definitely willing to put in. With good discipline, concentration and desire to accomplish in focus here, you can even slip into the workaholic role if not careful. Career frustrations could affect your health (or your body might "break down" to force you to take a break). Business skills are likely to increase; you may deal with any field involving the physical world and tangible results.

7th: Your initial focus in a career was on responsibility and the authority role. Your relocation brings more attention to teamwork and sharing. You may also have to balance work and relationship demands in terms of time and energy. Your likely assets include logic, rationality, and common sense.

8th: You can be a superb organizer. Management is a potential skill here, with your talent for focus, concentration and follow-through being highlighted. You need security (physical and emotional) in your career. Taking charge may come naturally to you.

9th: Your desire to do what is necessary is likely to be raised to a higher and higher power. You can achieve a great deal, but beware of demanding too much of yourself. Focus on assets as well as flaws. Your visions can enhance your pragmatism, if you keep a balance between them.

11th: You are learning to blend the old and the new, the conventional and the unconventional, the rebel and the traditionalist in your work. You may change existing structures or build new structures, but need the best from what is and has been as well as what is possible and could be.

12th: In this locale, you are putting together ideals and reality in some form. If you focus too much on shortcomings or blocks, you will be frustrated. If you dream impossible dreams, you will be disappointed. The best of both allows you to set your sights high, but take practical steps to manifest your visions.

Midheaven (10th House) Rulers: from 11th to...

1st: Innovation and individuality are significant in your work in this area. You need freedom of action and may be inclined to leave (or get fired) if you feel confined or tied down. You can work well in unusual fields, with different hours, unconventional approaches, or other nonstandard techniques. You are probably creative here.

2nd: Your (natal) desire for independence and uniqueness in your work shifts toward being grounded and concerned with results and material manifestation (in this location). You may still thrive on vocational challenges and changes, but now seek a bit more security and stability. Your resources could be enhanced through unconventional, new age, technological, humanitarian or intellectual means.

3rd: Variety is highlighted in your work in this region. You probably thrive in an atmosphere of mental stimulation. Communication skills are likely to increase, and you may need changes of scene, of routine, of people, of working environment, etc. You can be objective about your world.

4th: Individualism remains an important part of your career, but you are now (in this area) more focused on security needs. Your support system on the job becomes more central. Friends and/or family may affect your work. You might demonstrate networking skills, and can blend logic and emotions.

5th: Excitement and creativity are central in your career while living here. You probably need freedom in your work, to expand, to do more than has been done before. You can be a leader as well as a good team player, can balance enthusiasm and detachment in your endeavors. You could become quite a pioneer and groundbreaker.

6th: Your uniqueness and need for freedom are more grounded here. Your (natal) creativity and skill at innovative approaches are shifting to include a talent for details, organization and a natural desire to improve. Problem-solving may rise to new heights with your capacity to see alternatives and desire to repair and improve.

7th: You may have excellent skills for working with people, and can be quite objective about work routines and necessary duties in this region. You probably have a flair for communications and a natural sense of fair play and justice, willing to cooperate with others. Networking may come more easily to you; you need people and mental stimulation on the job.

8th: Equality and teamwork remain important skills of yours, but you may need more power and control in your work in this location. A sense of mastery is vital. You're apt to work best in a field you find intensely fascinating and absorbing. You can balance security demands with the impetus to change, integrate emotional intensity and detachment on the job.

9th: You tend to work best in fields that are open, have variety, are progressive, future-oriented, or involve humanitarian ideals. You need to be constantly growing and expanding in your career and may have a natural optimism about your work. You can be a good team player, but require lots of space and independence while in this area.

10th: Your innovative ideas and natural vocational independence must now be grounded in the crucible of reality. Your desire for change, the new, the different and modern must be blended with societal rules, vocational limits, authority demands and the constraints of making a living. You can change the structures in which you work, with patience and creativity.

12th: You can be a visionary in your work. You have potential talent for looking ahead, imagining, projecting, extrapolating into the future. You can work well in fields which involve a big picture, people at large. Your abilities may draw you toward abstractions, ideals, principles, the new and what is most inspirational.

Midheaven (10th House) Rulers: from 12th to...

1st: Your career here needs to involve a sense of ideals, inspiration, compassion, beauty, principles or visions. You can put much energy into the pursuit of your dreams. You are willing to seek the best and the highest in your professional activities.

2nd: You'll work best in pleasant and beautiful surroundings. You may strengthen your talent for aesthetic, artistic, or graceful work. You may sometimes seek the path of least resistance. You prefer to avoid unpleasantness and might sometimes be a bit passive. You can operate as a peacemaker and appreciate harmony.

3rd: Your multiplicity of interests could lead you to scatter your vocational talents. You are apt to be drawn in many directions, desiring to know, to learn, to grasp everything. You may seek more than is possible in your career, and need to set priorities so that what really matters does get accomplished. You'll be more able to blend logic and intuition in your world.

4th: Your intuition and ability to tune into others could be assets in your work in this locale. You probably function best in a sheltered environment and your work might even involve family. Since you wish to succor and assist, you might sometimes be taken advantage of on the job. Nurture yourself as well as others.

5th: You have potentially spellbinding talent. You could be a natural persuader, teacher, entertainer, promoter, comic, seller, etc. Casting a spell upon your audience and moving people with your emotions are highlighted in this area. Dramatic, romantic approaches to reality appeal.

6th: You are learning to bring your dreams down to earth. This location emphasizes grounding your visions, making your aesthetic or idealistic images tangible. You may be drawn to physical, mental, emotional or spiritual repair work. You see the highest potential, and can develop the practicality to help manifest what you envision.

7th: Your career in this locale could benefit from your feeling for grace, harmony, line, form and beauty. You may exhibit artistic, aesthetic talent, or a natural charm and diplomacy with others. You are apt to prefer easy tasks and pleasant surroundings and can bring enhanced gratification through your efforts.

8th: Your psychic understanding can be an asset in your career in this area. You are able to look beneath the surface and deal with hidden issues and unconscious motives. You can sense and work with people's "vibes" as well as the basic, underlying patterns in a vocation. You might put feelings to work.

9th: Idealism is an underlying theme in your vocation in this region. This could reflect the quest for the "perfect" job (perfect pay, hours, co-workers, etc.). It might indicate a desire to do your work flawlessly (perfectly). It could point to a high value placed on the work ethic, or laboring for a more ideal world. You can inspire others through your career.

10th: This location emphasizes finding a structure in which to live out your dream. The natal idealism prominent in your vocational needs must be grounded and applied responsibly to the world. You need to bring together inspiration and dedication, hopes and hard work.

11th: Your vocational drives may have a mystical, visionary streak in this area. You could be drawn toward work involving ideals, principles, the future, progress, humanitarian ideas or anything transpersonal—affecting the wider world. You are able to combine both logic and intuition in your efforts.

Stellia Changing Houses
A relocation may break up a natal stellium (from one house to two houses); move it into an entirely different house, or create a stellium by house where none existed before. This section provides a few keywords for the issues highlighted by stellia. [A stellium refers to three or more planets in one sign or in one house.]

If a stellium forms by relocation, give greater weight to the matters of that house. (See keyword listing.) If a stellium is broken up by a relocation, the matters of that house are no longer quite so central.

One could also look at planet-by-planet house changes, but there are a number of good books out on the subject of planets in houses, so we chose not to repeat such text here. (See, for example, *Easy Astrology Guide*.) Just remember that relocated house placements apply while you are living in that area (or interacting with people there). Natal placements last a lifetime.

Key Words for Houses

1ST HOUSE: personal identity, self-expression, instinctive action, desire for freedom, need to be first or on your own, self-consciousness, energy, self-will and drive, independence and integrity.

2ND HOUSE: sensuality, desire for comfort, preference for stability, self-earned money, tangible arts (e.g., sculpture), ability to relax, possessions and pleasures, indulgence, physical focus.

3RD HOUSE: communications, relatives, learning capacity, involvement with the media, relationship to immediate environment, curiosity, light-heartedness, dexterity, flexibility.

4TH HOUSE: home, family, nurturing parent, ability to care and be cared for, need for emotional security, attachment to the land, country, roots, or public; dependency; protective tendencies.

5TH HOUSE: creativity, desire to shine and be admired, drive for excitement, romantic needs and love affairs, children, urge to take risks, to do more than before, speculation for greater gain.

6TH HOUSE: job routines, co-workers, health habits, desire to function efficiently, ability to handle details, competence, flaw-finding in order to improve or repair, step-by-step focus.

7TH HOUSE: partner(s) and/or partnership, cooperation and competition, visual arts, litigation, appreciation of polarities, drive for equality and fair play, balance, harmony, teamwork.

8TH HOUSE: shared resources and possessions, joint pleasures including sexuality, intensity, digging into the psyche, intimacy instincts, ability to share power, obsessions, self-mastery issues.

9TH HOUSE: truth-seeking activities, beliefs and values, long-range goals, writing, teaching, dealings with law courts, churches, universities; long trips, broadening horizons, knowledge.

10TH HOUSE: career, executive power, sense of responsibility, dealings with rules and authority figures, realistic limits, structures, conscience, status, societal roles, duties, consequences (karma).

11TH HOUSE: groups, organizations, causes, friends, anything on the cutting edge of change, individuality, desire for freedom and independence, resistance to limits, rebellion, invention.

12TH HOUSE: mysticism, love of nature, quest for infinite love and beauty, escapist tendencies, compassion, desire to merge and experience Oneness, spiritual yearnings, idealism, imagination.

CHAPTER SIX

SIGN CHANGES ON THE SELF/OTHER ANGLES

With a relocation, our angles often change signs. Since the self/other angle pairs form axes (Ascendant/Descendant; Antivertex/Vertex and East Point/West Point), this section looks at those axes rather than separating the pairs of angles. Each sign combination is delineated, beginning with the natal pair and looking at the relocated pair—for the Ascendant/Descendant axis. (We recommend that readers working with the Antivertex/Vertex and East Point/West Point axes treat them as auxiliary Ascendant/Descendant axes — with parallel meanings.)

Please remember that planets are more important than signs. Thus, the planet ruling a sign will often modify the interpretation of the issues depicted by the sign. (That is why we looked at planetary aspects to angles first.) The placement (by house and sign) and aspects to the rulers of each angle should also be considered.

The Ascendant/Descendant Axis
East Point/West Point Axis
Antivertex/Vertex Axis

The self/other axes (Ascendant/Descendant; EP/WP, AV/V) are significant keys to issues you are learning to balance in terms of interpersonal relationships. The Ascendant (and, secondarily, East Point and Antivertex) signify qualities you tend to express yourself, through your personal action, while the Descendant (and, secondarily, West Point and Vertex) denote attributes you face in your relationships. Sometimes these attributes will be shared with a partner. Other times, another person may express the qualities of the Descendant (West Point or Vertex) which seem foreign to your being. The challenge is to balance the polar opposites of the ascending and descending signs. They point to inner needs that can polarize and seem at opposite ends, yet need each other as natural partners.

NATAL: ARIES/LIBRA

Natally you have **Aries rising and Libra setting**, putting a strong focus on the balance between self and others. You are learning to integrate assertion and accommodation, or personal needs and drives with relationship desires. Your desire to be independent, self-expressive, active, and on your own must be harmonized with your need to form a partnership, your desire for close relationships, and your attraction to other people. If you polarize between these issues, you could swing between extremes of aggression and effacement; from demanding things on your terms to giving in excessively to others; from being alone versus being swallowed up in a relationship, etc. Keep room to be yourself and still share with others.

Defining your independence, gaining a firm sense of personal identity, and being free to be yourself are more personally relevant to you. Issues of sharing, cooperation, harmony and grace will probably be faced more through your relationships. But the call is for balance.

In your **relocation chart**, you have **Taurus rising and Scorpio setting**, fine-tuning the focus to issues of "mine" versus "yours" or "mine" versus "ours." Though this is also a self-other polarity, its focus is on issues involving sensuality, sexuality, money and shared possessions. You could feel torn between self-indulgence (in terms of food, money, sex, etc.) and self-control. You might be ambivalent over earning your own way versus depending on someone else's income. You might slip into power struggles with a mate over issues of money, sex or other material pleasures. The challenge is to be comfortable giving, receiving and sharing in a balanced manner that brings pleasure to both people.

You will probably face the issues of indulgence, pleasure, comfort and security more directly in your own actions, and are likely to confront themes of self-mastery, self-discipline, self-control and power more through your relationships. Incorporate the best of both.

In your **relocation chart**, you have **Gemini rising and Sagittarius setting**, highlighting the issues of communication and beliefs in your relationships with others. The balancing act between self and other is likely to occur in a context of questions, values, trust, and a search for meaning in life. Assertion versus accommodation struggles may be lived out in terms of who is more articulate and verbal, whose beliefs more define the relationship, whose metaphysics is predominant, etc. A restless and mental focus could become more important in your personal expression and relationships. You may seek more knowledge, truth and intellectual stimulation in your associations. Tension may exist between curiosity for its own sake versus information which adds to a sense of direction and purpose in life. The challenge is to enjoy gathering knowledge as well as gaining an inspired sense of meaning in life. Family may also be important: siblings, in-laws, grandchildren.

You may personally center more around issues of curiosity, data exchange and communication. Questions of beliefs, values, and ideals may be experienced more through your relationships.

In your **relocation chart**, you have **Cancer rising and Capricorn** setting, suggesting that the balance between self and other will be played out around issues of dependency and dominance or compassion and pragmatism. You and a partner may polarize over time and energy demands between work and the family. Or, you may feel torn between the soft, gentle, supportive style versus a strong, controlling style. Parental issues could influence your relationships. Beware of turning a partner into a parent or trying to parent your mate. The challenge is to take turns caring for and being strong and responsible for one another, so there is an equal exchange of nurturing and achieving energy. Your role as a parent or unfinished business with a parent may be more significant for you in this area. You are learning to integrate caring and capability.

You may deal more directly with issues of dependency and nurturing, while themes of power, authority and control are brought in through your relationships.

In your **relocation chart,** you have **Leo rising and Aquarius setting,** highlighting the issues of love and detachment in your relationships with others. The polarity being faced involves the head versus the heart or the intellect versus passion. You and a partner might take opposite positions in terms of intensity versus objectivity, loved ones versus friends, or emotional attachments versus separation and detachment. Some ambivalence is possible in associations, particularly if you have not achieved some integration between "freedom" versus "closeness" drives. You could swing between feeling "hot" and "cold" in relationships, or attract partners who go back and forth. Decisions involving children may be more significant in this area (including the question of whether or not to have kids). You are learning to love with an open hand, to encourage uniqueness within yourself as well as your partner, to be passionately committed while totally respecting the individuality of those you care about.

You may deal more personally with themes of self-esteem, the need to be admired, the drive for love, attention, limelight and passion, while your relationships bring in issues of intellectual detachment, objectivity, the wider world, the unusual and the drive for tolerance.

In your **relocation chart,** you have **Virgo rising and Pisces** setting, pointing to a focus on "ideal versus real" issues in your associations with others. You are learning to blend dreams and visions with the practical demands of achievement. This polarity is often active where people are involved in artistic activities or projects requiring craftsmanship. This opposition is also common when helping or healing associations are part of the picture (psychologists, astrologers, social workers, doctors, etc.). A negative form is savior/victim personal relationships (e.g., marrying an alcoholic, psychotic, drug addict—or looking to someone to make everything perfect for you). The challenge is to pursue a dream for something higher, better or more beautiful— in a practical, grounded way which will reap tangible results.

You are likely to be more personally involved with issues of reality, fact-finding, analysis, discrimination and the need to do a good job. You might also focus more on health or nutrition, and you need to be wary of too much self-criticism. Your partnerships are likely to bring up issues of fantasy, imagination, rose-colored glasses and the quest for infinite love and beauty.

In your **relocation chart,** you have **Libra rising and Aries setting**—the exact reverse of your natal ascending and descending signs. The focus remains intense on issues of self versus other, assertion versus accommodation, and personal versus interpersonal drives and desires. This location puts your relationship needs in higher focus, yet you are still dealing with harmonizing partnership drives with your loner instincts. Beware of falling into seesawing relationships: getting swallowed up and then running away, being overwhelmed and then fighting to assert your independence; avoiding people and then becoming a doormat. The challenge is to keep time for yourself as well as for the people you care about.

Issues of sharing, harmony, grace and beauty will be more personally relevant for you here. You have the opportunity to test your balance of your natal polarity. If you have truly integrated this opposition, you will maintain a strong sense of self while still enjoying attachments to a significant other. You will assert yourself when appropriate, compromise when necessary, and generally consider both your needs and the needs of other people. You will demonstrate mastery of diplomacy **and** self-expression.

In your **relocation chart,** you have **Scorpio rising and Taurus setting,** fine-tuning the focus to issues of "mine" versus "yours" or "mine" versus "ours." This self-other polarity is more concerned with issues involving sensuality, sexuality, money and shared possessions. You could feel torn between self-indulgence (in terms of food, money, sex, etc.) and self-control. You might be ambivalent over earning your own way versus depending on someone else's income. You might slip into power struggles with a mate over issues of money, sex or other material pleasures. The challenge is to be comfortable giving, receiving and sharing in a balanced manner that brings pleasure to both people.

You will probably face issues of self-mastery, self-discipline, self-control and power urges in terms of your own actions and drives. Your relationships may bring in issues around indulgence, pleasure, comfort and security. Incorporate the best of both!

In your **relocation chart,** you have **Sagittarius rising and Gemini setting,** highlighting the issues of communication and beliefs in your relationships with others. The balancing act between self and other is likely to occur in a context of questions, values, trust and a search for meaning in life. Assertion versus accommodation struggles may be lived out in terms of who is more articulate and verbal, whose beliefs more define the relationship, whose metaphysics is predominant, etc. A restless and mental focus becomes more important in your personal expression and relationships. You seek knowledge, truth and intellectual stimulation in your associations. Tension may exist between curiosity for its own sake versus information which adds to a sense of direction and purpose in life. The challenge is to enjoy gathering knowledge as well as gaining an inspired sense of meaning in life. Family may also be important: siblings, in-laws, grandchildren, etc.

You may be more personally concerned with questions of belief, values, ideals and truth—a spontaneous questing urge. Your relationships may bring in issues centering around pure curiosity, data exchange, communication and being casual about life.

In your **relocation chart,** you have **Capricorn rising and Cancer setting,** suggesting that the balance between self and other will be played out around issues of dependency and dominance or compassion and pragmatism. You and a partner may polarize over time and energy demands between work and the family. Or, you may feel torn between the soft, gentle, supportive style versus a strong, controlling style. Parental issues could influence your relationships. Beware of one-sidedly turning a partner into a parent or trying to parent your mate. The challenge is to take turns caring for and being strong and responsible for one another, so there is an equal exchange of nurturing and achieving energy. Your role as a parent or unfinished business with a parent may be very significant for you in this location. You are learning to integrate caring and capability.

You may deal more directly with themes of power, authority and control, while issues of dependency and nurturing are brought in through your relationships.

In your **relocation chart,** you have **Aquarius rising and Leo setting,** highlighting the issues of love and detachment in your relationships with others. The polarity being faced involves the head versus the heart or the intellect versus passion. You and a partner might take opposite positions in terms of intensity versus objectivity, loved ones versus friends, or emotional attachments versus separation and detachment. Some ambivalence is possible in associations, particularly if you have not achieved some integration between "freedom" versus "closeness" drives. You could swing between feeling "hot" and "cold" in relationships, or attract partners who go back and forth. Decisions involving children may be more significant in this area (including the question of whether or not to have kids). You are learning to love with an open hand, to encourage uniqueness within yourself as well as your partner, to be passionately committed while totally respecting the individuality of those you care about.

You may deal more personally with issues of intellectual detachment, objectivity, the wider world, the unusual, and a drive for tolerance, while themes of self-esteem, the need to be admired, the drive for love, attention, limelight, and passion emerge through your relationships.

In your **relocation chart,** you have **Pisces rising and Virgo setting**, pointing to a focus on "ideal versus real" issues in your associations with others. You are learning to blend dreams and visions with the practical demands of achievement. This polarity is often active where people are involved in artistic activities or projects requiring craftsmanship. This opposition is also common when helping or healing associations are part of the picture (psychologists, astrologers, social workers, doctors, etc.). A negative form is savior/victim personal relationships (e.g., marrying an alcoholic, psychotic, drug addict—or looking to someone to make everything perfect for you). Your challenge is to pursue a dream for something higher, better or more beautiful— in a practical, grounded way which will reap tangible results.

Your own actions and drives may be more directly connected to imagination, fantasy, rose-colored glasses, visions, Higher Wisdom and the need for infinite love and beauty. Your relationships are likely to trigger issues of reality, fact-finding, analysis, discrimination and the need to do a good job. They might also focus on health or nutrition and both you and any partners need to be wary of overdoing a critical approach. Make facts and fancy supportive of one another. Blend intuition and hard work.

NATAL: TAURUS/SCORPIO

Natally, you have **Taurus rising and Scorpio setting**, indicating a polarity between indulgence, comfort, stability, ease and self-control, facing the Shadow, transformation and intensity. You and/or a partner may feel torn between self-indulgence versus appetite mastery over food, drink, money, sexuality or other physical pleasures. You could feel ambivalent between earning your own way versus depending on (or providing for) someone else. You may fluctuate between a comfortable self-satisfaction and an intense, driving need to probe beneath the surface and ferret out hidden information and motives. You and a partner are likely to work out the balance together and may be susceptible to power struggles, particularly over money, sex and possessions. Your challenge is to learn to give, receive and share pleasures for mutual gratification, with a basic sense of equality.

You are more prone to experiencing the need for beauty, pleasure and relaxation through your own actions. Your relationships will probably bring in issues around intimacy, depth sharing, self-mastery.

In your **relocation chart,** you have **Aries rising and Libra setting,** indicating an intensified focus on the self/other polarity, or the balance between personal and interpersonal needs. Power struggles remain a potential hazard as you and associates strive to equalize assertion and accommodation, personal will with the needs of others. If the balance of power is skewed, one person may be the appeaser, giving in too much to the other. Or, an individual who feels threatened by the power of another could withdraw from relating, or attack others, feeling the only way to defend is to "get them first." Once power is shared, people can cooperate and learn to compromise. Negotiations can lead to win/win solutions. Healthy competition is another way people can test and build their strength through interactions with others. Many different relationship variants are possible, as you learn to balance your drives and desires with those of another person.

You may be more focused personally on issues of independence, assertion, spontaneity and self-expression. Your relationship(s) may bring in issues of sharing, cooperation, competition, harmony, equality and balance.

In your **relocation chart,** you have **Gemini rising and Sagittarius setting**, implying a mental overlay on the basic fixed polarity of your Ascendant/ Descendant. This suggests that you and a partner may deal with issues of mastery and indulgence more in the realm of the mind. You are likely to examine your beliefs and values around money and pleasures. You may question each other's assumptions concerning finances, gratification or the material/sensual world. You may spur each other's thinking, talking and collecting of information about the physical world. Rather than simple power struggles, you are likely to have discussions and concepts batted back and forth a lot. You have the opportunity to examine some of your old assumptions (particularly about "mine" and "ours") in this region, and may wish to alter some of your approaches to sensual, sexual and/or monetary matters. The "mental" approach to life lets us learn vicariously, through observing others.

You may find it natural to be more verbal, curious, flippant and interested in many things. Your relationships are likely to trigger issues of belief, faith, trust and values.

In your **relocation chart,** you have **Cancer rising and Capricorn setting** repeating the focus on earth and water in your interactions with others. Cancer/Capricorn suggest that parental influences may be significant here. Your handling of resources (especially money and sensual indulgences) may be influenced (positively **or** negatively) by parental figures. You and a partner could fall into parent-child interactions, rather than equalitarian exchanges. One may play the more dominant, controlling, power figure while the other is more sensitive, dependent, and emotional. Manipulation or power plays could affect the way you share resources and pleasures with one another. The challenge is to balance pragmatism and compassion in your handling of sex, money and resources. You and a partner could battle over financial and resource commitments to a profession or career versus contributions to the family or domestic arena. Both are essential; find compromises.

You may deal more personally with issues of emotional closeness, commitment and attachment, while partners bring in issues of control, authority, duties and the rules of the game.

In your **relocation chart,** you have **Leo rising and Aquarius setting**. Combined with your natal, this gives you the symbolism of a grand cross in fixed signs. There are several issues that could affect your relationships with others. One challenge is to integrate security and risk-taking needs. Natally, your approach (in terms of the Ascendant and Descendant only) is more security and safety-oriented. You want relationships to be dependable and known. Your **relocation** shows more of a willingness to take risks, to try something (or someone) new, to explore virgin territory. Since you are dealing with both urges, you need a balance of some basic commitment and safety while still open to new potentials and exciting, creative developments. Feelings are likely to be strong regarding sensual, sexual and financial issues. Recognize that neither you nor your partner want to be controlled, manipulated or told what to do in these areas. You can both be extremely strong-willed and resistant to outside influences. Battles and power struggles are possible, but a willingness to compromise will work wonders. It will be extra important for you and your associates to try to see each other's points of view.

You may deal more personally with issues of self-esteem, recognition, attention, charisma, excitement, and the drive to be noteworthy. Your partnership(s) may bring up the need to be unique, individualistic, independent and involved with a wider perspective (groups, networking, humanitarian causes, political action, etc.).

In your **relocation chart,** you have **Virgo rising and Pisces setting**. This "real versus ideal" polarity is likely to affect your handling of the basic Taurus/Scorpio push/pull between self-indulgence and self-control. One danger is falling into "savior-victim" scenarios in relationships—particularly when money or sex is involved. Your need to be helpful and compassionate could trap you into a martyr role. It is also possible to swing between the extremes of too much idealism (rose-colored glasses and lack of discrimination which can lead to confusion) versus too much nit-picking and critical judgment—especially where shared resources, finances and pleasures are concerned. You need a balance between seeing and visualizing the best that can be while also remaining practical and working hard to improve what **is**. Perfectionism awaits as a trap for you (if you demand too much in integrating your pull between appetite indulgence and appetite control) or for your relationships (if you or a partner consistently expects more than is reasonable). When positively channeled, your relationships can be constantly improving and growing as you are able to see the best and work to make it more real. You and a partner will be able to sensibly enjoy the material, financial world, with mutual pleasure—while maintaining moderation.

The Virgo qualities of analysis, discrimination, self-criticism and the need to improve things may be more personally relevant to you. Your partner(s) may bring up Piscean issues of dreams, visions, compassion, idealism and the quest for infinite love and beauty.

In your **relocation chart,** you have **Libra rising and Aries setting**, indicating an intensified focus on the self/other polarity, or the balance between personal and interpersonal needs. Power struggles remain a potential hazard as you and associates strive to equalize assertion and accommodation, personal will with the needs of others. If the balance of power is skewed, one person may be the appeaser, giving in too much to the other. Or, an individual who feels threatened by the power of another could withdraw from relating or attack others, feeling the only way to defend is to "get them first." Once power is shared, people can cooperate and learn to compromise. Negotiations can lead to win/win solutions. Healthy competition is another way people can test and build their strength through interactions with others. Many different relationship variants are possible, as you learn to balance your drives and desires with those of another person.

You may be more focused personally on issues of sharing, cooperation, competition, harmony, equality and balance. Your relationship(s) may bring in issues of independence, assertion, spontaneity and self-expression.

In your **relocation chart,** you have **Scorpio rising and Taurus setting**, repeating the natal polarity focus. You are likely to intensify the focus on learning to give, receive and share pleasures with other people. The strongest learning tends to come through the relationship to a mate. Appetite mastery versus appetite indulgence remains a theme, whether the focus revolves more around dieting versus overeating; smoking versus not smoking; alcohol versus abstaining; spending versus saving; sex versus celibacy, etc. Ambivalence in regard to who earns the money, who owns what, who supports whom, and how the purse strings affect emotional matters could arise. Power struggles are quite possible as you strive to develop a sense of mastery and control, but learn to direct your power inward rather than toward others.

You are likely to be more personally concerned with issues of intimacy, transformation, hidden depths, and the drive for transcendence. You retain your natal focus on beauty, pleasure and relaxation, but may also meet those themes increasingly through partner(s). An intense drive to understand the basic motivations of yourself and others is likely, to seek out root causes and hidden motives.

In your **relocation chart,** you have **Sagittarius rising and Gemini setting**, implying a mental overlay on the basic fixed polarity of your Ascendant/Descendant. This suggests that you and a partner may deal with issues of mastery and indulgence more in the realm of the mind. You are likely to examine your beliefs and values around money and pleasures. You may question each other's assumptions concerning finances, gratification or the material/sensual world. You may spur each other's thinking, talking and collecting of information about the physical world. Rather than simple power struggles, you are likely to have discussions and concepts batted back and forth a lot. You have the opportunity to examine some of your old assumptions (particularly about "mine" and "ours") in this region, and may wish to alter some of your approaches to sensual, sexual and/or monetary matters. You will be encouraged to learn vicariously through observing other people.

You may find yourself more personally concerned with issues of belief, faith, values, trust and the meaning of life. You may be drawn to anything which broadens your horizons (philosophy, education, travel, etc.). Your relationship(s) may trigger communication, curiosity, flippancy and the desire to learn many different things. Partner(s) may help you develop objectivity and the capacity to be more lighthearted.

In your **relocation chart,** you have **Capricorn rising and Cancer setting** repeating the focus on earth and water in your interactions with others. Cancer/Capricorn suggest that parental influences may be significant here. Your handling of resources (especially money and sensual indulgences) may be influenced (positively **or** negatively) by parental figures. You and a partner could fall into parent-child interactions, rather than equalitarian exchanges. One may play the more dominant, controlling, power figure while the other is more sensitive, dependent and emotional. Manipulation or power plays could affect the way your share resources and pleasures with one another. The challenge is to balance pragmatism and compassion in your handling of sex, money and resources. You and a partner could battle over financial and resource commitments to a profession or career versus contributions to the family or domestic arena. Both are essential; find compromises.

You may deal more personally with issues of control, responsibility, duties, limits, rules of the game and structuring. Partnership(s) could bring up issues of emotional closeness, dependency, nurturing, commitment and roots.

In your **relocation chart,** you have **Aquarius rising and Leo setting.** Combined with the signs on your natal angles, this gives you the symbolism of a grand cross in fixed signs. There are several issues that could affect your relationships with others. One challenge is to integrate security and risk-taking needs. Natally, your approach (in terms of the Ascendant and Descendant only) is more security and safety-oriented. You probably want relationships to be dependable and known. Your **relocation** will encourage more of a willingness to take risks, to try something (or someone) new, to explore virgin territory. Since you are dealing with both urges, you need a balance of some basic commitment and safety while still staying open to new potentials and exciting, creative developments. Feelings are likely to be strong regarding sensual, sexual and financial issues. Recognize that neither you nor your partner want to be controlled, manipulated or told what to do in these areas. You can both be extremely strong-willed and resistant to outside influences. Battles and power struggles are possible, but a willingness to compromise will work wonders. It will be extra important for you and your associates to try to see each other's points of view.

You may deal more personally with the need to be unique, individualistic, independent and involved with a wider perspective (groups, networking, humanitarian causes, political action, etc.). Your partnership(s) may bring up issues of self-esteem, recognition, attention, charisma, excitement and the drive to lead and be noteworthy.

In your **relocation chart,** you have **Pisces rising and Virgo setting.** This "real versus ideal" polarity is likely to affect your handling of the basic Taurus/Scorpio push/pull between self-indulgence and self-control. One danger is falling into "savior-victim" scenarios in relationships—particularly when money or sex is involved. Your need to be helpful and compassionate could trap you into a martyr role. It is also possible to swing between the extremes of too much idealism (rose-colored glasses and lack of discrimination which can lead to confusion) versus too much nit-picking and critical judgment—especially where shared resources, finances and pleasures are concerned. You need a balance between seeing and visualizing the best that can be while also remaining practical and working hard to improve what **is**. Perfectionism awaits as a trap for you (if you demand too much in integrating the pull between appetite indulgence and appetite control) or for your relationships (if you or a partner consistently expects more than is reasonable). When positively channeled, your relationships can be constantly improving and growing as you are able to see the best and work to make it more real. You and a partner will be able to sensibly enjoy the material, financial world, with mutual pleasure—while maintaining moderation.

You are likely to want to personally be involved with creating beauty or helping and healing in the world. Piscean dreams, visions, compassion and idealism will be important forms of self-expression. The Virgo qualities of analysis, discrimination, flaw-finding and the need to improve things may be more relevant in your interactions with others.

NATAL: GEMINI/SAGITTARIUS

Natally you have **Gemini rising and Sagittarius setting,** putting a strong focus on learning and communication in relationships. You are naturally curious, drawn to many different interests and willing to discuss almost any question. You are likely to seek partners who are mentally stimulating and broaden your horizons. This polarity is associated with teaching and traveling, so your relationships could easily involve some of both. Your associations are teaching you to balance short-range interests with long-range needs, visions and ideals. You face issues of priorities: how much time and energy to invest in your various projects and interests. You can easily be overextended, and may have to drop some involvements in order to give sufficient importance to others. Logic comes easily to you and your objectivity can be an asset.

You are likely to be a natural communicator, eager to talk and share ideas with others. Gathering and disseminating information is important to you. Your partner(s) may stimulate your thinking in terms of philosophy, religion, or questions revolving around meaning, faith, truth and moral principles.

In your **relocation chart,** you have **Aries rising and Libra setting,** bringing issues of assertion and accommodation strongly into the picture. The focus is likely to remain in the mental realm. Such simple issues as who talks and who listens may crop up. One person may feel their ideas receive short shrift in the relationship. One individual may try to influence the other in regard to beliefs and world views. There may be a perceived difference in mental or communicative skills. It is vital that you maintain a balance in these areas. Both partners need to contribute ideas, ideals, and ethics in the relationship. Both need to be willing to communicate and to listen. Since the relocated and the natal polarities both involve fire-air, the accent is on a sense of humor and sociability. Relating to a number of different people is advisable. You grow through interactions (particularly verbal) with others.

With Aries rising, you may personally face more issues around verbal and mental assertion, self-expression and independence. Your partnership(s) could stimulate questions of balance, harmony, sharing and justice.

In your **relocation chart,** you have **Taurus rising and Scorpio setting**, bringing in a material and financial focus. Where your natal concern was primarily intellectual and abstract, you are now likely to focus on physical resources, monetary issues, and the question of shared pleasures. You may strive to apply some of your ideas and beliefs about life to the question of how to intimately relate to a mate. Sexual and sensual connections may be a testing ground for ideals and ideas. And each exploration can lead to more discussion and new concepts. You could find yourself a bit more oriented toward staying in one place, rather than wandering the world. Your mind is likely to be drawn to investigate and question all realms tied to the physical senses. You may be more focused in your mental pursuits, more inclined to be thorough rather than flitting from flower to flower.

Your personal focus will probably center more about comfort, security, beauty, pleasure, and enjoying the physical world (without forsaking your natal identification with the mind). Your relationship(s) may stimulate your dealing with intensity, buried feelings, hidden matters, addictions, and issues of sharing resources and pleasures equitably.

In your **relocation chart,** you have **Cancer rising and Capricorn setting,** bringing a parental theme to your natal focus on the mind. This could indicate issues of dominance versus dependency arising in terms of communication and the intellectual realm. Relationships may deal with issues of who controls the lines of communication and who is more passive/receptive. It is possible that the examples set by your parents might become more significant in terms of your personal action and relationships. You may replay, with a partner, some issues you first faced with a parent. You are likely to find your logic and detachment more mixed with emotions now; feelings and sensitivities receive more notice. You are apt to do more thinking, questioning and examining of your emotional support system, in terms of what provides you with security and safety. Your learning focus may center around the balance between warmth and pragmatism, compassion and rules, empathy and limitation.

Your personal focus is more apt to revolve around feelings, desire for emotional closeness, family issues, domestic needs and a yearning for security and safety. Your relationships may feature issues revolving around responsibility, power, control, authority, practicality and facing the "real" world.

In your **relocation chart,** you have **Leo rising and Aquarius setting,** extending the (natal) mental focus into exciting, risk-taking realms. You will be balancing passion and detachment in your relationships, keeping room for an adrenaline rush as well as an objective assessment of probabilities. You may feel torn between freedom and closeness drives, needing some of each. Your native quick-wittedness could be augmented with increased charisma, sparkle and enthusiasm. Entertainment comes more easily to you here, along with sales, promotion, teaching or other persuasive, on-stage styles of expression. You may do a lot of thinking and communicating about trying to balance time/energy demands for friends versus children, groups versus lovers, passions versus intellectual drives. Your questioning, inquiring mind is likely to explore ambiguities concerning loving and letting go, being attached without being owned, caring about someone while still maintaining a sense of independence.

Your personal focus is more apt to revolve around fun, sparkle, zest and good times. You may enhance your skill with repartee or entertaining anecdotes. You may shine through your mind.

Your partner is apt to stimulate issues of independence, innovation, individuality and the new. Relationships may become a bit unusual, different or progressive.

In your **relocation chart,** you have **Virgo rising and Pisces setting**, continuing the natal focus on the mind. Your quest for knowledge and information remains central, with an added pressure to put your knowledge to work in the world. You may find yourself torn between quantity and quality—part of you wanting to learn anything and everything, and another part wanting to be thorough and get things done with what you learn. Your interactions with other people are apt to stimulate the tension between realism and idealism. You and/or a partner could swing from wanting too much, expecting more than is possible, seeking a beautiful, ideal dream in relationships, to being logical, practical, sensible, grounded and realistic—sometimes to the point of criticism and flaw-finding. You could feel torn between rationality and intuition, thinking and feeling, or dreams and practicality. The combination of a desire to repair and fix things up, along with marked compassion and assisting tendencies can result in relationships based on "rescuing" another person. You or a partner might unconsciously attract people who need help (alcoholics, addicts, psychotics, individuals not quite managing their lives) and try to help them reach their higher potential. Too often, however, the savior ends up victimized or martyred in the relationship. The challenge is to **share** dreams (but also hard work) with a partner— each contributing to making a better or more beautiful world.

You are apt to be more personally involved with issues of thinking, communication, logic and rationality. Your relationship(s) are likely to stimulate issues around ideals, beauty, values, faith, trust, hope, and where one seeks perfection and utopia.

In your **relocation chart,** you have **Libra rising and Aries setting**, bringing issues of balance and harmony strongly into the picture. The focus is likely to remain in the mental realm. Such simple issues as who talks and who listens may crop up. One person may feel their ideas receive short shrift in the relationship. One individual may try to influence the other in regard to beliefs and world views. There may be a perceived difference in mental or communicative skills. It is vital that you gain a balance in these areas. Both partners need to contribute ideas, ideals, and ethics in the relationship. Both need to be willing to communicate and to listen. Since the relocated and the natal polarities both involve fire-air, the accent is on a sense of humor and sociability. Relating to a number of different people is advisable. You grow through interactions (particularly verbal) with others.

With Libra rising, you may personally face more issues around balance, harmony, beauty, sharing, justice and fair play. Your relationship(s) may stimulate thinking, talking and questioning in terms of verbal and mental assertion, self-expression and independence.

In your **relocation chart,** you have **Scorpio rising and Taurus setting,** bringing in a material and financial focus. Where your natal concern was primarily intellectual and abstract, you are now likely to focus more on issues of self-control, self-mastery, intensity, sexuality and shared resources and pleasures. You may strive to apply some of your ideas and beliefs about life to the question of how to intimately relate to a mate. Sexual and sensual connections could become a testing ground for ideals and ideas. And each exploration can lead to more discussion and new concepts. You could find yourself a bit more oriented toward staying in one place, rather than wandering the world. Your mind is likely to be drawn to investigate and question hidden realms and emotions that lie beneath the surface. You may develop more concentration in your mental pursuits, more inclined to be thorough rather than flitting from flower to flower.

Your personal focus will probably center more on intense emotions, a drive for self-control, appetite mastery, concentration, endurance and facing unconscious depths. Your relationship(s) may stimulate your thinking and discussions in terms of comfort, security, beauty, pleasure and enjoying the physical world.

In your **relocation chart,** you have **Sagittarius rising and Gemini setting,** the exact reverse of your natal polarity. A strong focus remains on learning and communicating in relationships. You are more likely to consider travel to other countries or cultures—or other avenues of broadening your horizons. Education, philosophy, religion or any avenue which offers a potential sense of truth, morality, ethics, meaning and purpose in life will appeal. Your partnerships will stimulate your curiosity, your wide range of interest and willingness to communicate about anything and everything. You need partner(s) who are mentally stimulating. This polarity is associated with the student and the teacher, so your relationships could easily involve some of both roles. Your people associations are teaching you to balance short-range interests with long-range needs, visions and ideals. You face issues of priorities: how much time and energy to invest in your various projects and interests. You can easily be overextended, and may have to drop some involvements in order to give sufficient importance to others. Self-confidence is probably more marked in this location, so you could find it easy to take on more than is reasonable. Optimism comes naturally, but you may want more than is humanly possible.

You are likely to be a natural philosopher or truth-seeker, ever trying to expand your physical and mental horizons, to reach out toward meaning and purpose in life. Your relationships are apt to emphasize communication, talking and sharing ideas with others. Gathering and disseminating information is important with partner(s).

In your **relocation chart,** you have **Capricorn rising and Cancer setting**, bringing a parental theme to your natal focus on the mind. This could indicate issues of dominance versus dependency arising in terms of communication and the intellectual realm. Relationships may deal with issues of who controls the lines of communication and who is more passive/receptive. It is possible that the examples of your parents become more significant in terms of your personal action and relationships. You may replay, with a partner, some issues you first faced with a parent. You are likely to find your logic and detachment more mixed with practicality; you want to put your mind to work in the world. You are apt to do more thinking, questioning and examining of your career or contribution to society, in terms of what provides you with security and safety. Your learning focus is likely to center around the balance between warmth and pragmatism, compassion and rules, empathy and limitation.

Your personal focus is apt to revolve more around issues of responsibility, power, authority, control, pragmatism, limits, and facing the "real" world. Your relationship(s) are apt to bring up feelings, desire for emotional closeness, family issues, domestic needs and a yearning for security and safety. Strive to ensure that any parenting done in your partnerships is shared—that you and the other party can take turns taking care of each other, so no one is "stuck" in the role of parent or child.

In your **relocation chart,** you have **Aquarius rising and Leo setting,** extending the (natal) mental focus into exciting, risk-taking realms. You will probably be balancing passion and detachment in your relationships, keeping room for an adrenaline rush as well as an objective assessment of probabilities. You may feel torn between freedom and closeness drives, needing some of each. Your native quick-wittedness is augmented with uniqueness, inventiveness and the capacity to view life from a new perspective. Networking may come more easily to you, along with group activities, interest in technology, progress, the new age or anything on the cutting edge of change. You may do a lot of thinking and communicating about trying to balance time/energy demands for friends versus children, groups versus lovers, passions versus intellectual drives. Your questioning, inquiring mind is likely to explore ambiguities concerning loving and letting go, being attached without being owned, caring about someone while still maintaining a sense of independence.

Your personal focus is more apt to revolve around thinking for yourself, exploring new mental territories, consolidating your freedom and enjoying the new, unusual, different and varied. Your relationship(s) are apt to stimulate your desire for fun, your zest, enthusiasm and sparkle. You and a partner might enjoy repartee or telling each other entertaining anecdotes. You may shine through your minds.

In your **relocation chart,** you have **Pisces rising and Virgo setting,** continuing the natal focus on the mind. Your quest for knowledge and information remains central, with more emphasis on seeking an understanding that goes beyond words. Issues of faith increase in importance as you seek a sense of connection to the Universe, experience the need for Oneness or Union with something higher in life. You may find yourself feeling torn between your logical, rational side and your intuitive, non rational side. Your interactions with other people are apt to stimulate the tension between realism and idealism. You and/or a partner could swing from wanting too much, expecting more than is possible, seeking a beautiful, ideal dream in relationships to being logical, practical, sensible, grounded and realistic—sometimes to the point of criticism and flaw-finding. You could feel torn between thinking and feeling, or dreams and practicality. The combination of a desire to repair and fix things up, along with marked compassion and assisting tendencies can result in relationships based on "rescuing" another person. You or a partner might unconsciously attract people who need help (alcoholics, addicts, psychotics, individuals not quite managing their lives) and try to help them reach their higher potential. Too often, however, the savior ends up victimized or martyred in the relationship. The challenge is to **share** dreams (but also hard work) with a partner— each contributing toward making better and more beautiful interactions.

You are apt to be more personally involved with the yearning for an experience of infinite inspiration, merging through art, beauty, healing, helping or assisting activities. Your relationship(s) continue to stimulate your desire for thinking, communication, logic and tangible accomplishments. You and any partner(s) are learning to balance faith, trust, mysticism and intuition with hard work, practicality, rationality, focused attention, and details.

NATAL: CANCER/CAPRICORN

Natally, you have **Cancer rising and Capricorn setting**. This puts a strong focus on dominance/dependency issues with other people. You may feel pulled between compassionate, caring protection and practical, sensible control. You may feel "reality" and survival issues curtail your capacity for closeness and emotional attachments, or you could feel that domestic needs and emotional vulnerabilities threaten career achievements and practical duties. You and a partner could relate more as parent to child than as peers. If one of you plays the role of the caring, protective "mother," the other might be a child or might be the dominating, controlling "father." You and a partner might polarize between gentleness and strictness, between dependency and dominance, between home and career or between emotional needs and practical (worldly) demands.

You are apt to be dealing more personally with issues of emotions, feelings, dependency and nurturing. You may have to contend with too much neediness or too much needing to be needed. Your partner is apt to stimulate feelings around pragmatism, achievement drives, ambition, status needs and the desire to be in control. Responsibility could be an issue between you. Both of you need to create a blend between unconditional acceptance and an insistence that certain standards of performance be met.

In your **relocation chart,** you have **Aries rising and Libra setting**. This suggests heightened ambivalence in terms of relationships and balancing the different parts of life. You are trying to make room for assertion as well as accommodation, for compassion and capability. You may feel torn between time and energy demands for yourself (and personal development and hobbies), for your partner (and important relationships), for your home and family, and for your career and worldly achievements. If you over-emphasize any part of life, your partner is likely to overdo the opposite extreme. The challenge is to integrate freedom and closeness needs, to be able to be separate and yet attached, committed and yet an individual, caring and yet firm, productive and still loving.

You are likely to personally face more issues around balancing what you want and your desire for emotional closeness with others (dependency/ nurturing). Your partner is likely to be working more on the balance between equality and control, sharing versus being solely responsible. The goal is to make room for all of the above.

In your **relocation chart,** you have **Taurus rising and Scorpio setting**. This suggests that the natal parent/child tendencies may surface in terms of financial, sexual and sensual issues. You and a partner might succumb to power struggles over money, possessions or pleasures. Either of you might be tempted to try to control or dominate the other in this area—or to use weakness and vulnerability as a weapon. The challenge is to be sensitive to each other's sensual and financial needs, while maintaining practicality. A willingness to compromise will work wonders! Security could be overvalued, so be willing to put people and feelings ahead of things and owning.

This is a sensual combination, so you may need more "touchy feely" experiences and physical gratification. You might become more involved with property or other sources of security. Your partner is apt to elicit control issues and you might unconsciously pick someone a bit dominating in order to learn to develop your own strength. If your partner is over controlled s/he could hold back to the point of inhibition. The relationship is teaching you both about discipline and endurance.

In your **relocation chart,** you have **Gemini rising and Sagittarius setting**. The balancing act between strength and softness may be played out more in the mental realm. You are apt to face issues around ideas and ideals in your relationships. Beliefs and values may become an important focus, especially where feelings around home, family, nurturing and career, hard work and discipline are concerned. Giving equal time and attention to each other's concepts could be a challenge. There might be dominance differences in terms of who speaks and who listens, who controls the intellectual and communication channels. Your natal focus on security could be lightened, with more capacity for humor and desire to explore, adventure, learn and share information.

Personally, you are can balance your native focus on emotions with logic and lightness. You may find it easier to express verbally and be more personally involved with communication and learning. Your relationships are apt to stimulate you in terms of world views, metaphysics and principles of right and wrong. You may find that expectations (too much or too little) are a challenge in partnerships. You are apt to seek inspiration and excitement in partners as well as responsibility and practicality.

In your **relocation chart,** you have **Leo rising and Aquarius setting**. A focus on closeness remains constant. Although nurturing issues were primary in your birth location, the desire to give and receive love is paramount here. Both placements emphasize a desire for home/family commitments and a willingness to be intensely emotionally involved with others. Relationships are apt to bring up wider issues, transpersonal concerns (historical, the broad perspective). Emotional intensity remains a theme in terms of your self-expression, while detachment and an ability to see what needs to be improved are likely to be highlighted in relationships.

You may find it easier to shine, to be noticed in this area. The watery self-effacement of your natal placement now has a fiery focus for more extroversion and confidence. Partners may trigger issues around change, innovation, the new, the different and individuality. You will be learning to balance the conventional and the unconventional in your associations.

In your **relocation chart,** you have **Virgo rising and Pisces setting**. A need to be needed is likely to persist in your nature. You have moved from a placement emphasizing emotional caretaking to one emphasizing tangible results and a "repairing" orientation. Either way, you are likely to be the one who tries to help, to assist, and to make things better. Family concerns may be less paramount as work-related matters move to the forefront in your self-expression. In terms of relationships, you are blending the "ideal" (of Pisces) with the "real" (of Capricorn). Constructive combinations include seeing the best in others, while still being practical about what needs improvement. Less comfortable combinations include wanting more than is possible, living chronically frustrated because the real world does not measure up to one's dreams, overdoing rose-colored glasses or critical judgment.

You are likely to face more practical, down-to-earth drives yourself, while your relationships elicit issues revolving around beauty, idealism, mysticism and the quest for ultimate perfection.

In your **relocation chart,** you have **Libra rising and Aries setting.** This suggests heightened ambivalence in terms of relationships and balancing the different parts of life. You are trying to make room for assertion as well as accommodation, for compassion and capability. You may feel torn between time and energy demands for yourself (and personal development and hobbies), for your partner (and important relationships), for your home and family, and for your career and worldly achievements. If you overemphasize any part of life, your partner is likely to overdo the opposite extreme. The challenge is to integrate freedom and closeness needs, to be able to be separate and yet attached, committed and yet an individual, caring and yet firm, productive and still loving.

You are likely to personally face more issues around compassion, concern for others, and your desire for emotional closeness (dependency/nurturing). Your partner is likely to be working more on the balance between personal will and the limits of society, regulations and authority figures. The goal is for both of you to blend caring and control, closeness and competence, warmth and practicality.

In your **relocation chart,** you have **Scorpio rising and Taurus setting.** This suggests that the natal parent/child tendencies may surface in terms of financial, sexual and sensual issues. You and a partner might succumb to power struggles over money, possessions or pleasures. Either of you might be tempted to try to control or dominate the other in this area—or to use weakness and vulnerability as a weapon. The challenge is to be sensitive to each other's sensual and financial needs, while maintaining practicality. A willingness to compromise will work wonders! Security could be overvalued, so be willing to put people and feelings ahead of things and owning. You have moved from one water sign rising to another, so still tend to keep some feelings hidden and to check inside before risking outside actions.

This is a strong-willed combination, so constructive outlets (such as competitive sports, games or business) can be helpful. You are apt to face control issues with other people and may sometimes feel a need to withdraw in order to maintain a sense of mastery in a difficult situation. Your partner may elicit issues around indulgence, money, property or other sources of security. The relationship is teaching you both about discipline and endurance.

In your **relocation chart,** you have **Sagittarius rising and Gemini setting.** The balancing act between strength and softness may be played out more in the mental realm. In your relationships, you are apt to face issues around ideas, communication, and the ability to take some things lightly. Beliefs and values may be an important focus for you personally, especially where feelings around home, family, nurturing and career, hard work and discipline are concerned. Giving equal time and attention to each other's concepts may be a challenge. There might be dominance differences in terms of who speaks and who listens, who controls the intellectual and communication channels. Your natal focus on security is lightened, with more capacity for humor and a desire to explore, adventure, learn and share information.

Personally, you can balance your native focus on emotions with humor and venturesomeness. You may incline more toward searching and seeking activities—anything which expands your horizons and contributes to a sense of life's meaning. Your relationships are apt to stimulate you mentally and verbally, and could draw you toward communication and learning, especially knowledge that can help you understand the world around you.

In your **relocation chart,** you have **Capricorn rising and Cancer setting**. This is the exact reverse of your natal placements. The dominance/dependency polarity continues to be a strong focus in terms of self-expression and relationships with others. You have the opportunity to experience both sides of this polarity: the compassionate, caring, protective, emotional side and the practical, sensible, strong and ambitious side. If you have not yet gained a sense of "owning" both potentials, you may feel that exterior ("real world") demands or authority figures limit your capacity for closeness and emotional attachments. Or, you may believe that family duties and the emotional needs of those closest to you threaten your potential accomplishments in terms of career and the wider world. You and a partner could fall into parent/child interactions, rather than equal sharing as peers. Either of you might slip into the role of the caring, protective "mother," or the dominating, controlling "father." You and a partner might polarize between gentleness and strictness, between dependency and dominance, between home and career, or between emotional needs and practical (worldly) demands. Keep room for both!

In this area, you may face issues of achievement, status, responsibility and control more in your personal behavior and feelings. Emotional issues, feelings, dependency and nurturing could come up as relationship concerns. You may have to contend with too much neediness or too much needing to be needed. Either you or a partner might overdo or underdo responsibility. Both of you need to experience a blend between unconditional love (valuing a person for who they **are**) versus conditional love (valuing someone for **what** they **do**).

In your **relocation chart,** you have **Aquarius rising and Leo setting.** Although nurturing issues were primary in your birth location, issues around personal independence and uniqueness receive more focus here. You may be dealing with a balancing act between the desire for emotional closeness/commitment and the desire for freedom and space. You might feel torn between family and friends until a balance is attained. With integration, you can be compassionate on a wide scale, but sufficiently detached to not be overwhelmed by everyone's needs.

You may find it easier to be original, unique and creative in this area. Intuitive leaps are possible. You can combine feeling and thinking for optimum results. Partners may trigger issues around the limelight, attention, recognition, and self-esteem. If overdone, other people might seem too ambitious or power-oriented. In moderation, your relationships focus on excitement, doing more than has been done before and achieving the most that is possible.

In your **relocation chart,** you have **Pisces rising and Virgo setting.** A strong emotional thread persists within your basic identity. You have moved from one water sign rising to another. Your natal orientation was toward home and family, taking care of those close to you. In this area, you may feel the urge to save the whole world. Either way, rescuing tendencies could come to the fore. (Or, your personal sensitivities could feel overwhelming.) In terms of relationships, you are still dealing with the issue of "reality" and facing facts. Partners may bring up work needs, or criticism, and practical responsibilities could be important in your associations. A focus on the flaws might be overdone by you, or by a partner. If your partner lives out the earthy accomplishment focus of Capricorn (natal) and Virgo (relocated), s/he might seem the doer and achiever, while you focus more on emotional matters. Mutual satisfaction can be gained by shared efforts, shared responsibilities and a blend between the caring of water and the competence of earth.

You are likely to face feelings, impressions, wishes, dreams, and yearnings more directly in your self-expression, while your relationships elicit issues revolving around achievement, duties, essentials and what is necessary to cope with the material world.

NATAL: LEO/AQUARIUS

Natally you have **Leo rising and Aquarius setting,** bringing the focus on the polarity between passion and intellect, excitement and detachment, love relationships and friendships, or between closeness and freedom. This polarity may play out as delays in establishing long-term love relationships or having children. It can indicate a push/pull between the need for emotional excitement and intensity versus the desire to rely on logic, objectivity, and the mind. You may feel torn between the desire to be special, on stage, number one and noticed, versus the belief that everyone is equal and no one should "lord it over" others. You may feel that friends and your interest in the wider world take you away from loved ones (and vice versa). The challenge is to keep room for children and lovers as well as friends and causes; to balance the head and the heart.

You are likely to have some natural charisma, with a sparkle and an ability to entertain others. You can touch the inner child in yourself and other people, able to sway others emotionally. You need an arena in which to shine and receive positive feedback. You are likely to face issues around freedom, objectivity, the intellect and the need for space through partners and relationships.

In your **relocation chart,** you have **Aries rising and Libra setting.** This highlights the push/pull between freedom and closeness drives in your nature. Relationships may bounce from one extreme to the other, as you try to balance personal and interpersonal needs. Self-expression remains very significant as you have a fire sign rising natally and in this location. Extroversion, energy, and an urge to express yourself are vital. Impatience is possible as you are eager to move, to do. Excitement probably appeals to you; you are drawn toward the adrenaline rush. Relationships bring in the air (cool, detached) side of life: reminding you that sometimes it is necessary to contemplate rather than act, to consider rather than rushing in. You are working on the balance between immediate emotional response versus objective, logical thinking.

Personally you are more apt to deal directly with issues of confidence, action, the need for a "high" in life and the urge to break new ground. Through relationships you are apt to face issues of detachment, equality and the balance between personal independence and the desire to share life with another person.

In your **relocation chart,** you have **Taurus rising and Scorpio setting.** This means that your natal and relocated angles create a fixed cross, highlighting issues of sensuality, sexuality, possessions, pleasures and money. You are learning to balance giving and receiving in relationships, especially where finances and physical pleasures are concerned. You may feel torn between self-indulgence and self-control. Because fixity indicates an enduring will, you are likely to be focused on doing what you want, when you want, and how you want to do it. You tend to be resistant to the influences of other people. You may stubbornly oppose what you feel is someone else's attempt to control you or make you do what they want. This area will further encourage your natural strength and endurance.

You are also apt to be dealing with a push/pull between needs for security and your desire to take risks. Your new area will support a safe, dependable approach to life, guarding what you have and not taking chances. Your natural inclination (shown by the natal chart) is oriented more toward risk-taking, pioneering, adventures, and living on the edge. You need to make peace between (have room for both) creativity, change, innovation and safety and solidity.

In your **relocation chart,** you have **Gemini rising and Sagittarius setting.** This accentuates the sense of humor and restlessness of your natal placements. Your self-other polarity is still a fire-air combination, highlighting lightness, laughs, and a need for variety. You are apt to have a youthful air, with a freshness and a fun-loving spirit. The creativity of your natal placements may be channeled toward the mind in this location. Your thinking may be more original and innovative. You may be drawn to travel, to study, to learn and to share information with others. You may glory in collecting "trivia"— fascinating facts with which to impress others.

Freedom issues are a focus through relationships. If shared, you and a partner may encourage each other's uniqueness, stimulate each other's minds and enjoy some times apart, each pursuing his/her own adventures and explorations. If you deny the freedom side of your own nature, a partner might overdo it (gone a lot, not willing to make a commitment, unavailable, etc.). The people you associate with will heighten your awareness of transpersonal issues—the big picture, ultimate meaning, the wider world.

In your **relocation chart,** you have **Cancer rising and Capricorn setting**. Emotional warmth and closeness are in focus for your personal identity and self-expression. This combination suggests strong caring and usually a desire for home, family or close, emotional ties with others. You may have talent for dealing with the public, with an intuitive sense of what people need and want. Mood swings are possible if you switch between the extroverted, expressive fire of Leo to the inward, protective water of Cancer. With a strong feeling nature, you are apt to approach life from an emotional stance.

Relationships are likely to focus on balancing the conventional (Capricorn) and the unconventional (Aquarius). You may feel torn between choosing someone individualistic (and perhaps a bit strange or unusual) versus getting involved with pillars of the community who are oriented toward hard work and success. Your relationships are apt to bring up transpersonal issues of the world at large and societal demands, while you are more personally focused on warmth and one-to-one exchanges.

In your **relocation chart,** you have **Virgo rising and Pisces setting**. This is a place to put your (natal) Leo flair to work! This area focalizes your desire for competence and tangible results. You are apt to seek to express yourself through some form of accomplishment (such as your job), to strive for recognition and applause through your professional efforts. If you have tendencies toward self-criticism, this location is likely to exacerbate the trend. You need to remember to count assets as well as flaws. Often, however, this fire-earth combination (natal Leo; relocated Virgo) is highly productive. It combines the spark of leadership, initiative and creativity, along with the willingness to follow through, handle details and get the job done.

Relationships are apt to revolve around humanitarian and idealistic issues. Partners may stimulate your thinking around new age, philanthropic or progressive concepts, or they may seem a bit distant due to involvement in activities in the wider world. Partners will emphasize dreaming and visualizing; you will feel more of a need to do, to accomplish.

In your **relocation chart,** you have **Libra rising and Aries setting**. This highlights the push/pull between freedom and closeness drives in your nature. Relationships may bounce from one extreme to the other, as you try to balance personal and interpersonal needs. A need for others is highlighted, with the Leo desire for love blending with Libra's need for partnership. Your natural (Leo) charisma may be enhanced by the sweetness and charm of Libra. You are likely to expand your natural sparkle, a fire-air capacity to see the funny side in life, to communicate easily, to be drawn to many different interests and activities. You may be a bit susceptible to the opinions of others: this combination can be too ego vulnerable to how others see them. You need relationships and can help others to enjoy life, while gaining important support and validation for yourself.

Personally you are more apt to deal directly with issues of emotional closeness, sharing and commitment. Your relationships are apt to bring in issues of freedom, independence and space. If balance is lacking, your partners might be unavailable, unwilling to commit or off doing their own thing. The goal is to have sufficient warmth and attachment for relationship commitments, while still respecting the separateness and individuality of your partner (and of yourself).

In your **relocation chart,** you have **Scorpio rising and Taurus setting**. This means that your natal and relocated angles create a fixed cross, highlighting issues of sensuality, sexuality, possessions, pleasures and money. You are learning to balance giving and receiving in relationships, especially where finances and physical pleasures are concerned. You may feel torn between self-control and self-indulgence. Ambivalence in regard to who earns the money, who owns what, who supports whom, and how the purse strings affect emotional matters could arise. Because fixity indicates an enduring will, you are likely to be focused on doing what you want, when you want, and how you want to do it. You tend to be resistant to the influences of other people. You may stubbornly oppose what you feel is someone else's attempt to control you or make you do what they want. This area will further encourage your natural strength and endurance.

You are also apt to be dealing with a push/pull between needs for security and your desire to take risks. Your new area (shown in the relocated chart) will support the safe, dependable approach to life, guarding what you have and not taking chances. Your natural inclination (shown by the natal chart) is oriented more toward risk-taking, pioneering, adventures, and living on the edge. You need to make peace between (have room for both) creativity, change, innovation and safety, solidity, the familiar.

In your **relocation chart,** you have **Sagittarius rising and Gemini setting**. This accentuates the sense of humor and restlessness of your natal placements. Your self-other polarity is still a fire-air combination, highlighting lightness, laughs, and a need for variety. You have double fire for the Ascendant (Leo and Sagittarius), accenting a need for excitement, a willingness to risk, to seek an adrenaline rush, to be active and expressive. You may be courageous, charismatic and willing to lead the way. You could sometimes be impulsive, extravagant and inclined toward "too much, too fast." You are likely to have a good sense of humor, high vitality and an optimistic approach to life.

The mind is an important focus in your relationships. If the air (Aquarius and Gemini) theme is shared, you and any partners are likely to stimulate each others' minds, enjoy communicating, and be generally sociable. Your associations will bring up issues of objectivity and detachment. If shared, you and a partner can both step back and examine a situation logically when called for. If out of balance, you might overdo emotional impulses, while a partner is too cool, aloof and intellectually detached. By integrating this polarity, you can have both excitement and logical analysis in your relationships.

In your **relocation chart**, you have **Capricorn rising and Cancer setting**. Power and ambition are important themes for this combination. The "royal" urges of Leo rising are now backed by achievement-oriented Capricorn. You need to amount to something, to strive, to rise to the top. Your leadership ability needs an outlet. Competitive games, business or fighting for causes can allow you to channel your "managing" instincts into a healthy arena. Otherwise, you might be tempted to take control in relationships, rarely an optimum response. This fire-earth combination is potentially highly effective, indicating a blend of initiative and follow-through.

Relationships are likely to focus on balancing the closeness needs (Cancer) and the freedom drives (Aquarius). You may feel torn between choosing someone individualistic (and perhaps a bit too independent or unavailable) versus getting involved with someone very caring (but perhaps clinging as well). As long as you and a partner are both balanced, and allow some of each, you can love with an open hand, care without possessing, nurture each other's uniqueness and encourage one another to be true to inner needs while still able to love in a committed, emotional attachment.

In your **relocation chart**, you have **Aquarius rising and Leo setting**, an exact reverse of your natal placements. The focus remains on the polarity between passion and intellect, excitement and detachment, love relationships and friendships, or between closeness and freedom. You retain your natal charisma, but may become more personally focused on issues of freedom and individuality. As you continue to work on the blend between excitement and objectivity, you are likely to express more of whichever side you neglected in the past. You may feel torn between humanitarian causes, new age groups, friends, or progressive involvements— versus loving and being loved, your emotional commitments to lovers and/or children. Your leadership instincts may compete with your equalitarian principles. Your interest in transpersonal issues (humanity, science, causes, new and different ideas and groups) may pull you away from those you love (or vice versa). Your heart (passions, intensity, feelings) may war with your head (logic, objectivity and the rational intellect).

Your fun-loving spirit remains and you can truly sparkle with other people. Until balance is achieved, however, you may feel torn between freedom versus closeness in relationships. Whichever side you deny, a partner is apt to overdo (and vice versa). With integration, both of you can love each other's differences, cherish one another's special qualities, enjoy each other's minds, and find each other exciting as well.

In your **relocation chart,** you have **Pisces rising and Virgo setting.** The natural charisma of your (natal) Leo Ascendant is heightened with the magic of Pisces rising in this location. The combination is talented in entertainment, the arts, promotion, sales—anything which involves persuading and swaying others. You know how to make an emotional impact! You may tend toward mood swings—up with the extroversion of the fire, and down with the introversion of the water, but are likely to be extremely warm and caring. If the dramatic, persuasive talents of this blend are not channeled into the world, you may succumb to the temptations of the martyr role, over dramatizing suffering. With a focus on the positive, you can be a true inspirer of other people—envisioning wonderful possibilities, and motivating others to become involved in the process.

Relationships are apt to bring up issues of practicality and logic. Where the personal focus is emotional, the relationship focus is rational. An integration will work well. If balance is lacking, you and a partner might polarize between thinking and feeling, between impulsivity and planning, between dreaming and doing, or between idealism and practicality. You need both!

NATAL: VIRGO/PISCES

Natally you have **Virgo rising and Pisces setting,** highlighting the polarity of "the real" versus "the ideal." Virgo concentrates on doing; Pisces focuses on dreaming. Virgo is practical and uses common sense. Pisces is visionary and uses rose-colored glasses. Since the Ascendant/Descendant involve relationships, you will be working to balance these two sides of life in your associations with other people. One danger is falling into savior/ victim associations. This can be any relationship where one individual tries to "rescue" or "take care of everything" for the other. One party may be alcoholic, a drug addict, or simply not quite able to cope in some area. The other person's "need to be needed" or desire to help goes overboard.

If the idealistic side wins out in relationships, you could be attracted to spacey people, or view things unrealistically, falling for a fantasy, only to be disillusioned later. If the realistic side wins out, you might be too critical and judgmental. Flaws could be magnified. An integrated blending means you can be forgiving of insignificant foibles, glossing over human errors that are unimportant, seeing the best in a partner overall, but practical and sensible enough to pay attention to significant problems so you can work to improve relationships.

In your **relocation chart,** you have **Aries rising and Libra setting**. This places the "real versus ideal" focus firmly on the issue of assertion versus accommodation. You and partners will be reworking the balance between personal and interpersonal needs. You may feel torn between self-assertion and self-sacrifice. Part of the necessary discrimination will be deciding how much and when to put yourself first, and how much and when to consider the other person and give in for his/her sake. The challenge is to avoid extremes on either path.

You are more likely to be the "enabler," the doer, the fixer-upper with the strength of Aries rising (relocated) and the efficiency focus of (natal) Virgo rising. Your partnerships will help you to deal with issues of beauty, grace, idealism and the quest for perfection. Expecting a partner to be perfect, or trying to make everything ideal for another person, is doomed to disappointment. Sharing artistic activity, or mystical ideas, or philanthropic or healing tendencies with a partner can be very constructive.

In your **relocation chart,** you have **Taurus rising and Scorpio setting**. This places the "real versus ideal" focus on the issue of self-indulgence versus self-control. You and partners will be reworking the balance between appetite indulgence (whether around food, drinking, smoking, drugs, money, etc.) versus appetite control. Part of the necessary discrimination will be deciding how much and when to indulgence yourself, when to give (financially, materially, etc.), when to receive, and when to exercise self-mastery and discipline. Addiction issues may be faced personally or through relationships. The challenge is to enjoy the material, sensual world without being ruled by it.

You are likely to be more focused on practical issues with a double earth Ascendant (natal Virgo and relocated Taurus). Your partnerships may bring in more emotional issues, particularly themes that tend to get buried and are not easy to face. These "heavy" combinations can incline toward taking the self and life too seriously, feeling burdened at times. The best of both, however, involves the compassion of water and the capability of earth.

In your **relocation chart,** you have **Gemini rising and Sagittarius setting**. This combination makes a "grand cross" in the mutable signs when added to your natal Ascendant/Descendant. The initial challenge of the mutables is to deal with a multiplicity of interests. You may find yourself pulled in many different directions, particularly where relationship issues are concerned. You may explore various ideas, concepts and possibilities, and be unsure about what is most effective or practical. Perfectionism is also a challenge with mutability. You may set your sights too high in relationships, wanting more than is possible from another human being. Or, you could talk yourself into believing you have found the ideal mate only to be disappointed later when s/he turns out human and fallible. Criticism (of self or others) might be carried too far. The challenge is to be practical about people, while still striving to create the best of all possible partnerships. Your associations are likely to stimulate you mentally, and particularly to trigger your thinking in terms of goals, values, ethics and the purpose of life. You may rethink your world view or be influenced in how you view the truth and ultimate meaning.

In your **relocation chart,** you have **Cancer rising and Capricorn setting**. This combination heightens the challenge of equalitarian relationships. The (natal) polarity of Virgo-Pisces is susceptible to savior-victim associations, while the (relocated) polarity of Cancer-Capricorn is susceptible to parent-child relationships. Truly sharing the power with another person is likely to be a challenge. It is easy for you to slip into (1) a dependent, self-critical role, seeking a strong, inspiring parent to take care of you, **or** (2) a capable, compassionate, "mother earth" facilitating role, unconsciously attracting someone who needs assistance, who leans on your strength. Integration requires that each of you be aware of your own power and have arenas in which to be the strong, responsible one who is working toward a vision or goal. Each of you also needs some times in which you can be dependent and receive assistance from the other. The key is a capacity to take turns: **interdependency,** rather than one person being stuck perpetually in a parental role. The need to be needed may be quite marked, and fulfillment can come through blending warmth and caring with competence and achievement.

In your **relocation chart,** you have **Leo rising and Aquarius setting.** This puts the "real versus ideal" focus squarely on the issue of freedom versus closeness and the head versus the heart. A reasonable integration insures that you and a partner can have independence of action, express your uniqueness, and yet maintain close, emotional ties. With a healthy balance, you can be passionate, loving and exciting, but capable of logic, rationality and objectivity when appropriate. In your associations, any theme which you undervalue is apt to be overdone by a partner and vice versa. One of you may clutch and try to submerge or "rescue" the other. One of you may run away, avoid, retreat from any emotional entanglements in order to protect cherished independence. One of you may live out the intense, volatile emotionality, while the other expresses calm, cool, collected detachment. You could swing from seeing each other very clearly (sometimes ultra critically) to being overly idealistic, succumbing to wishful thinking and imagining that everything will be beautiful if we just visualize it so. With balance, you can be highly effective, able to initiate and persevere. Your relationships can broaden your view of the world, stimulate your mystical side, and help you make the most of your individuality.

You are most apt to personally express the need to do and accomplish, while partnerships are apt to bring up themes of imagination and visualization.

In your **relocation chart,** you have **Libra rising and Aries setting.** This places the "real versus ideal" focus firmly on the issue of assertion versus accommodation. You and partners will be reworking the balance between personal and interpersonal needs. You may feel torn between self-assertion and self-sacrifice. Part of the necessary discrimination will be deciding how much and when to put yourself first, and how much and when to consider the other person and give in for his/her sake. The challenge is to avoid extremes on either path.

You may incline a bit toward procrastination, as your (natal) Virgo rising wants to analyze everything in order to do everything right, while (relocated) Libra wants to see both sides to every issue. The combination may keep on collecting more and more information, and putting off decisions. You will be personally learning about the balance between love and work, as your identification is tied to both competence and the desire to share. Relationships are apt to revolve around the integration of self-assertion and self-sacrifice as you and partners learn to balance a personal focus (meeting your own needs) with concern for and looking after the other person. You may be more practical and sensible, while relationships bring in themes of emotionality and intense reactions.

In your **relocation chart,** you have **Scorpio rising and Taurus setting.** This places the "real versus ideal" focus firmly on the issue of self-indulgence versus self-control. You and partners will be reworking the balance between appetite indulgence (whether around food, drinking, smoking, drugs, money, etc.) versus appetite control. Part of the necessary discrimination will be deciding how much and when to indulgence yourself, when to give (financially, materially, etc.), when to receive, and when to exercise self-mastery and discipline. Addiction issues may be faced personally or through relationships. The challenge is to enjoy the material, sensual world without being ruled by it.

You are likely to be more focused on issues of control and discipline (natal Virgo and relocated Scorpio can encourage obsessive-compulsive tendencies). Your partnerships may bring in themes of indulgence and escapism (natal Pisces and relocated Taurus). Pointing fingers and telling another person "You should be more like me" won't solve anything. Both you and your partners need to achieve appetite mastery, to see the physical world as a pleasurable source of gratification, but one you choose to enjoy—not something that runs your lives. Beauty and pleasure are important relationship themes that need constructive outlets (not simple hedonism). Your organizational skills can help you plan your pleasures so the end result is most deeply satisfying and constructive.

In your **relocation chart,** you have **Sagittarius rising and Gemini setting.** This combination makes a "grand cross" in the mutable signs when added to your natal Ascendant/Descendant. The initial challenge of the mutables is to deal with a multiplicity of interests. You may find yourself pulled in many different directions, particularly where relationship issues are concerned. You may explore various ideas, concepts and possibilities, and be unsure about what is most effective or practical. Perfectionism is also a challenge with mutability. You may sets your sights too high in relationships or in self-expression, wanting more than is possible from another human being (or from yourself). Or, you might talk yourself into believing you have found the ideal mate only to be disappointed later when s/he turns out human and fallible. Criticism (of self or others) might be carried too far. The challenge is to be practical about people, while still striving to create the best of all possible partnerships. Your associations are likely to stimulate you mentally, and particularly to trigger your thinking in terms of communication and information dispersal. You may modify your speaking or thinking style due to concepts emerging in your partnership. You need a partner who is fascinating and enlarges your understanding of people and life.

In your **relocation chart,** you have **Capricorn rising and Cancer setting.** This combination heightens the challenge of equalitarian relationships. The (natal) polarity of Virgo-Pisces is susceptible to savior-victim associations, while the (relocated) polarity of Cancer-Capricorn is susceptible to parent-child relationships. Truly sharing the power with another person is likely to be a challenge. It is easy for you to slip into a capable, focused parental style, being the "enabler," the "rescuer" the fixer-upper, unconsciously attracting someone who needs assistance, who leans on your strength. Integration requires that you and a partner be aware of your own power and have arenas in which to be the strong, responsible one who is working toward a vision or goal. Each of you also needs some times in which you can be dependent and receive assistance from the other. The key is a capacity to take turns: **interdependency,** rather than one person being stuck perpetually in a parental role. The need to be needed may be quite marked, and fulfillment can come through blending warmth and caring with competence and achievement.

In your **relocation chart,** you have **Aquarius rising and Leo setting.** This puts the "ideal versus real" focus squarely on the issue of freedom versus closeness and the head versus the heart. A reasonable integration insures that you and a partner can have independence of action, express your uniqueness, and yet maintain close, emotional ties. With a healthy balance, you can be passionate, loving and exciting, but capable of logic, rationality and objectivity when appropriate. In your associations, any theme which you undervalue is apt to be overdone by a partner and vice versa. One of you may clutch and try to submerge or "rescue" the other. One of you may run away, avoid, retreat from any emotional entanglements in order to protect cherished independence. One of you may live out the intense, volatile emotionality, while the other expresses calm, cool, collected detachment. You could swing from seeing each other very clearly (sometimes ultra critically) to being overly idealistic, succumbing to wishful thinking and imagining that everything will be beautiful if we just visualize it so. With balance, you can combine a practical, objective outlook with dramatic, romantic experiences in relationships.

You are most apt to personally express the need to be sensible and logical, while partnerships are apt to bring up themes of magic, charisma, fantasy and dreams.

In your **relocation chart,** you have **Pisces rising and Virgo setting,** the exact reverse of your natal polarity. You are continuing to face the issue of "the real" versus "the ideal." If you have reached a reasonable balance in your relationships, you will be able to visualize and see the best potentials, and work practically toward achieving them. If you are still working on the integration, whichever side has been more ignored is likely to come up now. You will be looking at the relationship between dreaming and doing; between visions and practicalities, between wholistic images and nitty-gritty details. This could be lived out with partners, often through savior/victim associations. If you fall into the savior role, you try to "rescue" to "take care of" to "make it all better" for someone else. If you succumb to the victim role, you will unconsciously seek someone who seems perfect, all-giving, all-loving to be your savior (or provide for you that ideal image— "heaven on earth").

Too much idealism in relationships can lead you into fantasies, rose-colored glasses, disillusionment and disappointment. Too much realism can lead to excessive criticism and flaw-finding. By blending the best of both, you are able to see the Higher Self in your partner (and within yourself) and to work toward the best potentials in each of you, but remain practical about significant shortcomings and challenges in the relationship. Both people need to work, to labor at the relationship, while still visualizing the best possible outcomes.

NATAL: LIBRA/ARIES

Natally, you have Libra rising and Aries setting, putting a strong focus on the balance between self and other. You are learning to integrate assertion and accommodation, or personal needs and drives with relationship desires. Your desire to be independent, self-expressive, active, and on your own must be harmonized with your need to form a partnership, your desire for close relationships, and your attraction to other people. You are learning to harmoniously combine acting and reacting. If you polarize between these issues, you could swing between extremes of aggression and effacement; from demanding things on your terms to giving in excessively to others; from being alone versus being swallowed up in a relationship, etc. Keep room to be yourself and still share with others.

Your personal focus is apt to center around sharing, cooperation, beauty, grace and the desire for ease and harmony. You are likely to identify yourself partially through your relationships with others. Partners will stimulate your capacity to define your personal independence and to determine how you identify yourself. They may teach you about issues of freedom, assertion, self-expression, spontaneity or courage.

In your relocation chart, you have **Aries rising and Libra setting**—the exact reverse of your natal ascending and descending signs. The focus remains intense on issues of self versus other, assertion versus accommodation, and personal versus interpersonal drives and desires. This location puts your independence needs in higher focus, yet you are still dealing with the need to harmonize partnership drives with your loner instincts. Beware of falling into seesawing relationships: getting swallowed up and then running away, being overwhelmed and then fighting to assert your independence; avoiding people and then becoming a doormat. The challenge is to keep time for yourself as well as for the people you care about.

Issues of self-expression, freedom, assertion and personal will could be relevant for you in this location. You have the opportunity to test your ability to balance your natal polarity. If you have truly integrated this opposition, you will maintain a strong sense of self while still enjoying an attachment to a significant other. You will assert yourself when appropriate, compromise when necessary, and generally consider both your needs and the needs of other people. You will demonstrate mastery of diplomacy **and** self-expression.

In your **relocation chart,** you have **Taurus rising and Scorpio setting,** fine-tuning the focus to issues of "mine" versus "yours" or "mine" versus "ours." The self-other polarity is going to be more concerned with issues involving sensuality, sexuality, money and shared possessions. You could feel torn between self-indulgence (in terms of food, money, sex, etc.) and self-control. You might be ambivalent over earning your own way versus depending on someone else's income (or "having" to support someone else). You might slip into power struggles with a mate over issues of money, sex or other material pleasures. The challenge is to be comfortable giving, receiving and sharing in a balanced manner that brings pleasure to both people.

You will face the issues of indulgence, pleasure, comfort and security more directly in your own actions, and are likely to confront themes of self-mastery, self-discipline, self-control and power more through your relationships. Incorporate the best of both.

In your **relocation chart,** you have **Gemini rising and Sagittarius setting,** highlighting the issues of communication and beliefs in your relationships with others. The balancing act between self and other is likely to occur in a context of questions, values, trust and a search for meaning in life. Assertion vs. accommodation struggles may be lived out in terms of who is more articulate and verbal, whose beliefs more define the relationship, whose metaphysics is predominant, etc. A restless and mental focus becomes more important in your personal expression and relationships. You seek knowledge, truth and intellectual stimulation in your associations. Tension may exist between curiosity for its own sake versus information which adds to a sense of direction and purpose in life. The challenge is to enjoy gathering knowledge about the world immediately around you as well as gaining an inspired sense of meaning in life which can help you set clear priorities.

You may personally center more around issues of curiosity, data exchange and communication. Questions of beliefs, values, and ideals may be experienced more through your relationships.

In your **relocation chart**, you have **Cancer rising and Capricorn setting**, suggesting that the balance between self and other will be played out around issues of dependency and dominance or compassion and pragmatism. You and a partner may polarize over time and energy demands between work and the family. Or, you may feel torn between the soft, gentle, supportive style versus a strong, controlling style. Parental issues could influence your relationships. Beware of turning a partner into a parent or trying to parent your mate. The challenge is to take turns caring for and being strong and responsible for one another, so there is an equal exchange of nurturing and achieving energy. Your role as a parent or unfinished business with a parent may be more significant for you in this area. You are learning to integrate caring and capability.

You may deal more directly with issues of dependency and nurturing, while themes of power, authority and control are brought in through your relationships.

In your **relocation chart**, you have **Leo rising and Aquarius setting**, highlighting the issues of love and detachment in your relationships with others. The polarity being faced involves the head versus the heart or the intellect versus passion. You and a partner might take opposite positions in terms of intensity versus objectivity, loved ones versus friends, or emotional attachments versus separation and detachment. Some ambivalence is possible in associations, particularly if you have not achieved some integration between "freedom" versus "closeness" desires. You could swing between feeling "hot" and "cold" in relationships, or attract partners who go back and forth. Decisions involving children may be more significant in this area (including the question of whether or not to have kids). You are learning to love with an open hand, to encourage uniqueness within yourself as well as your partner, to be passionately committed while totally respecting the individuality of those you care about.

You may deal more personally with themes of self-esteem, the need to be admired, the drive for love, attention, the limelight and passion, while your relationships bring in issues of intellectual detachment, objectivity, the wider world, the unusual and the drive for tolerance.

In your **relocation chart**, you have **Virgo rising and Pisces setting,** pointing to a focus on "real versus ideal" issues in your associations with others. You are learning to blend dreams and visions with the practical demands of achievement. This polarity is often active where people are involved in artistic activities or projects requiring craftsmanship. This opposition is also common when helping or healing associations are part of the picture (psychologists, astrologers, social workers, doctors, etc.). A negative form is savior/victim roles in personal relationships (e.g., marrying an alcoholic, psychotic, drug addict—or looking to someone to make everything perfect for you). The challenge is to pursue a dream for something higher, better or more beautiful— in a practical, grounded way which will reap tangible results.

You are likely to be more personally involved with issues of reality, fact-finding, analysis, discrimination and the need to do a good job. You might also focus more on health or nutrition and you need to be wary of too much self-criticism. Your partnerships are likely to bring up issues of fantasy, imagination, rose-colored glasses and the quest for infinite love and beauty.

In your **relocation chart**, you have **Scorpio rising and Taurus setting**, fine-tuning the focus to issues of "mine" versus "yours" or "mine" versus "ours." Your self-other polarity is going to be more concerned with issues involving sensuality, sexuality, money and shared possessions. You could feel torn between self-indulgence (in terms of food, money, sex, etc.) and self-control. You might be ambivalent over earning your own way versus depending on someone else's income (or "having to" support someone else). You might slip into power struggles with a mate over issues of money, sex or other material pleasures. The challenge is to be comfortable giving, receiving and sharing in a balanced manner that brings pleasure to both people.

You will probably face issues of self-mastery, self-discipline, self-control and power urges in terms of your own actions and drives. Your relationships may bring in issues around indulgence, pleasure, comfort and security. Incorporate the best of both!

In your **relocation chart**, you have **Sagittarius rising and Gemini setting**, highlighting the issues of communication and beliefs in your relationships with others. The balancing act between self and other is likely to occur in a context of questions, values, trust and a search for meaning in life. Assertion versus accommodation struggles may be lived out in terms of who is more articulate and verbal, whose beliefs more define the relationship, whose metaphysics is predominant, etc. An restless and mental focus becomes more important in your personal expression and relationships. You seek knowledge, truth and intellectual stimulation in your associations. Tension may exist between curiosity for its own sake versus information which adds to a sense of direction and purpose in life. The challenge is to enjoy gathering knowledge about the world immediately around you as well as gaining an inspired sense of meaning in life which can help you set clear priorities.

You may be more personally concerned with questions of belief, values, ideals and truth—a spontaneous questing urge. Your relationships may bring in issues centering around pure curiosity, data exchange, communication and being casual about life.

In your **relocation chart**, you have **Capricorn rising and Cancer setting**, suggesting that the balance between self and other will be played out around issues of dependency and dominance or compassion and pragmatism. You and a partner may polarize over time and energy demands between work and the family. Or, you may feel torn between the soft, gentle, supportive style versus a strong, controlling style. Parental issues could influence your relationships. Beware of turning a partner into a parent or trying to parent your mate. The challenge is to take turns caring for and being strong and responsible for one another, so there is an equal exchange of nurturing and achieving energy. Your role as a parent or unfinished business with a parent may be very significant for you in this location. You are learning to integrate caring and capability.

You may deal more directly with themes of power, authority and control, while issues of dependency and nurturing are brought in through your relationships.

In your **relocation chart**, you have **Aquarius rising and Leo setting**, highlighting the issues of love and detachment in your relationships with others. The polarity being faced involves the head versus the heart or the intellect versus passion. You and a partner might take opposite positions in terms of intensity versus objectivity, loved ones versus friends, or emotional attachments versus separation and detachment. Some ambivalence is possible in associations, particularly if you have not achieved some integration between "freedom" versus "closeness" desires. You could swing between feeling "hot" and "cold" in relationships, or attract partners who go back and forth. Decisions involving children may be more significant in this area (including the question of whether or not to have kids). You are learning to love with an open hand, to encourage uniqueness within yourself as well as your partner, to be passionately committed while totally respecting the individuality of those you care about.

You may deal more personally with issues of intellectual detachment, objectivity, the wider world, the unusual and the drive for tolerance, while themes of self-esteem, the need to be admired, the drive for love, attention, the limelight and passion emerge through your relationships.

In your **relocation chart**, you have **Pisces rising and Virgo setting**, pointing to a focus on "real versus ideal" issues in your associations with others. You are learning to blend dreams and visions with the practical demands of achievement. This polarity is often active where people are involved in artistic activities or projects requiring craftsmanship. This opposition is also common when helping or healing associations are part of the picture (psychologists, astrologers, social workers, doctors, etc.). A negative form is savior/victim roles in personal relationships (e.g., marrying an alcoholic, psychotic, drug addict—or looking to someone to make everything perfect for you). The challenge is to pursue a dream for something higher, better or more beautiful— in a practical, grounded way which will reap tangible results.

Your own actions and drives may be more directly connected to imagination, fantasy, rose-colored glasses, visions, Higher Wisdom and the need for infinite lover and beauty. Your relationships are likely to trigger issues of reality, fact-finding, analysis, discrimination and the need to do a good job. They might also focus on health or nutrition and both you and any partners need to be wary of overdoing a critical approach. Make facts and fancy supportive of one another. Blend intuition and hard work.

NATAL: SCORPIO/TAURUS

Natally, you have **Scorpio rising and Taurus setting,** indicating a polarity between indulgence, comfort, stability, ease and self-control, facing the Shadow, transformation and intensity. You and/or a partner may feel torn between self-indulgence versus appetite mastery over food, drink, money, sexuality or other physical pleasures. You could feel ambivalent between earning your own way versus depending on someone else — or supporting someone else. You may fluctuate between a comfortable self-satisfaction and an intense, driving need to probe beneath the surface and ferret out hidden information and motives. You and a partner are likely to work out the balance together and may be susceptible to power struggles, particularly over money, sex and possessions. The challenge is to learn to give, receive and share pleasures for mutual gratification, with a basic sense of equality.

You are apt to deal personally with issues of intense emotions, secrecy, intimacy, self-mastery and a strong desire to control your own life. You may experience your need for beauty, pleasure, and relaxation through your relationships. Partners may elicit feelings around hedonism, sensuality, finances or comfort.

In your **relocation chart,** you have **Aries rising and Libra setting,** indicating an intensified focus on the self/other polarity, or the balance between personal and interpersonal needs. Power struggles remain a potential hazard as you and associates strive to equalize assertion and accommodation, personal will with the needs of others. If the balance of power is skewed, one person may be the appeaser, giving in too much to the other. Or, an individual who feels threatened by the power of another could withdraw from relating or attack others, feeling the only way to defend is to "get them first." Once power is shared, people can cooperate and learn to compromise. Negotiations can lead to win/win solutions. Healthy competition is another way people can test and build their strength through interactions with others. Many different relationship variants are possible, as you learn to balance your drives and desires with those of another person.

You may be more focused personally on issues of independence, assertion, spontaneity and self-expression. Your relationship(s) may bring in issues of sharing, cooperation, competition, harmony, equality and balance.

In your **relocation chart**, you have **Taurus rising and Scorpio setting**, repeating the natal polarity focus. You are likely to intensify the focus on learning to give, receive and share pleasures with other people. The strongest learning tends to come through dealing with sensuality. Appetite mastery versus appetite indulgence remains a theme, whether the focus revolves more around dieting versus overeating; smoking versus not smoking; drinking versus going on the wagon; spending versus saving; sex versus celibacy, etc. Ambivalence around earning your own way, versus being supported by someone else, or providing for another financially, is likely. Power struggles are quite possible as you strive to develop a sense of mastery and control. In relationships with team members, power needs to be directed inward rather than toward others.

Your natal concentration on intimacy, transformation, hidden depths and self-mastery remains, but indulgence is more of a focus here. In some way, your hedonistic side is in higher focus—through pleasures, possessions, money or artistic activities. You may personally confront issues of relaxation, comfort and stability.

In your **relocation chart**, you have **Gemini rising and Sagittarius setting**, implying a mental overlay on the basic fixed polarity of your Ascendant/Descendant. This suggests that you and a partner may deal with issues of mastery and indulgence more in the realm of the mind. You are likely to examine your beliefs and values around money and pleasures. You may question each other's assumptions concerning finances, gratification or the material/sensual world. You may spur each other's thinking, talking and collecting of information about the physical world. Rather than simple power struggles, you are likely to have discussions and concepts batted back and forth a lot. You have the opportunity to examine some of your old assumptions (particularly about "mine" and "ours") in this region, and may wish to alter some of your approaches to sensual, sexual and/or monetary matters.

You may find it natural to be more verbal, curious, flippant and casually interested in many things. Your relationships are likely to trigger issues of belief, faith, trust and values.

In your **relocation chart**, you have **Cancer rising and Capricorn setting**, repeating the focus on earth and water in your interactions with others. Cancer/Capricorn suggest that parental influences may be significant. Your handling of resources (especially money and sensual indulgences) may be influenced (positively **or** negatively) by parental figures. You and a partner could fall into parent-child interactions, rather than equalitarian exchanges. One may play the more dominant, controlling, power figure while the other is more sensitive, dependent and emotional. Manipulation or power plays could affect the way you share resources and pleasures with one another. The challenge is to balance pragmatism and compassion in your handling of sex, money and resources. You and a partner could battle over financial and resource commitments to a profession or career versus contributions to the family or domestic arena. Both are essential; find compromises.

You may deal more personally with issues of emotional closeness, commitment and attachment, while partners bring in issues of control, authority, duties and the rules of the game.

In your **relocation chart**, you have **Leo rising and Aquarius setting**. Combined with your natal angles, this gives you the effect of a grand cross in fixed signs. There are several issues that could affect your relationships with others. One challenge is to integrate security and risk-taking needs. Natally, your approach (in terms of the Ascendant and Descendant only) is more security and safety-oriented. You want relationships to be dependable and known. Your **relocation chart** shows more of a willingness to take risks, to try something (or someone) new, to explore virgin territory. Since you are dealing with both urges, you need a balance of some basic commitment and safety while still staying open to new potentials and exciting, creative developments. Feelings are likely to be strong regarding sensual, sexual and financial issues. Recognize that neither you nor your partner want to be controlled, manipulated or told what to do in these areas. You can both be extremely strong-willed and resistant to outside influences. Battles and power struggles are possible, but a willingness to compromise will work wonders. It will be extra important for you and your associates to try to see each other's points of view.

You may deal more personally with issues of self-esteem, recognition, attention, charisma, excitement and the drive to be noteworthy. Your partnership(s) may bring up the need to be unique, individualistic, independent and involved with a wider perspective (groups, networking, humanitarian causes, political action, etc.).

In your **relocation chart**, you have **Virgo rising and Pisces setting**. This "real versus ideal" polarity is likely to affect your handling of the basic Taurus/ Scorpio push/pull between self-indulgence and self-control. One danger is falling into "savior-victim" scenarios in personal relationships—particularly when money or sex is involved. Your need to be helpful and compassionate could trap you into a martyr role. It is also possible to swing between the extremes of too much idealism (rose-colored glasses and lack of discrimination) versus too much nit-picking and critical judgment—especially where shared resources, finances and pleasures are concerned. You need a balance between seeing and visualizing the best that can be while also remaining practical and working hard to improve what **is**. Perfectionism awaits as a trap for you (if you demand too much in integrating your pull between appetite indulgence and appetite control) or for your relationships (if you or a partner consistently demands more than is reasonable). When positively channeled, your relationships can be constantly improving and growing as you are able to see the best and work to manifest it. With integration, you and a partner are able to sensibly enjoy the material, financial world, with mutual pleasure—while maintaining moderation.

The Virgo qualities of analysis, discrimination, self-criticism and the need to improve things may be more personally relevant to you. Your partner(s) may bring up Piscean issues of dreams, visions, compassion, idealism and the quest for infinite love and beauty.

In your **relocation chart**, you have **Libra rising and Aries setting**, indicating an intensified focus on the self/other polarity, or the balance between personal and interpersonal needs. Power struggles remain a potential hazard as you and associates strive to equalize assertion and accommodation, personal will with the needs of others. If the balance of power is skewed, one person may be the appeaser, giving in too much to the other. Or, an individual who feels threatened by the power of another could withdraw from relating or attack others, feeling the only way to defend is to "get them first." Once power is shared, people can cooperate and learn to compromise. Negotiations can lead to win/win solutions. Healthy competition is another way people can test and build their strength through interactions with others. Many different relationship variants are possible, as you seek compromises between your drives and desires and those of another person.

You may be more focused personally on issues of sharing, cooperation, competition, harmony, equality and balance. Your relationship(s) may bring in issues of independence, assertion, spontaneity and self-expression.

In your **relocation chart**, you have **Sagittarius rising and Gemini setting**, implying a mental overlay on the basic fixed polarity of your Ascendant/Descendant. This suggests that you and a partner may deal with issues of mastery and indulgence more in the realm of the mind. You are likely to examine your beliefs and values around money and pleasures. You may question each other's assumptions concerning finances, gratification or the material/sensual world. You may spur each other's thinking, talking and collecting of information about the physical world. Rather than simple power struggles, you are likely to have discussions and concepts batted back and forth a lot. You have the opportunity to examine some of your old assumptions (particularly about "mine" and "ours") in this region, and may wish to alter some of your approaches to sensual, sexual and/or monetary matters.

You may find yourself more personally concerned with issues of belief, faith, values, trust and the meaning of life. You may be drawn to anything which broadens your horizons (philosophy, education, travel, etc.). Your relationship(s) may trigger communication, curiosity, flippancy and the desire to learn a little about many different things. Partner(s) may help you develop objectivity and the capacity to be more lighthearted.

In your **relocation chart**, you have **Capricorn rising and Cancer setting**, repeating the focus on earth and water in your interactions with others. Cancer/Capricorn suggest that parental influences may be significant. Your handling of resources (especially money and sensual indulgences) may be influenced (positively **or** negatively) by parental figures. You and a partner could fall into parent-child interactions, rather than equalitarian exchanges. One may play the more dominant, controlling, power figure while the other is more sensitive, dependent and emotional. Manipulation or power plays could affect the way your share resources and pleasures with one another. The challenge is to balance pragmatism and compassion in your handling of sex, money and resources. You and a partner could battle over financial and resource commitments to a profession or career versus contributions to the family or domestic arena. Both are essential; find compromises.

You may deal more personally with issues of control, responsibility, duties, limits, rules of the game and structuring. Partnership(s) could bring up issues of emotional closeness, dependency, nurturing, commitment and roots.

In your **relocation chart**, you have **Aquarius rising and Leo setting**. Combined with your natal, this gives you the effect of a grand cross in fixed signs. There are several issues that could affect your relationships with others. One challenge is to integrate security and risk-taking needs. Natally, your approach (in terms of the Ascendant and Descendant only) is more security and safety-oriented. You want relationships to be dependable and known. In your new area, you may become more willing to take risks, to try something (or someone) new, to explore virgin territory. To deal with both urges, you need a balance of some basic commitment and safety while still staying open to new potentials and exciting, creative developments. Feelings are likely to be strong regarding sensual, sexual and financial issues. Recognize that neither you nor your partner want to be controlled, manipulated or told what to do in these areas. You can both be extremely strong-willed and resistant to outside influences. Battles and power struggles are possible, but a willingness to compromise will work wonders. It will be extra important for you and your associates to try to see each other's points of view.

You may deal more personally with the need to be unique, individualistic, independent and involved with a wider perspective (groups, networking, humanitarian causes, political action, etc.). Your partnership(s) may bring up issues of self-esteem, recognition, attention, charisma, excitement and the drive to lead and be noteworthy.

In your **relocation chart**, you have **Pisces rising and Virgo setting**. This "ideal versus real" polarity is likely to affect your handling of the basic Taurus/Scorpio push/pull between self-indulgence and self-control. One danger is falling into "savior-victim" scenarios in personal relationships—particularly when money or sex is involved. Your need to be helpful and compassionate could trap you into a martyr role. It is also possible to swing between the extremes of too much idealism (rose-colored glasses and lack of clarity) versus too much nit-picking and critical judgment—especially where shared resources, finances and pleasures are concerned. You need a balance between seeing and visualizing the best that can be while also remaining practical and working hard to improve what **is**. Perfectionism awaits as a trap for you (if you demand too much in integrating the pull between appetite indulgence and appetite control) or for your relationships (if you or a partner consistently demands more than is reasonable). When positively channeled, your relationships can be constantly improving and growing as you are able to see the best and work to manifest it. With integration, you and a partner will be able to sensibly enjoy the material, financial world, with mutual pleasure—while maintaining moderation.

You are likely to want to personally be involved with creating beauty or helping and healing in the world. Piscean dreams, visions, compassion and idealism can be important forms of self-expression. The Virgo qualities of analysis, discrimination, flaw-finding and the need to improve things may be more relevant in your interactions with others.

NATAL: SAGITTARIUS/GEMINI

Natally, you have **Sagittarius rising and Gemini setting**, putting a strong focus on learning and communication in relationships. You are naturally optimistic, drawn to many different interests and willing to explore many avenues to understanding. You are likely to seek partners who are mentally stimulating and broaden your horizons. This polarity is associated with teaching and traveling, so your relationships could easily involve some of both. Your people associations are teaching you to balance short-range interests with long-range needs, visions and ideals. You face issues of priorities: how much time and energy to invest in your various projects and interests. You can easily be overextended, and may have to drop some involvements in order to give sufficient importance to others. You tend to see the big picture and might incline toward big dreams.

You are likely to be a natural philosopher, truth-seeker and searcher. You may deal personally with issues of ethics, morality, faith, truth and the quest for meaning in life. Your partners are apt to stimulate your need for communication, for sharing knowledge and information, for being open to many sources of data.

In your **relocation chart**, you have **Aries rising and Libra setting**, bringing issues of assertion and accommodation strongly into the picture. The focus is likely to remain in the mental realm. Such simple issues as who talks and who listens may crop up. One person may feel their ideas receive short shrift in the relationship. One individual may try to influence the other in regard to beliefs and world views. There may be a perceived difference in mental or communicative skills. It is vital that you maintain a balance in these areas. Both partners need to contribute ideas, ideals, and ethics in the relationship. Both need to be willing to communicate and to listen. Since the relocated and the natal polarities both involve fire-air, the accent is on a sense of humor and sociability. Relating to a number of different people is advisable. You grow through interactions (particularly verbal) with others.

With Aries rising here, you may personally face more issues around verbal and mental assertion, self-expression and independence. Your partnership(s) could stimulate questions of balance, harmony, sharing and justice.

In your **relocation chart**, you have **Taurus rising and Scorpio setting**, bringing in a material and financial focus. Where your natal concern was primarily intellectual and abstract, you are now more focused on physical resources, monetary issues and the question of shared pleasures. You may strive to apply some of your ideas and beliefs about life to the question of how to intimately relate to a mate. Sexual and sensual connections may be a testing ground for ideas and ideals. And each exploration can lead to more discussion and new concepts. You could find yourself a bit more oriented toward staying in one place, rather than wandering the world. Your mind is likely to be drawn to investigate and question all realms tied to the physical senses. You may be more focused in your mental pursuits, more inclined to be thorough rather than flitting from flower to flower.

Your personal focus will probably center more about comfort, security, beauty, pleasure and enjoying the physical world (without forsaking your natal identification with the mind). Your relationship(s) may stimulate your dealing with intensity, buried feelings, hidden matters, addictions, and issues of sharing resources and pleasures equitably.

In your **relocation chart**, you have **Gemini rising and Sagittarius setting**, the exact reverse of your natal polarity. A strong focus remains on learning and communicating in relationships. You may find yourself pulled in even more different directions, with an urge to learn anything and everything. You and a partner might consider travel to other countries or cultures—or other avenues of broadening your horizons. Education, philosophy, religion or any avenue which offers a potential sense of truth, morality, ethics, meaning and purpose in life could appeal—especially when shared with others. You need partner(s) who are mentally stimulating. This polarity is associated with the student and the teacher, so your relationships could include both roles. Your people associations are teaching you to balance short-range interests with long-range needs, visions and ideals. You face issues of priorities: how much time and energy to invest in your various projects and interests. You can easily be overextended, and may have to drop some involvements in order to give sufficient importance to others. Objectivity is a bit more likely in this location, so you can be more lighthearted (even flippant). Optimism comes naturally in relationships, but you may want more than is humanly possible.

This region will encourage your communication skills and a fresh, childlike approach to life that is interested in everything. Your relationships may stimulate thinking in terms of philosophy, travel, truth-seeking or any quest for understanding life's deeper meaning, for beliefs which let you determine priorities and goals.

In your **relocation chart**, you have **Cancer rising and Capricorn setting**, bringing a parental theme to your natal focus on the mind. This could indicate issues of dominance versus dependency arising in terms of communication and the intellectual realm. Relationships may deal with issues of who controls the lines of communication and who is more passive/receptive. It is possible that the examples of your parents will become more significant in terms of your personal action and relationships. You may replay, with a partner, some issues you first faced with a parent. You are likely to find your logic and detachment more mixed with emotions now; feelings and sensitivities receive more notice. You are apt to do more thinking, questioning and examining of your emotional support system, in terms of what provides you with security and safety. Your learning focus may center around the balance between warmth and pragmatism, compassion and rules, empathy and limitation.

Your personal focus is more apt to revolve around feelings, desire for emotional closeness, family issues, domestic needs and a yearning for security and safety. Your relationships may feature issues revolving around responsibility, power, control, authority, practicality and facing the "real" world.

In your **relocation chart**, you have **Leo rising and Aquarius setting**, extending the (natal) mental focus into exciting, risk-taking realms. You may need to balance passion and detachment in your relationships, keeping room for an adrenaline rush as well as an objective assessment of probabilities. You may feel torn between freedom and closeness drives, needing some of each. Your native quick-wittedness could be augmented with some charisma, sparkle and enthusiasm. Entertainment skills may be developed further, along with sales, promotion, teaching or other persuasive, on-stage styles of expression. You may do a lot of thinking and communicating about trying to balance time-and-energy demands for friends versus children, groups versus lovers, passions versus intellectual drives. Your questioning, inquiring mind is likely to explore ambiguities concerning loving and letting go, being attached without being owned, caring about someone while still maintaining a sense of independence.

Your personal focus is more apt to revolve around fun, sparkle, zest and good times. You may be skilled at repartee or entertaining anecdotes. You may shine through your mind. Your partner is apt to stimulate issues of independence, innovation, individuality and the new. Relationships may be a bit unusual, different or progressive.

In your **relocation chart**, you have **Virgo rising and Pisces setting**, continuing the natal focus on the mind. Your quest for knowledge and information remains central, with an added pressure to put your knowledge to work in the world. You may find yourself torn between the real and the ideal. You and/or a partner could swing from wanting too much, expecting more than is possible, seeking a beautiful, ideal dream in relationships to being logical, practical, sensible, grounded and realistic—sometimes to the point of criticism and flaw-finding. You could feel torn between rationality and intuition, thinking and feeling, or dreams and practicality. The combination of a desire to repair and fix things, along with marked compassion and assisting tendencies can result in personal relationships based on "rescuing" another person. You or a partner might unconsciously attract people who need help (alcoholic, addict, psychotic, someone not quite managing his/her life) and try to help them reach their higher potential. Too often, however, the savior ends up victimized or martyred in the relationship. The challenge is to **share** dreams (but also hard work) with a partner— each contributing to making a better or more beautiful world. If we want to help people, we can do it professionally (with office hours).

You are apt to be more personally involved with issues of competence, facing facts, dealing with what is necessary. Your relationship(s) are likely to stimulate issues around ideals, beauty, values, faith, trust, hope and where one seeks perfection and utopia.

In your **relocation chart**, you have **Libra rising and Aries setting,** bringing issues of balance and harmony strongly into the picture. The focus is likely to remain in the mental realm. Such simple issues as who talks and who listens may crop up. One person may feel their ideas receive short shrift in the relationship. One individual may try to influence the other in regard to beliefs and world views. There may be a perceived difference in mental or communicative skills. It is vital that you gain a balance in these areas. Both partners need to contribute ideas, ideals, and ethics in the relationship. Both need to be willing to communicate and to listen. Since the relocated and the natal polarities both involve fire-air, the accent is on a sense of humor and sociability. Relating to a number of different people is advisable. You grow through interactions (particularly verbal) with others.

With Libra rising, you may personally face more issues around balance, harmony, beauty, sharing, justice and fair play. Your relationship(s) may stimulate thinking, talking and questioning in terms of verbal and mental assertion, self-expression and independence.

In your **relocation chart**, you have **Scorpio rising and Taurus setting,** bringing in a material and financial focus. Where your natal concern was primarily intellectual and abstract, this region will encourage more concern with issues of self-control, self-mastery, intensity, sexuality and shared resources and pleasures. You may strive to apply some of your ideas and beliefs about life to the question of how to intimately relate to a mate. Sexual and sensual connections may be a testing ground for ideas and ideals. And each exploration can lead to more discussion and new concepts. You could find yourself a bit more oriented toward staying in one place, rather than wandering the world. Your mind is likely to be drawn to investigate and question hidden realms and emotions that lie beneath the surface. You may be more focused in your mental pursuits, more inclined to be thorough rather than flitting from flower to flower.

Your personal focus will probably center more on intense emotions, a drive for self-control, appetite mastery, concentration, endurance and facing unconscious depths. Your relationship(s) may stimulate your thinking and discussions in terms of comfort, security, beauty, pleasure and enjoying the physical world.

In your **relocation chart**, you have **Capricorn rising and Cancer setting**, bringing a parental theme to your natal focus on the mind. This could indicate issues of dominance versus dependency arising in terms of communication and the intellectual realm. Relationships may deal with issues of who controls the lines of communication and who is more passive/receptive. It is possible that the examples of your parents will become more significant in terms of your personal action and relationships. You may replay, with a partner, some issues you first faced with a parent. You are likely to find your idealism more mixed with practicality; you want to ground your visions. You are apt to do more thinking, questioning and examining of your career and contribution to society, in terms of what provides you with security and safety. Your learning focus is likely to center around the balance between warmth and pragmatism, compassion and rules, empathy and limitation.

Your personal focus is more apt to revolve more around issues of responsibility, power, authority, control, pragmatism, limits, and facing the "real" world. Your relationship(s) are apt to bring up feelings, desire for emotional closeness, family issues, domestic needs and a yearning for security and safety. Strive to ensure that any parenting done in your partnerships is shared—

that you and the other party can take turns taking care of each other, so no one is "stuck" in the role of parent or child.

In your **relocation chart**, you have **Aquarius rising and Leo setting**, extending the (natal) mental focus into exciting, risk-taking realms. You will be called to balance passion and detachment in your relationships, keeping room for an adrenaline rush as well as an objective assessment of probabilities. You may feel torn between freedom and closeness desires, needing some of each. You can augment your native quick-wittedness with uniqueness, inventiveness and the capacity to view life from a new perspective. Networking may come more easily to you, along with group activities, interest in technology, progress, the new age or anything on the cutting edge of change. You may do a lot of thinking and communicating about trying to balance time/energy demands for friends versus children, groups versus lovers, passions versus intellectual drives. Your questioning, inquiring mind is likely to explore ambiguities concerning loving and letting go, being attached without being owned, caring about someone while still maintaining a sense of independence.

Your personal focus is more apt to revolve around thinking for yourself, exploring new mental territories, consolidating your freedom and enjoying the new, unusual, different and varied. Your relationship(s) are apt to stimulate your desire for fun, your zest, enthusiasm and sparkle. You and a partner might enjoy repartee or telling each other entertaining anecdotes. You may shine through your minds.

In your **relocation chart**, you have **Pisces rising and Virgo setting**, continuing the natal focus on the mind. Your quest for knowledge and information remains central, with more emphasis on seeking an understanding that goes beyond words. Issues of faith increase in importance as you seek a sense of connection to the Universe, to experience the need for Oneness or Union with something higher in life. You may find yourself feeling torn between your logical, rational side and your intuitive, non rational side. Your interactions with other people are apt to stimulate the tension between realism and idealism. You and/or a partner could swing from wanting too much, expecting more than is possible, seeking a beautiful, ideal dream in relationships to being logical, practical, sensible, grounded and realistic—sometimes to the point of criticism and flaw-finding. You could feel torn between thinking and feeling, or dreams and practicality. The combination of a desire to repair and fix things, along with marked compassion and assisting tendencies can result in personal relationships based on "rescuing" another person. You or a partner might unconsciously attract people who need help (alcoholic, addict, psychotic, someone not quite managing his/her life) and try to help them reach their higher potential. Too often, however, the savior ends up victimized or martyred in the relationship. The challenge is to **share** dreams (but also hard work) with a partner— each contributing toward making better and more beautiful interactions.

You are apt to be more personally involved with the yearning for an experience of infinite inspiration, merging through art, beauty, healing, helping or assisting activities. Your relationship(s) continue to stimulate your desire for thinking, communication, logic and rationality. You and any partner(s) are learning to balance faith, trust, mysticism and intuition with hard work, practicality, rationality, focused attention, and tangible accomplishments.

NATAL: CAPRICORN/CANCER

Natally, you have **Capricorn rising and Cancer setting**. This puts a strong focus on dominance/ dependency issues with other people. You may feel pulled between compassionate, caring, protection and practical, sensible control. You may feel "reality" and survival issues curtail your capacity for closeness and emotional attachments, or you could feel that domestic needs and emotional vulnerabilities threaten career achievements and practical duties. You and a partner could relate more as parent to child than as peers. If one of you plays the role of the caring, protective "mother," the other might be a child or might be the dominating, controlling "father." You and a partner might polarize between gentleness and strictness, between dependency and dominance, between home and career or between emotional needs and practical (worldly) demands until you achieve balance.

You are apt to be dealing more personally with issues of pragmatism, achievement drives, ambition, status needs and the desire to be in control. Responsibility could be an important focus. Your relationships are likely to evoke issues around emotions, feelings, dependency and nurturing. You may have to contend with too much neediness or too much needing to be needed. Both you and a partner need to create a blend between unconditional acceptance and an insistence that certain standards of performance be met.

In your **relocation chart**, you have **Aries rising and Libra setting**. This combination suggests heightened ambivalence in terms of relationships and balancing the different parts of life. You are trying to make room for assertion as well as accommodation, for both compassion and capability. You may feel torn between time and energy demands for yourself (and personal development and hobbies), for your partner (and important relationships), for your home and family, and for your career and worldly achievements. If you overemphasize any part of life, your partner is likely to overdo the opposite extreme. The challenge is to integrate freedom and closeness needs, to be able to be yourself and yet attached, committed and yet an individual, caring and yet firm, productive and still loving.

You are likely to personally face more issues around balancing what you want and what the world demands (self-will versus societal limits and restrictions). Your partner is likely to be working more on the balance between equality and dependence, peer relationships versus nurturing or being nurtured. The goal is to make room in your life for all of the above.

In your **relocation chart**, you have **Taurus rising and Scorpio setting**. This suggests that the natal parent/child tendencies may surface in terms of financial, sexual and sensual issues. You and a partner might succumb to power struggles over money, possessions or pleasures. Either of you might be tempted to try to control or dominate the other in this area—or to use weakness and vulnerability as a weapon. The challenge is to be sensitive to each other's sensual pleasure and financial needs, while maintaining practicality. A willingness to compromise will work wonders! Security could be overvalued, so be willing to put people and feelings ahead of things and owning.

This is a sensual combination, so you need more "touchy feely" experiences and physical gratification. You may become more involved with property or other sources of security. Your partner is apt to elicit control issues and you might unconsciously pick someone a bit dominating in order to learn to develop your own strength. If your partner is over controlled s/he could hold back to the point of inhibition. The relationship is teaching you both about discipline and endurance.

In your **relocation chart**, you have **Gemini rising and Sagittarius setting**. The balancing act between strength and softness may be shifted here so it is played out more in the mental realm. You are apt to face issues around ideas and ideals in your relationships. Beliefs and values may be an important focus, especially where feelings around home, family, nurturing versus career, hard work, discipline are concerned. Giving equal time and attention to each other's concepts may be a challenge. There might be dominance differences in terms of who speaks and who listens, who controls the intellectual and communication channels. Your natal focus on security is lightened, with more capacity for humor and desire to explore, adventure, learn and share information.

Personally, you will be invited to balance your native focus on control/responsibility with logic and lightness. You may find it easier to express verbally here and be more personally involved with communication and learning. Your relationships are apt to stimulate you in terms of world views, metaphysics and principles of right and wrong. You may find that expectations (too much or too little) are a challenge in partnerships. Emotional intensity is likely in your people associations. You are apt to seek inspiration and excitement in partners in addition to your normal attraction to warmth and caring.

In your **relocation chart**, you have **Cancer rising and Capricorn setting**. This is the exact reverse of your natal placements. The dominance/dependency polarity continues to be a strong focus in terms of self-expression and relationships with others. You have the opportunity to experience both sides of this polarity: the compassionate, caring, protective, emotional side and the practical, sensible, strong and ambitious side. If you have not yet gained a sense of balance, you may feel that exterior ("real world") demands or authority figures limit your capacity for closeness and emotional attachments. Or, you may believe that family duties and the emotional needs of those closest to you threaten your potential accomplishments in terms of career and the wider world. You and a partner could fall into parent/child interactions, rather than equal sharing as peers. Either of you might slip into the role of the caring, protective "mother," or the dominating, controlling "father." You and a partner might polarize between gentleness and strictness, between dependency and dominance, between home and career, or between emotional needs and practical (worldly) demands. Keep room for both and avoid excessive criticism, including self-criticism!

In this area, you may face issues of achievement, status, responsibility and control more in your relationships, while emotional issues, feelings, dependency and nurturing could come up as personal concerns. You may have to contend with too much neediness or too much needing to be needed. Either you or a partner might overdo or underdo responsibility. Both of you need to experience a blend between unconditional love (valuing a person for who they **are**) versus conditional love (valuing someone for **what** they **do**). You two can create a blend of caring and competence.

In your **relocation chart**, you have **Leo rising and Aquarius setting**. A focus on power remains constant. Although parental issues were primary in your birth location, the desire to give and receive love which is emphasized here may be intensified through several types of relationships. Both natal and local signs emphasize a desire for home/family commitments and a willingness to be intensely emotionally involved with others. Relationships are apt to bring up wider issues, transpersonal concerns (historical, the broad perspective). A need for personal power remains a theme in terms of your self-expression, while freedom-closeness issues are likely to be highlighted in relationships. You and partners will work on the balance of emotional attachment and individuality.

You may find it easier to shine, to be noticed in this area. The self-critical tendencies of your natal placement now have a fiery focus for more extroversion and confidence. Partners may trigger issues around change, innovation, the new, the different and individuality. You will be learning to balance conventional versus unconventional in your associations, detachment versus emotions, the wider world versus home and family needs.

In your **relocation chart**, you have **Virgo rising and Pisces setting**. A need to be needed is likely to persist in your nature. You have moved from a placement emphasizing responsibility and taking charge to one emphasizing tangible results and a "repairing" orientation. Either way, you are likely to be the one who tries to help, to assist, and to make things better. Family concerns may be less paramount as work-related matters are at the forefront in your self-expression. In terms of relationships, you are dealing with emotional issues (with both Cancer and Pisces on the Descendant). Partners may be sensitive, inward, dreamy or spacey, silly, secretive. Constructive combinations include truly empathizing with others, while still being practical about what needs improvement. Less comfortable combinations include excessive criticism, withdrawing as a self-protective measure, or playing Atlas to helpless people in what should be peer relationships.

You are likely to face more practical, down-to-earth drives yourself, while your relationships elicit issues revolving around beauty, idealism, mysticism and the quest for ultimate perfection.

In your **relocation chart**, you have **Libra rising and Aries setting**. This suggests heightened ambivalence in terms of relationships and balancing the different parts of life. You are trying to make room for assertion as well as accommodation, for both compassion and capability. You may feel torn between time and energy demands for yourself (and personal development and hobbies), for your partner (and important relationships), for your home and family, and for your career and worldly achievements. If you overemphasize any part of life, your partner is likely to overdo the opposite extreme. The challenge is to integrate freedom and closeness needs, to be able to be yourself and yet attached, committed and yet an individual, caring and yet firm, productive and still loving.

You are likely to personally face issues around the balance between control and equality, love and work. Your partner is likely to stimulate your ambivalence between freedom and closeness, between going it alone versus depending on others or taking care of them, between society's regulations and authority figures and unique individuals. The goal is for both of you to blend caring and control, closeness and competence, warmth and practicality, personal rights and responsibilities.

In your **relocation chart**, you have **Scorpio rising and Taurus setting**. This suggests that the natal parent/child tendencies of your Capricorn/Cancer may surface in terms of financial, sexual and sensual issues. You and a partner might succumb to power struggles over money, possessions or pleasures. Either of you might be tempted to try to control or dominate the other in this area—or to use weakness and vulnerability as a weapon. The challenge is to be sensitive to each other's sensual pleasure and financial needs, while maintaining practicality. A willingness to compromise will work wonders! Security could be overvalued, so be willing to put people and feelings ahead of things and owning. You have moved from an earth sign rising to a water sign, but both earth and water tend to be cautious. They can keep some feelings hidden and check security before risking action so sometimes need to take things a bit more lightly.

This is a strong-willed combination, so constructive outlets (such as competitive sports, games or business) can be helpful. You are apt to face control issues with other people and may sometimes feel a need to withdraw in order to maintain a sense of mastery in a difficult situation. Your partner may elicit issues around indulgence, money, property or other sources of security. The relationship is teaching you both about discipline, endurance, and the appropriate times to pamper one another.

In your **relocation chart**, you have **Sagittarius rising and Gemini setting**. The balancing act between strength and softness may be played out more in the mental realm. You are apt to face issues around ideas, lightness and communication in your relationships. Beliefs and values may be an important focus for you personally, especially where feelings around home, family and nurturing versus career, hard work and discipline are concerned. Giving equal time and attention to each other's concepts may be a challenge. There might be dominance differences in terms of who speaks and who listens, who controls the intellectual and communication channels. Your natal focus on security is lightened, with more capacity for humor encouraged plus a desire to explore, adventure, learn and share information.

Personally, you can move toward balancing your native focus on duties and responsibilities with humor and venturesomeness. You may incline more toward searching and seeking activities—anything which expands your horizons and contributes to a sense of life's meaning. Your relationships are apt to stimulate you mentally and verbally, and could draw you toward more casual or eclectic learning, as well as knowledge that can be applied to help protect or care for others in some fashion.

In your **relocation chart**, you have **Aquarius rising and Leo setting**. Although responsibility and career issues were primary in your birth location, issues around personal independence and uniqueness receive more focus here. You may be dealing with a balancing act between the desire for emotional closeness and commitment versus the desire for freedom and space. You might feel torn between family and friends until a balance is attained. With integration, you can be compassionate on a wide scale, but sufficiently detached to not be overwhelmed by everyone's needs.

You may find it easier to be original, unique and creative in this area. Intuitive leaps are possible. You can combine feeling and thinking for optimum results. Partners may trigger issues around the limelight, attention, recognition, and self-esteem. If overdone, other people might seem too ambitious or power-oriented. In moderation, your relationships can focus on excitement, mutal admiration, a strong family focus, and great emotional warmth.

In your **relocation chart**, you have **Pisces rising and Virgo setting**. You may find a strong emotional thread developing within your basic identity. You have moved from a practical, responsible sign rising to a rescuing one. Your natal orientation was toward work, duty, power and control, taking care of business. In this area, you may feel the urge to save the whole world or to make it more beautiful. (Or, your self-criticism and high personal standards could feel overwhelming.), In terms of relationships, you are still facing the themes of realistic caretaking. Partners may bring up work issues, or criticism, and practical responsibilities could be important in your associations. A focus on the flaws might be overdone by you, or by a partner. If your partner lives out the emotional nurturing focus of Cancer (natal) and Virgo (relocated), s/he might seem very protective (self-protective or determined to look after others). The key is shared efforts, shared responsibilities and a blend between the caring of water and the competence of earth.

You are likely to face feelings, impressions, wishes, dreams, and yearnings directly in your self-expression, with the need to integrate mystical/idealistic wishes with practical achievement drives. Your relationships will elicit issues revolving around competence, health, common sense and capability along with empathy, compassion and sensitivity. These blends are potentially very supportive and helpful, as long as you and partner(s) manage to avoid taking the world or yourselves too seriously and avoid carrying everything on your back.

NATAL: AQUARIUS/LEO

Natally, you have **Aquarius rising and Leo setting,** bringing a focus on the polarity between passion and intellect, excitement and detachment, love relationships and friendships, or between closeness and freedom. This polarity may play out as delays in establishing long-term love relationships or having children. It can indicate a push/pull between the need for emotional excitement and intensity versus the desire to rely on logic, objectivity and the mind. You may feel torn between the desire to be special, on stage, number one and noticed, versus the belief that everyone is equal and no one should "lord it over" others. You may feel that friends and your interest in the wider world take you away from loved ones (and vice versa). The challenge is to keep room for children and lovers as well as friends and causes; to balance the head and the heart.

You are likely to need some personal space, independence and ability to be unique or unconventional. This area encourages your ability to be objective and to let your self-expression flow naturally into mental channels. Your relationships are apt to highlight charisma, excitement, dynamism and the need for zest and sparkle in life.

In your **relocation chart,** you have **Aries rising and Libra setting.** Your need for personal independence will be reinforced here, highlighting the push/pull between freedom and closeness drives in your nature. Relationships may bounce from one extreme to the other, as you try to balance personal and interpersonal needs. Self-expression remains very significant as you have an air sign rising natally and a fire sign in this location. Variety, extroversion, and an urge to express yourself are vital. Impatience is possible as you are eager to move, to do. Excitement may become more appealing to you for an adrenaline rush. Relationships bring in the air (cool, detached) side of life which can complement your natal Aquarius rising and remind you that we need to both contemplate and act. You are working on the balance between immediate emotional response versus objective, logical thinking.

Personally you are more apt to deal directly with issues of personal freedom, independence and the need to do your own thing in the world. Your relationships are apt to focus on empathy, family, nurturing, loving and close emotional ties. If balance is lacking, either you or a partner might be unavailable, unwilling to commit or off doing his/her own thing. The goal is to have sufficient warmth and attachment for relationship commitments, while still respecting the separateness and individuality of your partner and of yourself.

In your **relocation chart**, you have **Taurus rising and Scorpio setting**. This means that your natal and relocated angles create a fixed cross, highlighting issues of sensuality, sexuality, possessions, pleasures and money. You are learning to balance giving and receiving in relationships, especially where finances and physical pleasures are concerned. You may feel torn between self-indulgence and self-control. Because fixity indicates an enduring will, you are likely to be focused on doing what you want, when you want, and how you want to do it. You tend to be resistant to the influences of other people. You may stubbornly oppose what you feel is someone else's attempt to control you or make you do what s/he wants. You probably have great strength and endurance.

You are also apt to be dealing with a push/pull between needs for security and your desire to take risks. One part of your nature (the relocated placements) prefers the safe, dependable approach to life, guarding what you have and not taking chances. The other part of your nature (the natal placements) is oriented toward risk-taking, exploring, adventures, and living on the edge. You need to make peace (and room for both) between creativity, change, innovation and safety and solidity.

In your **relocation chart**, you have **Gemini rising and Sagittarius setting**. This accentuates the sense of humor and restlessness of your natal placements. Your self-other polarity is still a fire-air combination, highlighting lightness, laughs, and a need for variety. You are apt to have a youthful air, with a freshness and a fun-loving spirit. The originality of your natal placements may be channeled toward the mind in this location. Your thinking may be more inventive and innovative. You may increase your urge to travel, to study, to learn and to share information with others. You may glory in collecting "trivia"— fascinating facts with which to impress others.

Excitement is a focus through relationships. If shared, you and a partner may have positive channels to pursue the adrenaline rush, to seek a "high" in life. If out of balance, strife, or excesses, or other negative forms of excitement are possible. One of you might overdo gambling, speculating, risk-taking or ego-centered behavior, until a balanced perspective is achieved which maintains a clear and logical intellect as well as passion and fun.

In your **relocation chart**, you have **Cancer rising and Capricorn setting**. Emotional warmth and closeness need to be integrated with your detached Aquarian personal identity and self-expression. This area encourages strong caring and usually a desire for home, family or close, emotional ties with others. You may expand your talent for dealing with the public, with an intuitive sense of what people need and want added to your intellect. Freedom-closeness issues are possible if you switch between the independent, airy Aquarius to the inward, protective water of Cancer. Both feeling and thinking are important.

Relationships are likely to revolve around issues of power and ambition. Partners may bring up issues of control, authority or leadership for you. Personally, you will be working on the balance between closeness needs (relocated Cancer rising) and the urge for independence (natal Aquarius rising). You may turn family into friends and/or friends into family as you learn to blend warm and empathy with logic, detachment and individuality.

In your **relocation chart**, you have **Leo rising and Aquarius setting**, an exact reverse of your natal placements. The focus remains on the polarity between passion and intellect, excitement and detachment, love relationships and friendships, or between closeness and freedom. You retain your natal uniqueness and individuality, but may now be more personally focused on the desire for recognition, applause and creativity. As you continue to work on the blend between excitement and objectivity, you are likely to express more of whichever side you neglected in the past. You may feel torn between humanitarian causes, new age groups, friends or progressive involvements versus loving and being loved, your emotional commitments to lovers and/or children. Your leadership instincts may compete with your equalitarian principles. Your interest in transpersonal issues (humanity, science, causes, new and different ideas and groups) may pull you away from those you love (or vice versa). Your heart (passions, intensity, feelings) may war with your head (logic, objectivity and the rational intellect).

Your openness to new ideas remains and you can be quite tolerant of others. Until balance is achieved, however, you may feel torn between freedom versus closeness in relationships. Whichever side you deny, a partner is apt to overdo (and vice versa). With integration, both of you can love each other's differences, cherish one another's special qualities, enjoy each other's minds and find each other exciting as well.

In your **relocation chart**, you have **Virgo rising and Pisces setting**. You may seek and find a unique job to put your (natal) Aquarian inventiveness to work! This area encourages your desire for competence and tangible results. You are apt to seek independence and uniqueness in your job, and may be pulled between variety and the desire to be thorough and handle all the details. If you have tendencies toward self-criticism, this location might exacerbate the trend. You need to remember to count assets as well as flaws. Often, however, this earth-air combination (natal Aquarius; relocated Virgo) is very sensible, logical, rational and may be scientifically minded. You can learn to combine theory and practice, logic and common sense. You can see the wide perspective and also handle the nitty-gritty details.

Relationships are apt to revolve around romantic and idealistic issues. Partners may stimulate your starry-eyed side, or might overdo an emotional approach to life. Positively, relationships could be exciting, magical and rouse intense feelings. Negatively, they might include savior/ victim associations, hysteria, or tremendous mood swings. You and partners are learning to balance the practical and rational side of life with the intuitive and emotional side.

In your **relocation chart**, you have **Libra rising and Aries setting**. This highlights the push/pull between freedom and closeness drives in your nature. Relationships may bounce from one extreme to the other, as you try to balance personal and interpersonal needs. A need for others is highlighted, with the Aquarian desire for friends blending with Libra's need for partnership. This double-air combination emphasizes a personal focus on communication, objectivity and the desire to relate to others on an equal level, but Aquarius thrives on being unique and individualistic, while Libra wants to blend in with the crowd. You may feel pulled between the two. The focus in relationships is on fire (Leo and Aries): a strong drive for excitement, open expression, charisma, spontaneity and the adrenaline rush. If personal and interpersonal needs are not combined constructively, you might feel tension between head and heart needs, between emotional impulses and rational decisions, between detachment and immediacy. Optimally, these combinations can be quite sociable and fun loving.

Personally you are more apt to deal directly with issues of communication, seeing both sides and using your head. Your relationships are apt to bring up issues of dynamism, magnetism, extroversion and the desire for immediate action. If freedom and closeness drives are not blended, your partners might be unavailable, unwilling to commit, off doing their own thing, or strong-willed and reluctant to compromise. The goal is to have sufficient warmth and attachment for relationship commitments, while still respecting the separateness and individuality of your partner (and of yourself).

In your **relocation chart**, you have **Scorpio rising and Taurus setting**. This means that your natal and relocated angles create a fixed cross, highlighting issues of sensuality, sexuality, possessions, pleasures and money. You are learning to balance giving and receiving in relationships, especially where finances and physical pleasures are concerned. You may feel torn between self-control and self-indulgence. Because fixity indicates an enduring will, you are likely to be focused on doing what you want, when you want, and how you want to do it. You tend to be resistant to the influences of other people. You may stubbornly oppose what you feel is someone else's attempt to control you or make you do what s/he wants. You probably have great strength and endurance.

You are also apt to be dealing with a push/pull between needs for security and your desire to take risks. One part of your nature (the relocated placements) prefers the safe, dependable approach to life, guarding what you have and not taking chances. The other part of your nature (the natal placements) is oriented toward risk-taking, exploring, adventures, and living on the edge. You need to make peace (and room for both) between creativity, change, innovation and safety, solidity, the familiar.

In your **relocation chart**, you have **Sagittarius rising and Gemini setting**. This accentuates the sense of humor and restlessness of your natal placements. Your self-other polarity is still a fire-air combination, highlighting lightness, laughs, and a need for variety. You have a double freedom focus for the Ascendant (Aquarius and Sagittarius), accenting a need for independence, uniqueness, exploration and many alternatives. You may pioneer, explore new territory, or be on the cutting edge of life. You are apt to have broad, transpersonal interests and involvements. You could be humanitarian or idealistic and probably have a vision of the "ideal future" you would like to see.

The mind and people are important in your relationships. If the fire-air (Leo and Gemini) theme is shared, you and any partners are likely to stimulate each others' minds, find one another exciting, and may also have other relatives or family members be a part of the picture. Your associations will bring up issues of lightness, adaptability and fun-lovingness. If shared, you and a partner can both laugh at life, enjoy people and sparkle in communication. You can help keep each other young.

In your **relocation chart**, you have **Capricorn rising and Cancer setting**. This combination calls for balancing the conventional and the unconventional. You may feel torn between the desire to be unique, independent and progressive versus the desire to take control, be responsible and follow the rules. Your perspective is likely to be broad, with a good capacity for understanding systems and the overview. You may structure new ideas and approaches, or revolutionize current structures. You have the opportunity to take the best of each from the old and the new.

Relationships are likely to focus on emotional warmth and caring. The Leo/Cancer combination is strongly drawn toward home, family and emotional attachments. You are seeking a sense of connection through your relationships. If the balance is off, you could be more detached and impersonal, while partners emphasize caring and commitment (or vice versa). If you make room for both sides, you can love with an open hand, care without possessing, nurture each other's uniqueness and encourage one another to be true to inner needs and outer-world ambitions and principles, while still able to care and commit to an emotional attachment.

In your **relocation chart**, you have **Pisces rising and Virgo setting**. The humanitarianism of your (natal) Aquarian Ascendant is heightened with the idealism of Pisces rising in this location. The combination is likely to have a strong urge to heal and improve the world. You may be drawn toward new age involvements or group activities, especially anything which offers a better way. You are likely to have increasing talent in visualization, the ability to imagine alternatives and possibilities. This air-water combination (Aquarius/Pisces) can bring together conscious and unconscious insights, blending logic and intuition. You can be involved with inspirational activities which are on the cutting edge of change.

Relationships are apt to bring up issues of recognition and accomplishment. The relationship focus is fire-earth (Leo/Virgo), indicating a need for results which involve others and in which you can take pride. Initiative and perseverance are suggested. **Doing** is highlighted where partnership is concerned. If not integrated, you and a partner might feel torn between dreaming and doing or between idealism and accomplishment. The challenge is for each of you to do some of both!

NATAL: PISCES/VIRGO

Natally, you have **Pisces rising and Virgo setting**, highlighting the polarity of "the ideal" versus "the real." Virgo concentrates on doing; Pisces focuses on dreaming. Virgo is practical and uses common sense. Pisces is visionary and uses rose-colored glasses. Since this polarity involves relationships, you will be working on balancing both in your associations with other people. One danger is falling into savior/ victim associations in your personal life. This can be any personal relationship where one individual tries to "rescue" or "take care of everything" for the other. One party may be alcoholic, a drug addict, or simply not quite able to cope in some area. The other person's "need to be needed" or desire to help goes overboard. Work as a helping professional can provide a constructive outlet.

If the idealistic side wins out in personal relationships, you could be attracted to spacey people, or view things unrealistically, falling for a fantasy, only to be disillusioned later. If the realistic side wins out, you might be too critical and judgmental. Flaws could be magnified. An integrated blending means you can be forgiving of insignificant foibles, glossing over human errors that are unimportant, seeing the best in a partner overall, but practical and sensible enough to pay attention to significant problems and can work at improving relationships.

In your **relocation chart**, you have **Aries rising and Libra setting**. This places the "real versus ideal" focus firmly on the issue of assertion versus accommodation. You and partners will be reworking the balance between personal and interpersonal needs. You may feel torn between self-assertion and self-sacrifice. Part of the necessary discrimination will be deciding how much and when to put yourself first, and how much and when to consider other people and give in for their sake. This could include finding a balance between holding in (natal Pisces) versus expressing feelings immediately (relocated Aries). You may feel torn between self-assertion and self-sacrifice.

Your partnerships will bring in issues of efficiency, teamwork, productive efforts, practicality, comparing, contrasting and weighing possibilities and choices. If carried too far, the (natal) Virgo urge to get the "right" answer combined with Libra's fence-sitting tendencies can lead to procrastination (endlessly collecting more data)—by you or a partner. Natal Virgo plus relocated Libra calls for a compromise between love and work. Your challenge in relationships is to know when to exert effort and when to relax; when to focus on a task and when to share quality time with a partner.

In your **relocation chart**, you have **Taurus rising and Scorpio setting**. This places the "real versus ideal" focus firmly on the issue of self-indulgence versus self-control. You and partners will be reworking the balance between appetite indulgence (whether around food, drinking, smoking, drugs, money, etc.) versus appetite control. Part of the necessary discrimination will be deciding how much and when to indulge or control yourself, when to give (financially, materially, etc.), when to receive, and when to share possessions and pleasures. Addiction issues may be faced personally or through relationships. The challenge is to enjoy the material, sensual world without being ruled by it.

You are likely to be more focused on beauty, grace and pleasure personally with your Ascendant in Pisces natally and relocated to Taurus. Artistic outlets could be rewarding. Relationships may revolve around issues of perseverance and finishing up. Dealing with things completely and thoroughly may be a challenge. These "heavy" earth-water combinations can incline toward taking the self and life too seriously, feeling burdened at times unless you have faith in something beyond the physical world. An effective integration includes the compassion of water and the capability of earth.

In your **relocation chart**, you have **Gemini rising and Sagittarius setting**. This combination makes a "grand cross" in the mutable signs with your natal angles. The initial challenge of the mutables is to deal with a multiplicity of interests. You may find yourself pulled in many different directions, particularly where relationship issues are concerned. You may explore various ideas, concepts and possibilities, and be unsure about what is most effective or practical. Perfectionism is also a challenge with mutability. You may sets your sights too high in relationships, wanting more than is possible from another human being, from yourself, or from the relationship. Or, you could talk yourself into believing you have found the ideal mate only to be disappointed later when s/he turns out human and fallible. Criticism (of self or others) might be carried too far.

The challenge is to be practical about people, while still striving to create the best of all possible partnerships. Your associations are likely to stimulate you mentally, and particularly to trigger your thinking in terms of goals, values, ethics and the purpose of life. You may rethink your world view or be influenced in how you view the truth and ultimate meaning.

In your **relocation chart**, you have **Cancer rising and Capricorn setting**. This combination heightens the challenge of achieving equalitarian relationships. The (natal) polarity of Virgo-Pisces is susceptible to savior-victim associations, while the (relocated) polarity of Cancer-Capricorn is susceptible to parent-child relationships. Truly sharing the power with another person will be a challenge. It is easy for you to slip into (1) a dependent, needy role, seeking a strong, capable parent to take care of you, **or** (2) a sensitive, nurturing, "mother earth" facilitating role, unconsciously attracting someone who needs assistance, who relies on your compassion.

Integration requires that each of you be aware of your own power and have arenas in which to be the strong, responsible one who is working toward a vision or goal. Each of you also needs some times in which you can be dependent and receive assistance from the other. The key is a capacity to take turns: **interdependency**, rather than one person being stuck perpetually in a parental, caretaking role. The need to be needed may be quite marked, and you and your mate can learn to blend warmth and caring with competence and achievement.

In your **relocation chart**, you have **Leo rising and Aquarius setting**. This puts the "ideal versus real" focus squarely on the issue of freedom versus closeness and the head versus the heart. A reasonable integration insures that you and a partner can have independence of action, express your uniqueness, and yet maintain close, emotional ties. You can then be passionate, loving and exciting, but capable of logic, rationality and objectivity when appropriate. In your associations, any theme which you undervalue is apt to be overdone by a partner and vice versa. One of you may clutch and try to submerge or "rescue" the other. One of you may run away, avoid, retreat from any emotional entanglements in order to protect cherished independence. One of you may live out the intense, volatile emotionality, while the other expresses calm, cool, collected detachment. You could swing from seeing each other very clearly (sometimes ultra critically) to being overly idealistic, succumbing to wishful thinking and imagining that everything will be beautiful if we just visualize it so.

You are most apt to personally express the need for imagination, romance and excitement, while partnerships are apt to bring up themes of logic, common sense and detachment.

In your **relocation chart**, you have **Virgo rising and Pisces setting**, the exact reverse of your natal polarity. You are continuing to face the issue of "the real" versus "the ideal." If you have reached a reasonable balance in your relationships, you will be able to visualize and see the best potentials, and work practically toward achieving them. If you are still working on the integration, whichever side has been more ignored is likely to come up now. You will be looking at the relationship between dreaming and doing; between visions and practicalities, between wholistic images and nitty-gritty details. This could be lived out with partners, often through savior/victim associations. If you fall into the savior role, you try to "rescue" to "take care of" to "make it all better" for someone else. If you succumb to the victim role, you will unconsciously seek someone who seems perfect, all-giving, all-loving to provide for you that "heaven on Earth."

Too much idealism in relationships can lead you into fantasies, rose-colored glasses, disillusionment and disappointment. Too much realism can lead to excessive criticism and flaw-finding. By

blending the best of both, you are able to see the Higher Self in
your partner (and within you) and work toward the best potentials in each of you, while remaining practical about significant
shortcomings and challenges in the relationship. Both need to be
willing to work, to labor at the relationship, while still visualizing
the best possible outcomes and enjoying the journey, not waiting
til you achieve perfection to be happy.

In your **relocation chart**, you have **Libra rising and Aries
setting**. This places the "real versus ideal" focus firmly on the
issue of assertion versus accommodation. You and partners will
be reworking the balance between personal and interpersonal
needs. You may feel torn between self-assertion and self-sacrifice. Part of the necessary discrimination will involve deciding
how much and when to put yourself first, and how much and when
to consider the other person and give in for their sake. The challenge is to avoid extremes in either direction. You may have a
strong sense of beauty and could exhibit personal gracefulness
with aesthetic Pisces rising natally and relocated "lovely" Libra.
The combination tends to be drawn toward ease, the arts, beauty,
harmony and "niceness." You may incline toward romanticism, or
a tendency to put others first.

Relationships are apt to revolve around the need to accomplish. Initiative and accomplishment are highlighted in terms of
people associations. If balance is not attained, you and a partner
may be pulled between self-assertion and self-sacrifice, between
personal and interpersonal needs, between self-direction and an
orientation toward others. Strength and softness are both called
for, to attain a reasonable integration.

In your **relocation chart**, you have **Scorpio rising and
Taurus setting**. This places the "real versus ideal" focus firmly
on the issue of self-indulgence versus self-control. You and partners will be reworking the balance between appetite indulgence
(whether around food, drinking, smoking, drugs, money, etc.) versus appetite control. Part of the necessary discrimination will be
deciding how much and when to indulge or control yourself, when
to give (financially, materially, etc.), when to receive, and when
to share possessions and pleasures. Addiction issues may be faced
personally or through relationships. The challenge is to enjoy the
material, sensual world without being ruled by it.

You are likely to be more focused on emotional issues and
dealing with feelings (natal Pisces and relocated Scorpio). Your

partnerships may bring in themes of practicality or common sense. (natal Virgo and relocated Taurus). Pointing fingers and telling another person "You should be more like me" won't solve anything. Both you and your partners need to achieve appetite mastery, to see the physical world as a pleasurable source of gratification, but one you choose to enjoy—not something that runs your lives. Beauty and pleasure are important themes that need constructive outlets (not simple hedonism). An effective compromise between emotional needs and practical demands will bring deeply satisfying and constructive results.

In your **relocation chart**, you have **Sagittarius rising and Gemini setting**. This combination makes a "grand cross" in the mutable signs with your natal angles. The initial challenge of the mutables is to deal with a multiplicity of interests. You may find yourself pulled in many different directions, particularly where relationship issues are concerned. You may explore various ideas, concepts and possibilities, and be unsure about what is most effective or practical. Perfectionism is also a challenge with mutability. You may sets your sights too high in relationships or in self-expression, wanting more than is possible from another human being (or from yourself). Or, you might talk yourself into believing you have found the ideal mate only to be disappointed later when s/he turns out human and fallible. Criticism (of self or others) might be carried too far. The challenge is to be practical about people, while still striving to create the best of all possible partnerships.

Your associations are likely to stimulate you mentally, and particularly to trigger your thinking in terms of acquiring and using information. You may modify your speaking or thinking style due to concepts emerging in your partnership. You need a partner who is highly intelligent, who enlarges your understanding of people and life.

In your **relocation chart**, you have **Capricorn rising and Cancer setting**. This combination heightens the challenge of achieving equalitarian relationships. The (natal) polarity of Pisces-Virgo is susceptible to savior-victim associations, while the (relocated) polarity of Capricorn-Cancer is susceptible to parent-child relationships. Truly sharing the power with another person will be a challenge. It might be easy for you to slip into a capable, focused parental style, being the "enabler," the "rescuer" the fixer-upper, unconsciously attracting someone who needs assistance, who leans on your strength. Or, you might succumb to so much self-criticism and feelings of inadequacy that you look for another person to be competent and take care of you.

Integration requires that you and a partner be aware of your own power and have arenas in which to be the strong, responsible one who is working toward a vision or goal. Each of you also needs some times in which you can be dependent and receive assistance from the other. The key is a capacity to take turns: **interdependency**, rather than one person being stuck perpetually in a parental, caretaker role. The need to be needed may be quite marked, and you have the ability to help others by blending warmth and caring with competence and achievement. But guard against taking yourself and life too seriously or trying to play Atlas to the world. Plan for relaxation; work inner processing into your schedule.

In your **relocation chart**, you have **Aquarius rising and Leo setting**. This puts the "ideal versus real" focus squarely on the issue of freedom versus closeness and the head versus the heart. A reasonable integration insures that you and a partner can have independence of action, express your uniqueness, and yet maintain close, emotional ties. You can then be passionate, loving and exciting, but capable of logic, rationality and objectivity when appropriate. In your associations, any theme which you undervalue is apt to be overdone by a partner and vice versa. One of you may clutch and try to submerge or "rescue" the other. One of you may run away, avoid, retreat from any emotional entanglements, in order to protect cherished independence. One of you may live out the intense, volatile emotionality, while the other expresses calm, cool, collected detachment. You could swing from seeing each other very clearly (sometimes ultra critically) to being overly idealistic, succumbing to wishful thinking and imagining that everything will be beautiful if we just visualize it so.

You are most apt to personally express the need to envision future possibilities and deal with large-scale issues, while partnerships are apt to bring up themes of accomplishment, recognition and rewarding work which copes with the world next door. The challenge is to integrate the passive, dreamy, visionary side with the active desire to do something worth noticing in the world within your reach.

CHAPTER SEVEN

CHANGING SIGNS ON THE MIDHEAVEN

When angles change signs, you need to consider the nature of the relocated signs as overlays on the basic essence of the natal signs. You never lose your natal sign placements, but get additional themes and issues when your relocated angles change signs. This chapter will consider the issues you are facing through the signs on your Midheaven.

You must also consider the placements of planets ruling the angles, particularly when the relocated ruler occupies a different house than the natal ruler does. (The themes must be combined in such cases.) Furthermore, a relocation may change the aspects a house ruler makes (or does not make) to the angles of the horoscope. (Chapter 5 gave examples of rulers of the Ascendant and Midheaven changing house. Chapter 4 discussed aspects to rulers of the various houses.)

Midheaven Sign Changes

Aries to Taurus: You need to have your work under your own, personal control. Your gain most satisfaction from doing things when, where and how you choose. You may resist outside authority. You can be very strong, determined and forceful on the job. A desire for excitement and variety shifts more toward a focus on comfort, good pay and work which brings pleasure and/or beauty to yourself or others.

Aries to Gemini: Variety is the name of the game for you. You function best in an environment or with tasks that change. Your native pioneering spirit is apt to center around issues of communication, paperwork or mental prowess. You may test or sharpen your wits through your career. Coordination or dexterity could be a part of your work. Repetition repels you; you thrive on new challenges and learning experiences.

Aries to Cancer: You are apt to have strong feelings about your work. Beginning with a native courage, energy, and urge to break new ground, you are moving toward more caring, protectiveness and concern with security. You may feel torn between work which allows you freedom and independence versus work which satisfies emotional needs and a desire for safety. Balance competitive and compassionate instincts.

Aries to Leo: Excitement is the name of the game! You may be a natural mover and doer on the job. You thrive on activity and the adrenaline rush. Your career can be a focus for expressing vitality, enthusiasm and charisma. You can lead in your work. Talent is possible in sales, promotion or other "high energy" fields. You need to be creative in what you do and can provide the initiating "spark" of inspiration.

Aries to Virgo: "Doing your own thing" is increasingly measured in terms of productivity and tangible accomplishments. Your self-directed, independent natal focus is shifting toward more concern with results. You are likely to measure yourself in terms of what you do and must avoid extremes of criticism or judgment. Your initiating skills are now backed up with a willingness to endure and get the job done!

Aries to Libra: You are balancing personal and interpersonal issues in your work. Beginning with a natal focus on independence and self-direction, you have moved to more of a concern with teamwork and the needs of others. Your job may be more people-oriented (less solitary), or your style of working could be more balanced between self and others. Polarities may develop easily on the job.

Aries to Scorpio: You are prepared to be the authority or power center in your work; taking orders from others does not appeal. Your career is a focus for handling issues of assertion, anger, control and mastery. You are learning to balance your natal confrontation, directness and immediacy with relocated subtlety, appreciation of nuances and ability to look beneath the surface.

Aries to Sagittarius: You are probably ready to expand your vocational horizons! Excitement and action are doubly emphasized. You seek that adrenaline thrill. Where independence and self-direction were the primary natal focus, you are now drawn to disseminate knowledge, information, ideas, ideals in some form. You are ready to inspire, uplift, affect, or sway the world.

Aries to Capricorn: You are learning to temper your "I want what I want" focus with caution and a sensible assessment of the rules of the game. Rather than pushing too hard for your own way, you can see what is truly possible, and work within sensible limits. This includes practical dealings with authority figures (not confrontation or stress). You can be highly effective.

Aries to Aquarius: Independence is essential. You need to do your own thing on the job! Freedom is a watch word. Variety appeals to you, and anything which is unique, individualistic or innovative. You could be a natural pioneer and ground-breaker. Vocationally, you may be drawn to the cutting edge of change and technology, or anything stretching the limits of possibility.

Aries to Pisces: The ideal job for you would involve a personal vision. You need to do your own thing, but also make the world better or more beautiful in some fashion. You could fight for causes, be active artistically, or put your energy into helping and healing. Your assertive, direct focus (natally) is now more subtle and imaginative. You can envision as well as act.

Taurus to Aries: You want to do it **your** way! A laid-back style becomes more energetic and self-directed. Personal control of your career is more paramount. Your focus on enjoying what you do moves more into the realm of pioneering efforts, excitement or anything self-expressive. Resistance to outside authorities is likely. You can combine initiative and follow-through.

Taurus to Gemini: You want your work to be personally gratifying. Although the natal focus on pleasurable work was more stability-oriented, with artistic or financial overtones, you are currently more drawn toward work involving the mind, speech, dexterity or paperwork. You may even create beauty through language (music, song writing, lecturing). You can be relaxed and comfortable on the job and put others at ease.

Taurus to Cancer: You would probably prefer work that you enjoy, and a career that pays well. Stability and safety (financial and emotional) are important to you. You are likely to gravitate to secure positions, and might get involved with work through family members or examples. Your skills could involve monetary realms or basic resources of any kind: food, shelter, clothing, commodities, land and the public.

Taurus to Leo: Your willpower may well be evident in your professional approach. Not easily intimidated, you can be firm about controlling your own destiny and resisting other people's influences. Power struggles are possible if you are too set on maintaining the reins of control. Your natal placement emphasizes stability, comfort and a secure income, but the relocation suggests a risk-taking theme, a need to shine.

Taurus to Virgo: You probably want personal gratification and good remuneration for what you do. Enjoying your work is important, but this area emphasizes taking satisfaction in doing things well. Fields which provide measurable results are most pleasing: business, health, crafts, technical areas, etc. You can be quite organized and thorough. Consistency and endurance serve you well. Doing it **right** matters more and more to you.

Taurus to Libra: Beauty, comfort, and pleasure are highlighted in terms of your career. You may focus on earning power, financial fields, aesthetic vocations, work which gratifies others, or simply enjoying what you do. If overdone, a laid-back attitude might prevail. You may exercise charm or diplomacy at work, or deal in grace, beauty or art. A cooperative approach is natural.

Taurus to Scorpio: You may very well have business talent, or be drawn to fields involving money or physical manipulation (massage, physiotherapy, acupressure, chiropractic, etc.). You function best with security on the job and a large measure of personal control. You may feel torn between an indulgent, comfortable focus versus an intense, driving, demanding style. Find a middle ground.

Taurus to Sagittarius: Your natal focus on gratification, recompense, pleasure, beauty and tangible results through a career is shifting to a more idealistic focus. You may be more drawn toward metaphysical, spiritual, educational fields. You might wish to expand your vocational horizons. You are ready to do more, to risk more, to go further, than you have in the past. You need more mountains to conquer!

Taurus to Capricorn: You can make a virtue of fidelity, thoroughness, organization, endurance and commitment. Willing to pay your dues and earn your way to the top, you are likely to be a steady, dependable worker. You may have talent for business, or anything requiring some regular routines. You can be quite sensible and stable and are likely to appreciate success and be dedicated in your seeking of it.

Taurus to Aquarius: Your natal career focus revolved around money, stability, security, beauty and comfort. You may have settled for what was easy or paid reasonably well. You might also have enjoyed your work a lot! The relocation emphasizes a desire for more personal freedom in your work, and more variety. You may be willing to take risks to express your individuality in your vocation.

Taurus to Pisces: You can appreciate grace, beauty and a smooth flow on the job. You may be drawn to artistic/aesthetic fields, or adopt the role of the peacemaker at work. Since harmony appeals, you might sometimes be tempted to take the "easy" route, particularly if you can avoid discomfort. You prefer work that is gratifying, flowing, pleasant, financially rewarding, or involved with beauty.

Gemini to Aries: Mental stimulation is essential in your work. Doing something once is usually enough for you; repetition bores you. You may put your mind, tongue or hands to work, particularly in some fashion which is self-expressive or pioneering. Since your patience is limited, you tend to plow through work quickly, eager to move on to the next (hopefully new) task.

Gemini to Taurus: Dual or multiple careers were a natal possibility for you, but the current focus moves more toward stability and security. Mental stimulation remains vital for you in your work; you could use your eyes, mind, speech or fingers on the job. Now, however, the desire for pleasure and worthwhile remuneration become more important. You want to enjoy what you do and do what you enjoy.

Gemini to Cancer: Your natal versatility remains, but emotional security becomes more of a current focus. Your mental/communicative skills may be directed toward the public, toward a family enterprises or toward dealing with basic resources (food, shelter, clothing, etc.) or commodities. You probably want safety or warm feelings as well as mental stimulation through your work. Relatives could be in your career picture.

Gemini to Leo: Your sense of humor may be a vocational asset. You are likely to have talent for communication, especially of the persuasive type (advertising, promotion, sales, etc.). You might be drawn toward teaching, entertainment, or some forum in which you can shine with your mind or tongue. You may become a leader in training or in other forms of disseminating information. You need variety and excitement in your work.

Gemini to Virgo: Your breadth of interests may have led you into many vocational byways. You could have talent for anything involving the mind, communication, paperwork, dexterity or dealing with information. Although the natal tendency is for dual careers or becoming overextended, your relocated focus is on tangible results and a willingness to finish what you start. A grounded focus is of increasing importance to you.

Gemini to Libra: Your social skills may be important vocationally. You are likely to work with ideas and/or people. You need the stimulation of other minds, and the input from other people, to function best. Naturally equalitarian on the job, you can be a good team player; you are willing to meet people on their level. Mental and social stimulation are both important to you at work. Communication skills are likely to increase.

Gemini to Scorpio: Your natal approach emphasized mental stimulation, variety and a wide range of interests. Your relocation emphasizes the desire for completion and an intensity of focus. You may sometimes feel torn between depth and breadth. Your native communication skills can be honed to a sharper, more incisive mind (and tongue). You may dig deeper and probe further in your learning and sharing of information.

Gemini to Sagittarius: Teaching, traveling, preaching and communicating are likely prospects for your work. Your mind is highly emphasized, with a restless curiosity and eagerness to know and explore further. A need for variety is accentuated; lack of focus could lead to job-hopping. Clear priorities help you to have a variety of interests and skills, and still accomplish something (often with the mind or communication).

Gemini to Capricorn: Your natal focus on sociability, multiple interests, mental stimulation and a desire for variety is shifting (by relocation) toward ambition, control, focused attention and seriousness. You will have to compromise between the formal and the informal; sociability and nose to the grindstone; ideas and application; words and deeds. Each has something to contribute to the other if you keep room for both.

Gemini to Aquarius: Variety is the spice of life where your work is concerned. With your curiosity about anything and everything, the last thing you need is a set routine. Naturally friendly, you are most productive in an atmosphere of teamwork. Your job should involve ideas and/or people. Mental stimulation is essential. Changing scenes, co-workers, duties or projects keep your interest up and boredom down.

Gemini to Pisces: Settling on a single career may not be easy for you. You may have multiple talents, with skills in many mental areas as well as a feeling for beauty. Interested in many possibilities, choosing one or two to focus on is challenging. Integration means you can blend logic and intuition in your work; the conscious and unconscious. You are likely to be adaptable, versatile and flexible.

Cancer to Aries: Strong emotions are in focus for your career, but you may experience a push/pull between going inward versus letting it all hang out. Your natal placement emphasizes emotional safety and security, protectiveness, home, family and basic food, shelter, clothing, or public needs as a focus. Your relocated placement shows the desire for more excitement, activity, self-direction and independence.

Cancer to Taurus: Security, safety and stability are highlighted in terms of your career. You may have talent for dealing with the land, public, commodities, food, shelter, clothing or other basic resources. Financial fields could attract you. You may nurture or protect people through your work, in a practical, grounded way. Family members or family feelings could affect your profession.

Cancer to Gemini: Your natal focus on security and stability is moving toward an appreciation of variety and versatility. Your work might still involve family, emotional issues, land, the public or commodities, food, shelter, clothing, etc., but could increasingly bring in verbal skills, dexterity or the use of your mind. You can be more lighthearted about what you do, as well as more objective.

Cancer to Leo: Emotional warmth and caring are highlighted in your work. You might work with family, or in an assisting or supportive fashion. Your career might involve nurturing, the land, the public, food, clothing, shelter, or strong emotional reactions. Parenting roles or influences might be significant. You need an arena where your concern and caring can bring you recognition and applause.

Cancer to Virgo: Your nurturing spirit is directed toward work. Your sympathetic concern may lead you to select fields or circumstances where you can assist, rescue, look after, nourish or protect others in some fashion. You may do too much for those you work with, and could sometimes feel drained by the load which you shoulder. You are likely to be capable as well as compassionate, blending ability and empathy.

Cancer to Libra: You thrive in an atmosphere of emotional warmth. Talent for working with people is likely. You may sometimes fall into a parenting role, while other times equal sharing seems natural. Commitments to family as well as career matter to you; working in a family business is one way to integrate. Your vocation needs to have room for caring, compassion and empathy.

Cancer to Scorpio: You are more sensitive to the "vibes" around the work place than most. You probably have talent for understanding the underlying processes of life and may work in fields that use such knowledge, or that put your intuition to work. Skill in dealing with money or resources is also likely. You function best in a protected atmosphere, with the privacy to figure things out in your own way.

Cancer to Sagittarius: Your natal focus revolved around home, family, commodities and safety. Your relocated emphasis is on travel, far horizons, other cultures and adventures. You may be torn between security and risk-taking, between the familiar and the unknown. You might expand your base of operations. You are likely to reach beyond your vocational roots, to do something bigger and better.

Cancer to Capricorn: Your natal focus was more on protection, nurturing, home, family and safety. Your relocated emphasis highlights achievement, authority and reality demands. You may feel torn between family and career. You might choose to work in a family business, out of your home, or in a field involving land, the public, food, shelter, clothing, or protection/nurturing in some fashion. You are likely to seek security.

Cancer to Aquarius: Your natal focus on protection, security, safety and caretaking is broadening and universalizing. Where you might have been more home-centered, you may now be drawn toward including the world, and the future, in your work. You will get opportunities to change, to risk, to innovate and be creative. You need to incorporate the new along with the best of tradition. You can bring together logic and intuition.

Cancer to Pisces: Protection is an important vocational theme—whether you are protecting others or seeking a sheltered working environment. Gentleness may be a factor. You are likely to have a poetic or sensitive side which needs nourishment to flower fully. You might sacrifice too much on the job on occasion. You are likely to have intuitive ability and an instinctive understanding of emotions. You may develop aesthetic skills or a good capacity for visualization.

Leo to Aries: Being on stage is natural for you career-wise. This could range from the actor/actress to the salesperson, the promoter, the teacher, the comic, etc. You need to be on the move in your work. Restless, sitting still is **not** your forte. You thrive in creating excitement and stimulation in or through your work. You are probably skilled at beginning things and have leadership ability.

Leo to Taurus: Your natal desire to shine, to be noticed, to be recognized and applauded through your work is modified by an increasing focus on stability and security. A safe paycheck may become more important—or simple pleasure in what you do. Your risk-taking side is being modified by a desire for comfort. You can exhibit great strength of will and endurance in your vocational attainments.

Leo to Gemini: Your natural charisma may flow easily into verbal ability in this region. You could express your talent for leadership through mental fields or areas involving dexterity, transportation, paperwork, or communication of any kind. You are likely to become a skillful persuader with talent for sales, promotion, advertising or teaching. You need to sparkle on the job and can be an entertaining colleague.

Leo to Cancer: Your leadership and charisma may be channeled toward assisting and helpful work. You can be quite warm and caring on the job, and may be drawn to fields involving family members, emotional connections, teaching, coaching, or basic commodities: food, shelter, clothing, land, etc. You need to be proud of what you do, and increasingly value providing support (emotional, physical...) to the public.

Leo to Virgo: Your sparkle, dash and enthusiasm is drawn toward more productivity and tangible results in this area. You retain your need to shine, but probably want something measurable. You may take a leadership role in terms of efficiency, repairs, nutrition or anything which improves or enhances. You can channel your natural confidence and zest into practical accomplishments and solid successes.

Leo to Libra: Sparkle, enthusiasm, sociability, confidence, and charm are likely vocational assets for you. Charisma and magnetism are highlighted in this locale. Although leadership comes naturally to you, team playing is emphasized in this location. Your abilities might manifest in the creative arts, or any field that involves persuading or emotionally swaying other people. Entertainment is another possible area of focus.

Leo to Scorpio: Power and control are important issues for you at work. You probably function best when you are in charge. You are likely to choose vocations which arouse strong emotions, so make sure they are constructive. You are capable of great loyalty and perseverance, but detest others trying to tell you what to do. You can shine through digging up hidden information, knowledge, motives or issues at work.

Leo to Sagittarius: Your viewpoint is likely to be **large**. Oriented toward things on a grand scale, you may have trouble dealing with an ordinary job. You tend to want it bigger and better! You are likely to have good confidence, zest, enthusiasm, initiative, courage, and the spark of inspiration. You may become quite a salesperson, advertiser, persuader, teacher, trainer or motivator who sways others emotionally.

Leo to Capricorn: You are likely to prefer a position at the top of the vocational heap. A leadership role has appeal, but your patience may be stronger in this locale. Your natural charisma, dynamism and enthusiasm remain, but you have a further focus on responsibility, endurance, effort and doing what is necessary.

The combination can be highly capable. Ambition is probable, as is great achievement.

Leo to Aquarius: Your natal focus revolved around gaining attention, applause, admiration, excitement and recognition through your work. Your relocation emphasizes mental stimulation, change, detachment and the cutting edge (of technology, people, society, etc.). The combination suggests great creativity and inventiveness, but you must balance the emotions and intellect; approval-seeking and objectivity.

Leo to Pisces: Your natural charisma and magnetism is backed up by whimsical charm and an illusive, magical quality. You may increase your talent for sales, spellbinding, entertainment, comedy, teaching, promotion, advertising, politics or any kind of persuasion. You could be very creative artistically. You might sometimes slip into the martyr role. You need work which involves your emotions and ideals.

Virgo to Aries: Results continue to matter, but self-direction and personal independence become increasingly important to your career. Focused on a need for efficiency and productivity, you are also highly motivated to pursue your own vocational instincts. Your natal service orientation is overlaid with a desire for excitement and new challenges. You are ready to be on your own more, working for yourself.

Virgo to Taurus: Efficiency, productivity and tangible results matter to you. You probably feel greatest personal satisfaction in doing a good job and having measurable fruits for your labors. You can be quite organized, thorough and precise. You are likely to take pleasure in being accurate. Talent for many business fields could increase, or anything requiring an attitude of good craftsmanship: pride in your efficacy.

Virgo to Gemini: Your natal urge for efficiency, accomplishment and doing a good job remains. Your talents may center more around the mind; you may strengthen verbal or writing skills, a good capacity to deal with paperwork, numbers or information, dexterity or generate lots of ideas. Although you are motivated to achieve, you will find it easy to scatter in this location. You could be drawn in many different directions. Make priorities!

Virgo to Cancer: Your efficiency orientation remains, but this locale highlights the need to assist and care for others. Your productivity may become increasingly channeled into family duties, caretaking activities, emotional support or work that looks after others in some fashion. You could be very competent in terms of the land, the public, commodities and basic needs: food, shelter, clothing, etc. You are compassionate **and** capable.

Virgo to Leo: Your native desire for efficiency, productivity, and accomplishment is shifting toward a need for excitement, stimulation, dynamism and recognition. You leave the role of humble server and adopt the role of leader or center-stage personality. You are ready to be admired and applauded for what you do. Your pride in your work can grow. You may become a better promoter of your natural efficacy.

Virgo to Libra: Efficiency matters much to you. Your natal focus revolves around careful analysis, productivity, and a desire to repair, fix or improve through your work. This location highlights the drive for harmony, teamwork, aesthetics or people contact. You could be focused on good craftsmanship. You are likely to be logical in your work, with talent for objective assessment and a practical viewpoint.

Virgo to Scorpio: Your natal focus on analysis, discrimination, flaw-finding, productivity and efficiency can be strengthened and deepened in this locale. Finishing up is extra important to you; with tenacity and determination, you get to the bottom of things, clean them up, clear them out, and transform them into a healthier or more useful condition. Business skills may be enhanced, along with increased talent for research. You can be thorough and exacting.

Virgo to Sagittarius: The mind is a likely focus in your work. You need mental stimulation. Your natal focus on details, productivity, efficiency and doing things **just** right expands in this locale to a desire for more excitement, adventure, challenges and a broader perspective. You may find it easy to overextend. You are likely to want to do more, better, faster, higher, than before. Keep your priorities clear to accomplish the most.

Virgo to Capricorn: Efficiency, productivity and plain, old hard work are in high focus. This combination can point to the workaholic—the individual who takes on everything, for fear others won't do it, or won't do it **well**. Also possible is illness if the individual feels frustrated that they cannot do things **just** the way they feel things **ought** to be done. Fear of failure can block action. Moderation and being sensible about responsibility can bring much achievement!

Virgo to Aquarius: Your natal focus on details, efficiency, productivity and measurable results could shift (in this locale) toward more concern with principles, concepts, the overview and a need for variety. You may feel torn between focused attention on routine versus the desire for change and the new. (Keep some of both.) Logic and good problem-solving skills are likely assets. Scientific interests are possible.

Virgo to Pisces: You are learning to integrate the ideal and the real in your work. If at odds with each other, you might be too critical of yourself (as a worker) or of your career. You might demand that you do your work perfectly or want your work to make a more ideal (or more beautiful) world. The challenge is to bring dreams down to earth in some sensible, yet inspirational, fashion.

Libra to Aries: A balancing act is called for. You are working on a blend between personal needs and the needs of others. Beginning with a natal relationship (teamwork) orientation, you are feeling more and more need to do what truly matters to **you**. Empathy will not be forgotten, but you need to strike out, to initiate projects and opportunities that will be self-expressive.

Libra to Taurus: Grace, charm, beauty or pleasure could be a focus in your work. You may be drawn to artistic or aesthetic fields which allow scope for your feeling for beauty. You may seek work which involves finances or is monetarily rewarding. You might prefer work which is comfortable and easy, or function on a team. Your vocation could involve pleasing and gratifying others.

Libra to Gemini: You can function very well in an atmosphere of teamwork. Your orientation toward work is cooperative. Naturally sociable, you probably have flair for meeting people on their own level and for communication. Any work dealing with people or ideas is your métier. You deal best in an open framework— where everything is discussed and compromises are natural. Mental and/or social stimulation is essential.

Libra to Cancer: A profession involving people or beauty is likely for you. Your natural empathy and diplomatic talents could be useful in any relating capacity. You can be equalitarian and still nurture people, giving them a sense of acceptance. Your imaginative capacities could add to your artistic abilities. Warmth is important, so you may become more involved with work which nurtures or supports others in some fashion.

Libra to Leo: Grace, charm, diplomacy or social skills may be useful in your work. Your natural magnetism or charisma could be called upon. Although generally egalitarian, you may be feeling the desire for more of a starring (leadership) role. Aesthetic talents could beckon, especially artistic creativity. Persuasive abilities are likely; you can sell, promote, entertain, teach and deal well in any people field.

Libra to Virgo: People skills or aesthetic talents are possible in your career. You may use grace, charm, diplomacy, teamwork or beauty in your work. The current focus leans toward more careful analysis, skill with details, and tendency to focus on the flaws in order to fix and improve what is being examined. Logic is likely with a good capacity for logical assessment and sensible problem-solving.

Libra to Scorpio: People-work is natural for you. Teamwork may come easily; you are likely to have empathy and a feeling for the other person's point of view. Diplomacy, counseling, personnel or similar fields may appeal. You might also be drawn toward artistic/ aesthetic works which arouse strong emotions. Competitive fields are also possible, which stress one-to-one confrontations.

Libra to Sagittarius: Your sense of justice and fair play may be prominent in your work. Attraction to fields of law, politics, social causes, etc., is possible. Your desire to balance may be a factor. Your work could bring together people and ideals in some fashion, or expose people to wider viewpoints, expanded perspectives, or inspirational truths.

Libra to Capricorn: Your natal focus suggests a career involved with people, beauty or balance. Charm, a sense of justice, or aesthetic talents could be vocational assets. Your relocated focus suggests an increased concern with taking charge, being responsible, and being successful in traditional terms. You may have to balance equalitarian and control instincts.

Libra to Aquarius: Your work is likely to involve ideas and/or people. Intellectual skills are highlighted. Objective detachment is a likely talent. You can be an impartial observer, reporter or witness. This location emphasizes a need for more individuality, variety or stimulation, but the general focus is on justice, fair play, equal opportunity and communication in your work.

Libra to Pisces: Your feeling for beauty is highlighted. You may apply grace, harmony, ease, aesthetic capacities to your work. You are likely to prefer a pleasant atmosphere and may sometimes look for the "easy" way. Gentleness, compassion, sensitivity and a feeling for people could contribute to your vocational challenges and to your accomplishments in this locale.

Scorpio to Aries: Personal direction of what you do is probably advisable. You thrive in a working environment that you control. You may have intense feelings about your career. You are learning to balance your natal shrewdness, secrecy and caution with current forthrightness, immediate action and courage. Assertion or anger could be issues on the job. You have a great deal of strength of will.

Scorpio to Taurus: A sensual focus might be part of your work (through fields such as massage, chiropractic, physiotherapy, etc.). Or, you might be drawn into financial realms. You are likely to have good talent for business in almost any form. You are capable of great loyalty, but may feel torn between your natal intense, serious focus and your relocated orientation toward pleasure and easygoing gratification. Tremendous strength of will and purpose are highlighted.

Scorpio to Gemini: Your natal focus on depth, probing beneath the surface, and attraction to the hidden or taboo is shifting toward more general curiosity and eagerness to explore many vocational directions. You may feel a bit more scattered, with wide-ranging interests pulling at you. Your analytical mind could be applied to a multitude of ideas, paperwork, information, or the dissemination of knowledge.

Scorpio to Cancer: You are likely to dig beneath the surface in your vocation, and may be drawn to explore hidden or taboo areas. You could have an intuitive grasp of the life's underlying processes, as well as human motivations. You are probably sensitive to the "vibes" around you, and may use psychic insights in your job. Financial talent is possible; you appreciate security and may help others increase theirs.

Scorpio to Leo: Your all-or-nothing focus might mean that work is very good—or very bad. You are likely to choose vocational situations that arouse strong feelings. Generally, you do best being in charge yourself. Taking orders is not your style. Your strength, endurance, perseverance and loyalty work optimally in a situation where you can go all-out to uncover what you feel is significant—and then be recognized for your efforts.

Scorpio to Virgo: You can get intensely focused on what you do (perhaps even a bit obsessive at times). You may have great endurance with a real need to finish what you start. You are likely to enhance your organizational skills, flair for details, and talent for any kind of business or research work. You probably know how to take things apart, improve them, and put them back together in a more functional manner. You usually work carefully.

Scorpio to Libra: Your intense focus on work could be a valuable asset in figuring out people's motivations. You might further develop talent for psychotherapy, personnel work or other people-oriented professions. You may enjoy artistic activities which are deeply moving, and you could be drawn toward fields with a high degree of competition. You need to build and test your strength in relationship to others.

Scorpio to Sagittarius: You are likely to experience strong emotions in regard to your career. You could swing between high hopes and intense caution. You need a sense of both depth and breadth in what you do. Your natal focus on shared resources, possessions, taboo areas, or hidden matters is moving toward a broader perspective, an attraction toward knowledge, far horizons and the long-range view.

Scorpio to Capricorn: Business acumen is likely on your part. Organizational skills are suggested, with a keen sense for finances, and a willingness to work hard to accomplish. Your loyalty is probably very strong and you are committed to finishing whatever you start. You generally work best in a position of power and need security in your work. You can be intuitive as well as practical (shrewd).

Scorpio to Aquarius: Your natal sign suggests intense, focused work which involves hidden, taboo areas or shared finances and pleasures. The relocation sign suggests more concern with variety, innovation, the mind and detachment. You will have to balance security and risk-taking needs; the drive for power and your egalitarian instincts; emotionality and logic/rationality. You may learn to confront in inventive ways, and to put a strong emotional drive into creating the future.

Scorpio to Pisces: Your intuition may be a vocational tool. You are likely to be sensitive to the "vibes" at work, and may instinctively understand people's motives and drives. You can grasp the underlying processes of life and work in any field which identifies or studies them. You have an affinity for anything beneath the surface (literally and metaphorically).

Sagittarius to Aries: You are apt to be on the move literally! You need an expansive, increasing scope for your vocational skills. If a career or position seems too limited, you are apt to leave (or unconsciously arrange to be let go). You thrive on challenges, excitement, stimulation and the capacity to express yourself through your work. You probably prefer humor and independence in what you do.

Sagittarius to Taurus: Your natal focus on expansion, dissemination of ideas or ideals, and exciting work is still an underlying focus. You may continue to be drawn toward metaphysics, education, the law, travel or other truth-seeking avenues, but tangible results become more important to you in this location. This might include more desire for a good salary, or a need for measurable results from your work.

Sagittarius to Gemini: You can be an adventurer or explorer vocationally. Eager for variety, your interests may be broad. You have talent for almost anything involving the mind (and/or tongue). Teaching, preaching or traveling are particularly likely. You are drawn to far horizons, toward activities which stimulate the mind. Your restlessness needs an outlet; a routine will not do for you. Your body or mind must be on the go!

Sagittarius to Cancer: Your natal focus was on exploring, seeking the truth, broadening horizons and taking risks vocationally. Your relocation emphasizes safety, roots, family ties, and security. You might expand the public's horizons, or offer nurturing, homey, comforting qualities or products to the world. You will have to compromise between the spirit of the wheeler dealer and the desire to always have a nest egg tucked away.

Sagittarius to Leo: Excitement is important for you in your work. Ideally you seek an adrenaline rush through what you do! You may be a risk-taker in some form, or enjoy work which uses dynamism, magnetism, charisma, flair, humor, or persuasive abilities. You could enhance any talent for sales, promotion, teaching, preaching, travel fields or anything which expands people's horizons and possibilities. Your boredom threshold may be low!

Sagittarius to Virgo: The world of the mind is a likely focus in your career. You thrive on mental challenges. Your natal exploration and desire to affect the wider world is tuning into a finer focus in this location. It is likely to be more important to you to oversee the details, to be sure things are done just **right**, to see tangible results. Keep a balance between high expectations and what is truly possible.

Sagittarius to Libra: Your job could involve personal flair or charm. You may have natural magnetism and may well pursue justice or fair play professionally. You are likely to connect ideals with people in your career, and might be involved with the courts, the law, social causes, politics, etc. Your sense of humor, quick wits, high standards or interpersonal skills could become vocational assets.

Sagittarius to Scorpio: Your vocational hopes could range quite high at times (perhaps too much so). Your work is likely to involve intense emotions (yours or those of other people) and could relate to beliefs, values, sexuality, finances or other areas where people have strong feelings. Although your natal focus was broad, examining issues thoroughly and in depth is of increasing importance to you in this region.

Sagittarius to Capricorn: You are learning to blend the highest of hopes with the most demanding of judgments. If the integration is comfortable, much achievement and success is likely. If the blend is uncomfortable, you could be chronically dissatisfied (always wanting more, or wanting to do more, or better than you can/have). Remember to count assets as well as flaws!

Sagittarius to Aquarius: Your general outlook is progressive, forward-going, optimistic, intellectual and restless. You function best in an atmosphere of change, innovation, individuality, and broad horizons. Your work may become more transpersonal, new age, intellectually stimulating or in some way expanding people's options and choices. You function best when you can do your job in your own unique way.

Sagittarius to Pisces: The quest for perfection is a theme in your career. This might be the search for the "perfect" job, trying to do your work perfectly, idealizing the work ethic, working to make a more perfect (or more beautiful world), or faith tied to effort and accomplishment. You need to inspire, uplift, transcend, or sweep away in what you do.

or to do thing **well**. Integration means you are dedicated, hard-working, productive, and a high achiever (and still know when to relax as well).

Capricorn to Libra: Your natal focus suggests a strong sense of responsibility and a tendency to do things yourself (to be sure they get done right). The current location suggests an increasing concern with relationships and fair play. You may move from an authority role to a more equal stance. You may bring more beauty, grace, balance, people-work or sharing into your job.

Capricorn to Scorpio: You are probably suited to an executive role. Power and authority feel best to you. Business skills are quite likely. You may have talent for dealing with financial matters. You may be a very capable organizer, with a penchant for thoroughness and handling details. You finish what you start; endurance is marked. Practicality is high, but your intuitive side can be quite useful in this region.

Capricorn to Sagittarius: Your hard-headed, hard-nosed, hard-driving side is confronting your optimistic, visionary, expansive side. A reasonable blend means making your dreams real, manifesting your ideals in tangible form. Less comfortable combinations include chronic dissatisfaction (with your work, how you do it, the state of the world, etc.). Keep room for both idealism and realism.

Capricorn to Aquarius: Your natal and relocated placements are trying to combine the old and the new, the conventional and the unconventional. If these two sides fight each other, you may swing from one to the other, or do the worst of each, instead of the best. You may choose to revolutionize old structures, or to build new ones, but need to combine stability and change constructively.

Capricorn to Pisces: Your natal practicality and grounded focus is moving toward more intuition, sensitivity and idealism in this locale. You still need tangible results, but could be drawn to more involvement with inspirational, healing, helping, or artistic activities. You need dreams as well as practicalities. Your visionary side needs attention, along with your achievements.

Aquarius to Aries: Freedom remains a central thread in your professional life. You probably function best in an atmosphere of openness, variety, and stimulation. You could have good brainstorming talent and an ability to consider alternatives in your work. You work best on your own, in your own fashion, not bothered by authorities. You need constant challenge and regular activity in your job.

Aquarius to Taurus: Your natal focus revolved around individuality, freedom, variety, technology, friends and the new and different. Your relocation emphasizes a desire for more stability and security. You may want more tangible results and less experimentation. You may pay more attention to what you are earning, or incorporate more of your desire for pleasure, beauty or comfort into your work.

Aquarius to Gemini: Independence is apt to be important to you vocationally. With strong restlessness, you probably want to be free to move on if necessary. You need variety in your work, with changes of scene, people or job routines. You can get bored easily and need lots of mental and social stimulation. Your vocational style tends to be equalitarian, so you can be a good team player. Communication skills are likely to be strengthened in this locale.

Aquarius to Cancer: Your natal focus on independence, variety, the wider world and new technology or organizations is narrowing toward a more personal, supportive, empathic connection. You may want more emotional involvement in your work, closer family ties, or work which involves the land, the public or providing people's basic needs. You will be learning to balance security and risk-taking drives.

Aquarius to Leo: Your natal focus revolves around anything new, different, unusual, and a flair for detachment, objective judgment and dealing with large groups of people. Your relocation emphasizes passion, charisma, zest, enthusiasm and the desire for admiration. The combination suggests strong creativity and inventiveness, but you must balance the mind and emotions; teamwork versus a royal attitude.

Aquarius to Virgo: Your natal desire for innovation, change, variety, and a broad perspective is shifting (in this area) toward a desire for tangible results, a focus on details, and "fix-it" tendencies. You might feel torn between restlessness versus attention to the nitty-gritty. Scientific interests or skills are likely to increase. Logic can be one of your tools; talent for problem-solving is highlighted.

or to do thing **well**. Integration means you are dedicated, hard-working, productive, and a high achiever (and still know when to relax as well).

Capricorn to Libra: Your natal focus suggests a strong sense of responsibility and a tendency to do things yourself (to be sure they get done right). The current location suggests an increasing concern with relationships and fair play. You may move from an authority role to a more equal stance. You may bring more beauty, grace, balance, people-work or sharing into your job.

Capricorn to Scorpio: You are probably suited to an executive role. Power and authority feel best to you. Business skills are quite likely. You may have talent for dealing with financial matters. You may be a very capable organizer, with a penchant for thoroughness and handling details. You finish what you start; endurance is marked. Practicality is high, but your intuitive side can be quite useful in this region.

Capricorn to Sagittarius: Your hard-headed, hard-nosed, hard-driving side is confronting your optimistic, visionary, expansive side. A reasonable blend means making your dreams real, manifesting your ideals in tangible form. Less comfortable combinations include chronic dissatisfaction (with your work, how you do it, the state of the world, etc.). Keep room for both idealism and realism.

Capricorn to Aquarius: Your natal and relocated placements are trying to combine the old and the new, the conventional and the unconventional. If these two sides fight each other, you may swing from one to the other, or do the worst of each, instead of the best. You may choose to revolutionize old structures, or to build new ones, but need to combine stability and change constructively.

Capricorn to Pisces: Your natal practicality and grounded focus is moving toward more intuition, sensitivity and idealism in this locale. You still need tangible results, but could be drawn to more involvement with inspirational, healing, helping, or artistic activities. You need dreams as well as practicalities. Your visionary side needs attention, along with your achievements.

Aquarius to Aries: Freedom remains a central thread in your professional life. You probably function best in an atmosphere of openness, variety, and stimulation. You could have good brainstorming talent and an ability to consider alternatives in your work. You work best on your own, in your own fashion, not bothered by authorities. You need constant challenge and regular activity in your job.

Aquarius to Taurus: Your natal focus revolved around individuality, freedom, variety, technology, friends and the new and different. Your relocation emphasizes a desire for more stability and security. You may want more tangible results and less experimentation. You may pay more attention to what you are earning, or incorporate more of your desire for pleasure, beauty or comfort into your work.

Aquarius to Gemini: Independence is apt to be important to you vocationally. With strong restlessness, you probably want to be free to move on if necessary. You need variety in your work, with changes of scene, people or job routines. You can get bored easily and need lots of mental and social stimulation. Your vocational style tends to be equalitarian, so you can be a good team player. Communication skills are likely to be strengthened in this locale.

Aquarius to Cancer: Your natal focus on independence, variety, the wider world and new technology or organizations is narrowing toward a more personal, supportive, empathic connection. You may want more emotional involvement in your work, closer family ties, or work which involves the land, the public or providing people's basic needs. You will be learning to balance security and risk-taking drives.

Aquarius to Leo: Your natal focus revolves around anything new, different, unusual, and a flair for detachment, objective judgment and dealing with large groups of people. Your relocation emphasizes passion, charisma, zest, enthusiasm and the desire for admiration. The combination suggests strong creativity and inventiveness, but you must balance the mind and emotions; teamwork versus a royal attitude.

Aquarius to Virgo: Your natal desire for innovation, change, variety, and a broad perspective is shifting (in this area) toward a desire for tangible results, a focus on details, and "fix-it" tendencies. You might feel torn between restlessness versus attention to the nitty-gritty. Scientific interests or skills are likely to increase. Logic can be one of your tools; talent for problem-solving is highlighted.

Sagittarius to Virgo: The world of the mind is a likely focus in your career. You thrive on mental challenges. Your natal exploration and desire to affect the wider world is tuning into a finer focus in this location. It is likely to be more important to you to oversee the details, to be sure things are done just **right**, to see tangible results. Keep a balance between high expectations and what is truly possible.

Sagittarius to Libra: Your job could involve personal flair or charm. You may have natural magnetism and may well pursue justice or fair play professionally. You are likely to connect ideals with people in your career, and might be involved with the courts, the law, social causes, politics, etc. Your sense of humor, quick wits, high standards or interpersonal skills could become vocational assets.

Sagittarius to Scorpio: Your vocational hopes could range quite high at times (perhaps too much so). Your work is likely to involve intense emotions (yours or those of other people) and could relate to beliefs, values, sexuality, finances or other areas where people have strong feelings. Although your natal focus was broad, examining issues thoroughly and in depth is of increasing importance to you in this region.

Sagittarius to Capricorn: You are learning to blend the highest of hopes with the most demanding of judgments. If the integration is comfortable, much achievement and success is likely. If the blend is uncomfortable, you could be chronically dissatisfied (always wanting more, or wanting to do more, or better than you can/have). Remember to count assets as well as flaws!

Sagittarius to Aquarius: Your general outlook is progressive, forward-going, optimistic, intellectual and restless. You function best in an atmosphere of change, innovation, individuality, and broad horizons. Your work may become more transpersonal, new age, intellectually stimulating or in some way expanding people's options and choices. You function best when you can do your job in your own unique way.

Sagittarius to Pisces: The quest for perfection is a theme in your career. This might be the search for the "perfect" job, trying to do your work perfectly, idealizing the work ethic, working to make a more perfect (or more beautiful world), or faith tied to effort and accomplishment. You need to inspire, uplift, transcend, or sweep away in what you do.

Capricorn to Aries: You are working on the balance between rules and personal independence. Your natal placement emphasizes practicality, fitting in, and doing what is proper. Your current focus is more concerned with self-expression, self-direction and a career that is personally satisfying. You may take more chances vocationally, or opt for more action and excitement. You can still be highly competent.

Capricorn to Taurus: Although you have a natural executive drive, you also have considerable patience. You probably want to gain the role of expert, but are willing to get there through regular hard work. Business is an arena where your steady, dependable style is likely to pay considerable dividends. You can be very stable, sensible, and are likely to appreciate success as you work hard to earn it.

Capricorn to Gemini: Your natal placement emphasizes executive control, authority, responsibility and doing what is necessary. Your relocation is more concerned with equality, mental stimulation and the desire for variety. You need to compromise between flippancy and being too serious, between all-work and all-play. Integration means you can be very productive with your ideas, communications and paperwork. You are probably mentally responsible.

Capricorn to Cancer: Your natal focus on achievement, making it to the top, accomplishing and responsibility is shifting toward more concern with home, family and nurturing issues. You may feel torn between time/energy commitments to career versus the nest. You might want to work more from your home, with family, or in fields involving nurturing, the land, the public, or basic commodities (e.g., food, shelter).

Capricorn to Leo: You are likely to seek the executive role in your work, with natural leanings toward being the power figure. Your dedication and effort quotient are high, but the desire for recognition and applause may be stronger in this locale. You are ready to receive public attention for your accomplishments, and eager for some excitement and fun to follow the foundation of hard work and responsibility.

Capricorn to Virgo: Your desire to do things **right** is in high focus. One option is the individual who is afraid to try, lest efforts not measure up. Another possibility is the workaholic—taking all of the responsibility because one does not trust others to produce,

CHAPTER EIGHT

"INSTANT" RELOCATION FOR SPECIFIC QUESTIONS

People often inquire for a "quick, easy" way to read an *Astrolocality Map* (or a *Relocation Chart*) when they are interested in only one particular focus—such as, "Where are my best prospects for relationships?"

Following is a list of the astrological positions which are promising for a number of common questions. Please remember: **astrology offers no guarantees! Each planet means many different things**. Venus rules love and partnership, but is also connected to beauty and sensual pleasures, so can be a key to overeating. Moving to an area which accentuates your Venus does not guarantee you true love. You might just get fat, become involved with art (or express another side of Venus). But, a Venus aspect is your best bet astrologically, if you also do your part of seeking out potential partners and making yourself available.

It is not ever advisable to make a move based solely on astrological placements. You should consider significant life factors **first**—such as:

(1) Can I make a living in this area?

(2) Will I be too close/too far from family members in this area?

(3) Will I be comfortable with the climate in this area?

and so on.

Even though a certain planet may, in theory, be the one you wish to highlight for a certain focus, **if that planet has much** sible. You have aesthetic and imaginative talents which could be used to enhance your job.

Pisces to Scorpio: Your vocational idealism may lead you into fields which involve strong emotions. You may be tempted to rescue, assist or otherwise "save" people. You probably have an instinctive grasp of what lies beneath the surface (of the land, of people, of situations) and may work in related fields. Your inner wisdom (psychic ability) could be a vocational asset. You understand basic processes and patterns.

Pisces to Sagittarius: Your career is mixed with a theme of idealism. This might indicate a tendency to look for the perfect position (ideal hours, pay, co-workers, etc.). It might point to a desire to do one's work perfectly, or working in a field which improves (makes better or more beautiful) the world. It can highlight someone who idealizes work, believing effort can gain you almost anything. You need to inspire the world.

Pisces to Capricorn: Your natal idealism is being brought down to earth in this locality. You are learning to blend practicality and effort with dreams, hopes and inspirations. Beware of demanding more than is humanly possible—or giving up too soon. A constructive blend allows you to work sensibly toward making your wishes come true. You may work in a practical manner with ideals, healing, or art.

Pisces to Aquarius: Your logic and intuition may contribute jointly to your career. You can blend rationality and inner knowing, or the conscious and unconscious, to contribute to the future. Your perspective is likely to be broad; you may be visionary in your sense of humanity, abstraction, ideals and potentials. You can contribute in terms of new-age interests and insights.

Pisces to Taurus: Your vocational strengths probably lie in the realms of beauty, grace, ease and harmony. You may be drawn to artistic or aesthetic vocations. You could adopt the role of diplomat, peacemaker or appeaser on the job. You might sometimes be tempted by the role of least resistance (the "easy" way). You can ground your intuitive connection to grace, and manifest harmony through your work.

Pisces to Gemini: Beware of the temptation to seek the "perfect" job. There is no such thing, especially as you could consider so many different possibilities! You may have artistic/aesthetic leanings, but are also likely to possess communication skills and talent for many "mind" fields. You may be tempted to scatter, trying to cover many different vocational options. You will have to focus in on just a few.

Pisces to Cancer: Your idealistic nature may incline you to keep seeking the "perfect" job, or trying to do your work perfectly. Your "need to be needed" might be carried too far—until you become a martyr. You tend to operate better in a sheltered environment, where your sensitive, poetic, imaginative side can manifest fully. You may increase your intuitive skills and visionary capacities.

Pisces to Leo: You may sometimes try to be all things to all people. You can play many roles, combining the magic of illusions and grace with natural charisma and magnetism. You may be skilled in promotion, sales, entertainment, teaching, comedy, advertising, politics or other persuasive fields. You could be a highly creative artist. You function best in work with stirs your ideals and your passions.

Pisces to Virgo: Your career is somehow a focus for blending the ideal and the real. If you bounce between them, some vocational restlessness is likely. You might be seeking the "perfect" job that does not exist, expecting to do your work perfectly, or wanting your work to save the world. A reasonable blend means you can do something artistic, healing or assisting in a practical, down-to-earth fashion.

Pisces to Libra: Your idealistic urge for infinite love and beauty may express through your work. Grace, charm, sweetness and sensitivity may be vocational handicaps (if you seek expect things to come too easily or to be "perfect") or assets (if applied with some common sense). Aesthetic or assisting careers are quite pos-

Aquarius to Libra: Your need for individualistic work remains, but a strong sense of team spirit is likely. You're apt to have people skills and can function well in any sort of communication field. Ideas may be your forte with good capacity for intellectual detachment and objectivity. Your sense of fair play is marked and you may enjoy working with groups, or with people one-on-one.

Aquarius to Scorpio: Natally, your chart suggests a focus on change, innovation, intellectual detachment and a desire for independence. In the relocation, you are facing the need for intensity, involvement with hidden or taboo subjects, financial matters, sexual needs or issues of control/manipulation. You must balance between safety needs and the willingness to risk, between thinking and feeling.

Aquarius to Sagittarius: Transpersonal issues are one focus in your work; your career could be tied to, affect, or take place out in the wider world. You may have talent for anything progressive, new age, freedom-loving, on the cutting edge, or which expands people's choices and possibilities. You need a general atmosphere of freedom, tolerance, openness and change. You thrive on variety and intellectual stimulation.

Aquarius to Capricorn: The focus of your natal and relocated positions is on the balance between the new, unconventional, freewheeling and the old, traditional and solidly ensconced. Battles between these two sides solve nothing. You need to incorporate some flexibility or freedom inside old structures, or to build newer, more open structures. You also need to know when to take control and when to share equally.

Aquarius to Pisces: Your career may involve transpersonal themes (connection to the wider world). You are likely to have visionary skills, an ability to blend the conscious and unconscious. You can combine logic and intuition to deal with the future, ideals, principles, abstractions and humanity's needs. You may innovate in regard to beauty, mysticism, spirituality or healing.

Pisces to Aries: You might operate as the professional artist, savior or victim looking for extremely personal meaning. Your natal focus on idealism is drawn toward work that is healing, helping, artistic (or escapist). The relocation emphasizes more personal direction and alone time in your work. You must balance self-assertion and self-sacrifice in your work; action and imagination.

conflict in your natal chart, you should think twice about putting it in high focus in your relocation! In other words, if you are thinking of moving to put Jupiter conjunct your Midheaven for potential career opportunities, but Jupiter is part of a grand cross in your chart, consider focusing on a different planet—unless you are sure you have integrated the issues represented by the grand cross and are able to manifest them positively.

If you have dealt constructively with the issues represented by conflict patterns in your chart, then choose a planet you want to highlight. Otherwise, look for an alternative to your first choice!

Even though conjunctions are the strongest aspects, a significant number of people find that having a planet conjunct an angle pinpoints an area which is a bit **too intense** for them. **You may do better with sextiles and trines to the angles.** For highly competitive activities (e.g., sports, some businesses), squares are often fine as well.

Aspects to Angles

For the quickest summary, use an *Astrolocality Map* which shows you the planetary aspects to angles across a given continental area (e.g., U.S., Europe, South America, etc.). For your first step, you think in terms of the natural meanings of the planets: Sun for prominence, shining, attention, recognition; Moon for emotional focus, nesting; Mercury for intellectual emphasis and curiosity, etc. If you have a little more time, consider aspects to angles in terms of the house each planet rules (as opposed to that planet's natural meaning). For that, you need your *Relocation Chart* for a particular city. (Thus, you know for example, that Venus trines your Midheaven in a certain area and Venus rules your 6th and 11th houses, suggesting additional harmony in regard to work/health and friendships/future directions.)

Here's a quick guide for these first two steps.

Your Purpose	Astrological Possibilities
Marriage/Relationships:	Venus trine, sextile, conjunct Asc/Desc axis.
	Venus trine, sextile MC/IC axis
	Juno trine, sextile, conjunct Asc/Desc axis
	Juno trine, sextile MC/IC axis
	Planet ruling your 7th house trine, sextile, conjunct Asc/Desc axis
	Planet ruling 7th house trine, sextile MC/IC axis

Vitality/Well-Being:	Jupiter trine, sextile, conjunct Ascendant
	Sun trine, sextile, conjunct Ascendant
	Mars trine, sextile, conjunct Ascendant
	Vesta trine, sextile Ascendant
	Planet ruling Ascendant sextile, trine, or conjunct Ascendant
	Planet ruling your 6th house trine, sextile, or conjunct Ascendant
Success in Career:	Jupiter trine, sextile, conjunct MC/IC axis
	Sun trine, sextile, conjunct MC/IC axis
	Saturn trine or sextile MC/IC axis
	Pluto trine or sextile MC/IC axis
	Vesta trine or sextile MC/IC axis
	Ceres trine or sextile MC/IC axis
	Planet ruling 10th house trine, sextile, conjunct MC/IC axis
	Planets ruling 10th house trine or conjunct 6th house ruler
Monetary Gain:	Venus trine, sextile Midheaven
	Pluto trine, sextile Midheaven
	Jupiter trine, sextile Midheaven
	Planet ruling your 2nd and/or 8th cusps trine or sextile Midheaven
Knowledge/Education:	Mercury trine, sextile, conjunct Asc/Desc axis
	Mercury trine, sextile, conjunct MC/IC axis
	Jupiter trine, sextile, conjunct Asc/Desc axis
	Jupiter trine, sextile, conjunct MC/IC axis
	Chiron trine, sextile, conjunct Asc/Desc axis
	Chiron trine, sextile, conjunct MC/IC axis
	Planet ruling your 3rd and/or 9th cusps trine, sextile, or conjunct Asc/Desc axis or MC/IC axis.
Home/Family Focus:	Moon conjunct, trine, sextile IC.
	Moon trine, sextile Ascendant axis.
	Ceres conjunct, trine, sextile IC.
	Ceres trine, sextile Ascendant axis.
	Whichever planet(s) rule your 4th and/or 5th houses trine, sextile, or conjunct IC or Ascendant axis.

Spiritual Focus:	Neptune trine, sextile Ascendant axis.
	Neptune trine, sextile Midheaven axis.
	Jupiter trine, sextile Ascendant axis.
	Jupiter trine, sextile Midheaven axis.
	Chiron trine, sextile Ascendant axis.
	Chiron trine, sextile Midheaven axis.
	Planet(s) ruling 9th and/or 12th houses trine, sextile or conjunct Asc/Desc or MC/IC axis.
Artistic Involvement:	Venus trine, sextile, conjunct Ascendant axis.
	Venus trine, sextile, conjunct Midheaven axis.
	Neptune trine, sextile Ascendant or Midheaven.
Sports Focus:	Mars trine, sextile, conjunct, square Ascendant axis.
	Mars trine, sextile, conjunct, square MC/IC axis.
	Jupiter trine, sextile, conjunct, square Ascendant axis.
	Jupiter trine, sextile, conjunct, square Midheaven axis.
More Astrology in Your Life:	Uranus trine, sextile, conjunct Ascendant or Midheaven axis.
Increased Focus, Organizational Skills:	Saturn trine, sextile Asc/Desc axis
	Saturn trine, sextile MC/IC axis
	Vesta trine, sextile Asc/Desc axis
	Vesta trine, sextile MC/IC axis
	Pluto trine, sextile Asc/Desc axis
	Pluto trine, sextile MC/IC axis
Power Focus, Increased Ambition:	Saturn trine, sextile Asc/Desc axis
	Saturn trine, sextile MC/IC axis
	Pluto trine, sextile Asc/Desc axis
	Pluto trine, sextile MC/IC axis
	Sun trine, sextile Asc/Desc axis
	Sun trine, sextile MC/IC axis
More Independence:	Uranus trine, sextile Asc/Desc axis
	Mars trine, sextile Asc/Desc axis
	Jupiter trine, sextile Asc/Desc axis
	Chiron trine, sextile Asc/Desc axis
	Uranus trine, sextile MC/IC axis
	Mars trine, sextile MC/IC axis
	Jupiter trine, sextile MC/IC axis
	Chiron trine, sextile MC/IC axis

House Placements

If you wish to take the next step after considering aspects to angles, take a look at the house placements of the various planets. Remember, every placement has an "up" side and a "down" side. Astrology does not guarantee which side we will manifest; it merely mirrors our inner potentials. A brief summary of down-side possibilities is included here, along with the desired goals. It is up to us to express the best we can among our options.

Purpose	Astrological Placements	"Down" Side Possibilities
Marriage/Relationships:	Venus in 7th	too other directed, appeasing
	Juno in 7th	power issues in relationships
	7th house Ruler in 7th	passive
Vitality/Well-Being:	Sun in 1st, 5th, 9th	exaggerative, speculator
	Mars in 1st, 5th, 9th	focused on self
	Jupiter in 1st, 5th, 9th	grandiose, self-righteous
Success in Career:	Sun in 2nd	extravagant
	Sun in 10th	ego-involved in power
	Ruler of 10th in 1st, 2nd	work identified
	Ruler of 10th in 6th	overly responsible
	Ruler of 6th in 10th	workaholic
Monetary Gain:	Ruler of 2nd in 2nd, 8th	indulgent
	Ruler of 2nd in 10th	duty vs. pleasure
	Ruler of 8th in 2nd, 8th	feast versus famine
	Ruler of 8th in 10th	power issues
	Ruler of 10th in 1st, 2nd	love of power
	Ruler of 2nd, 8th in 1st	sensual focus
	4th, 8th, 12th connected to each other and 2nd	overindulgence
Knowledge/Education:	Jupiter in 3rd, 9th	restless
	Mercury in 3rd, 9th	scattered
	Chiron in 3rd, 9th	scattered
	Ruler of 3rd in 3rd, 9th	scattered
	Ruler of 9th in 3rd, 9th	scattered
Home/Family Focus:	Moon in 4th	too dependent/ too nurturing
	Sun in 4th	ego issues in home
	Venus in 4th	complacent
Spiritual Focus:	Jupiter in 9th, 12th	overly idealistic
	Neptune in 9th, 12th	wanting more than is possible
	Chiron in 9th, 12th	wanting more than is possible

Artistic Involvement:	Venus in 2nd, 5th, 7th, 12th	passive
	Neptune in 2nd, 5th, 7th, 12th	passive
Sports Focus:	Mars in 1st, 5th, 9th	self-focused
	Jupiter in 1st, 5th, 9th	self-righteous
	Sun in 1st, 5th, 9th	ego-involved
More Astrology in Your Life:	Uranus in 1st, 2nd	chaos; monetary unpredictibility
	Uranus in 6th, 10th	chaos; disruption in work
Increased Focus, Organizational Skills:	Vesta in 6th, 8th, 10th	workaholic
	Pluto in 6th, 8th, 10th	compulsive
	Saturn in 6th, 8th, 10th	over burdened
Power Focus, Increased Ambition:	Sun in 5th, 8th, 9th, 10th, 11th	power-hungry
	Pluto in 5th, 8th, 9th, 10th, 11th	"control freak"
	Saturn in 5th, 8th, 9th, 10th, 11th	dictatorial
More Independence:	Mars in 1st, 9th, 11th	impulsive
	Jupiter in 1st, 9th, 11th	over confident
	Uranus in 1st, 9th, 11th	chaotic, rebellious

Conclusion

We hope that this "quick guide" is useful in your consideration of different places to live. Astrology can be a helpful tool as long as we recall it is only **one** tool among many for living a fulfilling life. As always, the power and responsibility lie within our hands. May you have exciting, growth-filled years full of self-expression, pleasure, communication, nurturing, love and self-esteem, productivity, equality, shared insights, a satisfying belief system, realism and responsibility, uniqueness, and the ecstatic connection to something higher! May you and your clients make the most of your opportunities and overcome your challenges—everywhere on Earth you travel.

Your Personal Electronic Astrologers